BYRON'S GHOSTS

LIVERPOOL ENGLISH TEXTS AND STUDIES 62

BYRON'S GHOSTS

THE SPECTRAL,
THE SPIRITUAL
AND THE
SUPERNATURAL

EDITED BY GAVIN HOPPS

LIVERPOOL UNIVERSITY PRESS

First published 2013 by
Liverpool University Press
4 Cambridge Street
Liverpool
L69 7ZU

British Library Cataloguing-in-Publication data
A British Library CIP record is available

ISBN 978-1-84631-970-9

Typeset by Carnegie Book Production, Lancaster
Printed and bound by CPI Group (UK) Ltd, Croydon CR0 4YY

— I own my partiality for *Spirit*. —

Byron, 'Detached Thoughts'

Contents

Acknowledgements

The editor would like to thank all the contributors for their fine work and patience during the long editorial process.

Thanks are also due to Danny Gabelman for his work on the index; to Emma Woodhouse for her help with the typing; and to Anthony Cond at Liverpool University Press for his encouragement, advice and for overseeing the book's emergence into being.

The editor finally wishes to express gratitude to Dr Elizabeth Denlinger and The Carl H. Pforzheimer Collection of Shelley and His Circle, The New York Public Library, and the Astor, Lenox and Tilden Foundations for permission to use the cover image of 'Lord Byron in the other world'. This is taken from: W. Davenport, *The book of spirits, and tales of the dead: comprising 'Lord Byron in the other world', Weber and the heavenly choir, Talma in celestial spheres, The phantom ship, and other narrations of deep and awful interest* (London: William Charlton Wright, [1827?]).

Texts and Abbreviations

All quotations from Byron's poetry are taken from *Lord Byron: The Complete Poetical Works*, eds. Jerome J. McGann and Barry Weller, 7 vols. (Oxford: Clarendon Press, 1980–1993). All quotations from Byron's letters are taken from *Byron's Letters and Journals*, ed. Leslie A. Marchand, 13 vols. (London: John Murray, 1973–1994). All quotations from Keats's poetry are taken from: *The Poems of John Keats*, ed. Jack Stillinger (London: Heinemann, 1978). All quotations from Schiller's poetry are taken from: Friedrich Schiller, *Sämtliche Werke*, eds. Gerhard Fricke and Herbert G. Göpfert, vol. 1 (München: Carl Hanser Verlag, 1965). All quotations from P.B. Shelley's poetry are taken from: *The Poems of Shelley*, eds. Geoffrey Matthews and Kelvin Everest, vol. 1 (London: Longman, 1989). All quotations from William Wordsworth's poetry are taken from: *The Poetical Works of William Wordsworth*, eds. E. de Selincourt and H. Darbishire, 5 vols. (Oxford: Clarendon Press, 1940–1949).

BLJ	*Byron's Letters and Journals*, ed. Leslie A. Marchand, 13 vols. (London: John Murray, 1973–1994)
CHP	*Childe Harold's Pilgrimage*
CMP	*Lord Byron – The Complete Miscellaneous Prose*, ed. Andrew Nicholson (Oxford: Clarendon Press, 1991)
CPW	*Lord Byron: The Complete Poetical Works*, eds. Jerome J. McGann and Barry Weller, 7 vols. (Oxford: Clarendon Press, 1980–1993)
CWWH	*The Complete Works of William Hazlitt*, ed. P.P. Howe, 21 vols. (London: J.M. Dent, 1930–1934)
DJ	*Don Juan*
LJK	*The Letters of John Keats, 1814–1821*, ed. Hyder Edward Rollins, 2 vols. (Cambridge: Cambridge University Press, 1958)
LPBS	*The Letters of Percy Bysshe Shelley*, ed. Frederick L. Jones, 2 vols. (Oxford: Clarendon Press, 1964)
SWMS	*The Novels and Selected Works of Mary Shelley*, eds. Nora Crook and Pamela Clemit, 8 vols. (London: Pickering & Chatto, 1996)
WJR	*The Works of John Ruskin*, eds. E.T. Cook and Alexander Weddeburn, 39 vols. (London: George Allen, 1903–1912)

Introduction:
The Re-Enchantment of Romanticism

immaterialism's a serious matter
(Byron, *DJ*, XVI, 114)

'Grim reader! did you ever see a ghost?' (XV, 95). What relevance does
Don Juan's question have for contemporary readers of Byron? What is
to be gained from focusing attention on the spectral, the spiritual and
the supernatural in the work of this worldly and sceptical poet? As a
way of contextualizing this volume's concerns, ahead of an outline of
the individual chapters, this introduction seeks to explain why ghosts
are of interest in a postmodern world and why this surprising renewal
of interest is of significance for Romantic studies in general, and readers
of Byron in particular.

I

If the notion of being 'a little bit dead' was memorably ridiculed
by Monty Python's Parrot Sketch, it has been at least as effectively
redeemed by the writings of Jacques Derrida.[1] According to Derrida
– who claimed that 'the logic of spectrality' is 'inseparable from the
very motif [...] of deconstruction'[2] – the ghostly has hitherto eluded
the scholarly gaze, since a commitment to the categories of classical
ontology pre-emptively rules out its manner of appearing.[3] As Peter
Buse and Andrew Stott explain:

> the necessary distance of scholarly 'objectivity' [...] constitutes an avoidance
> of spectrality, since to figure the ghost in terms of fact or fiction, real or
> not-real, is to attribute to it a foundational ground, either a positive or
> negative facticity that the notion of ghostliness continually eludes.[4]

In adumbrating a modality that is irreducible to the alternatives of living and not living, presence and absence, real and imaginary etc., Derrida has hospitably made room for such ontological unhousedness.

Derrida is of course not alone in this newfound hospitality towards the ghostly.[5] Indeed, Theory – that amorphous, quasi-agentive apotheosis – is positively teeming with spectres, and it is possible to find evidence of the 'spectral turn' in most of the major movements and schools. Examples include: Lacan's psychoanalytical exposition of an uncanny site 'between two deaths'; Abraham and Torok's work on the haunting of transgenerational trauma; Žižek's meditations on the spectres of ideology and the 'symbolic efficiency' of fictional entities; Foucault's account of the 'phantasms of madness' that reside 'between the book and the lamp'; ruminations on the 'trace' and the presence of an absence in the writings of Levinas; Hélèna Cixous's conception of fiction as 'a secretion of death'; Vilashini Cooppan's postcolonial rethinking of the ontology of nation as a 'fantasmic object' that moves 'within, across, and beyond a series of spatial and temporal borders'; Judith Butler's exploration of the 'phantasmatic' effects of performatively constituted gender; and Carla Freccero's exegesis of 'queer spectrality'.[6] There is even a chapter solely devoted to 'Spectral Criticism' – and a related chapter on '(A)material Criticism' – in Julian Wolfreys's recent guide 'to current directions in literary criticism'.[7]

It is obviously no coincidence that this exponential increase of interest in the spectral has occurred alongside the emergence of a new kind of reality, which calls itself 'virtual' and has made possible a mode of being 'without' materiality.[8] Here is what Geoffrey Batchen has to say about this shadow reality, with a nod to the opening of Marx's *Manifesto*:

> A new spectre is haunting Western culture – the spectre of Virtual Reality. [...] Even the words themselves have a certain phantom quality. Virtual Reality – a reality which is apparently true but not *truly* True, a reality which is apparently real but not *really* Real.[9]

Manifestly, such spectres are not of the chandelier-rattling kind (though they evidently problematize our notions of 'real' and 'true'). As Fredric Jameson has been quick to point out, the profusion of spectres in contemporary discourse is not necessarily a matter of belief. He writes:

> Spectrality does not involve the conviction that ghosts exist or that the past (and maybe even the future they offer to prophesy) is still very much alive and at work, within the living present: all it says, if it can be thought to speak, is that the living present is scarcely as self-sufficient as it claims to

be; that we would do well not to count on its density and solidity, which might under exceptional circumstances betray us.[10]

This is a salutary point, which helps us to put into perspective what Roger Luckhurst refers to as the proliferation of 'Gothicized literary criticism'.[11] Nevertheless, one might question Jameson's confidence about what the haunting of contemporary reality does or does not involve. As Derrida rather more circumspectly cautions: '[L]et's not act as if we knew what a phantom or a phantasm was.'[12] In any case, the current hospitality towards the spectral is not simply a conceptual convenience or the flourishing of a particularly felicitous idiom, but is also bound up with wider epistemological shifts that are coextensive with the advent of postmodernity and which do – *pace* Jameson – reflect alterations in matters of belief. We can illustrate something of such underlying shifts with reference to a context traditionally associated with spirits and ghosts – namely, the religious.

In 1948, in *Kerygma und Mythos*, Rudolf Bultmann famously claimed: 'It is impossible to use electric light and the wireless and to avail ourselves of modern medical and surgical discoveries, and at the same time to believe in the New Testament world of spirits and miracles.'[13] And yet, as the new English translation of the Roman missal reveals – which came into use in 2011 – what may have seemed unthinkable in the 1940s and 1950s is once again being explicitly encouraged. Here are a couple of the more conspicuous changes: while previously the congregation was enjoined to respond to the celebrant's blessing with the words 'And also with you', the new, more accurate translation of the Latin is: 'And with your spirit' ('*Et cum spiritu tuo*'). Similarly, the words of the Centurion (Matthew 8: 8) uttered prior to Communion, which were previously translated as 'Lord, I am not worthy to receive you, but only say the word and I shall be healed', are now translated as follows: 'Lord, I am not worthy that you should enter under my roof, but only say the word and my soul shall be healed.' What this new translation of liturgical language suggests is that it is no longer 'impossible' to be comfortably cognizant of the latest technology and at the same time believe in a world of spirits and souls. How can we explain this epistemological shift?

One possibility that immediately suggests itself is that the contemporary hospitality towards the ghostly is part of a so-called 're-enchantment' of the world.[14] To summarize an already familiar story, what this refers to is a counter-reaction to the process of 'disenchantment' or '*Entzauberung*' famously associated by Max Weber with the constitutive outworking

of the Enlightenment agenda during the course of modernity.[15] While
Weber's notion of 'disenchantment' is usually traced back to Schiller's
poem 'Die Götter Griechenlandes' (1788),[16] its principal lineaments are
succinctly exhibited in Wordsworth's sonnet 'The world is too much
with us' (1807):

> The world is too much with us; late and soon,
> Getting and spending, we lay waste our powers:
> Little we see in Nature that is ours;
> We have given our hearts away, a sordid boon!
> This Sea that bares her bosom to the moon;
> The winds that will be howling at all hours,
> And are up-gathered now like sleeping flowers;
> For this, for everything, we are out of tune;
> It moves us not. – Great God! I'd rather be
> A Pagan suckled in a creed outworn;
> So might I, standing on this pleasant lea,
> Have glimpses that would make me less forlorn;
> Have sight of Proteus rising from the sea;
> Or hear old Triton blow his wreathèd horn.

Here we can see, in Wordsworth's nostalgic elegy for mythological
intermediaries, a sense that the much vaunted emancipation of the
Enlightenment – whose valorization of unassisted reason was supposed
to result in a knowable, controllable natural order – has brought
about a different kind of entrapment and a mode of alienation that
coincides with proximity: we are radically 'out of tune' with things
and yet the world is 'too much with us'. The 'filial bond' of which
Wordsworth speaks in *The Prelude* (II, 234) between man and nature
has been sundered or eclipsed, and the resulting autonomy of the
created order has displaced a sense of it as gifted or given ('Little we
see in Nature that is ours'). The poem also suggests that the scientific
method and emergence of '*homo economicus*' – implicated in the
paratactic hygiene of 'late and soon, / Getting and spending' – do
not in fact lead to an amelioration of the human condition.[17] Most
ardently, though, the sonnet mourns the passing of a divinely inhabited
cosmos, whose demystification has led not to a this-worldly heaven of
secular perfection, but rather a mechanistic 'universe of death' in which
all is *light* and comfortless. (The line break after 'I would rather be'
dramatically raises the stakes of this disenchantment in eliciting an
existential reference from the auxiliary verb 'to be'.) There is a further
complication, however. The invocation 'Great God!', which suggests the
persistence of a monotheistic worldview alongside the speaker's nostalgia

for a mythologically inhabited universe, indicates something of the complexities involved in the process of 'desacralization'. For while the valorization of reason and the corollary rise of the scientific method were conspicuously opposed to the superstition and mystery associated with the church, one of the crucial sources of demystification came from within religion itself in the shape of the Reformation. Indeed, the venture of separateness that was the Enlightenment project was vitally reinforced by the Protestant Reformation – even paradoxically as it sought to *restore* man's relationship with the divine – in that it fostered a more interiorized and transcendental religion, which, as Weber contended, helped to remove a sense of immanent holiness from the world.[18] This explains why Wordsworth's speaker can apparently retain a belief in the divine while mourning the advent of a desacralized sphere.

If this, as a crude and cursory summary, is roughly what is meant by a 'disenchantment of the world', in what sense are we witnessing its re-enchantment?

Most accounts of postmodern enchantment draw attention to a re-awakened sense of mystery in the world, both in terms of a corner around which we cannot peer as well as the kinds of entities that populate contemporary culture. One thinks, for example, of the extraordinary proliferation of vampires, aliens, androids and zombies – who widen the category of being 'a little bit dead' – in mainstream film and television series (such as *Twilight*, *True Blood*, *Being Human* or *Blade*); the insatiable craze for fantasy fiction (*The Lord of the Rings*, *Harry Potter*, *The Chronicles of Narnia* etc.);[19] the emergence of the 'uncanny' or 'metaphysical' soap opera (exemplified by *Twin Peaks*, *Life on Mars* and *Lost*); and the enormous popularity of graphic novels – by Neil Gaiman, Alan Moore and others – which combine magic, mysticism, contemporary serial killers and ancient mythology. Indeed, the gods whose apparently irrevocable passing is mourned in the poetry of Wordsworth and Schiller have returned with a vengeance in the worlds envisaged by Gaiman and Moore.[20] These are of course fictional representations of the world; yet as Žižek is fond of pointing out, a thing doesn't need to exist to have an effect. Moreover, as Elaine Graham has observed, such fictional representations are not simply portrayals of an imagined reality, sealed off from and opposed to 'that which is'. Rather, our sense of the real is reciprocally 'constructed through representational practices', which call into question the apparent finality or taken-for-grantedness of the known.[21] In his survey of contemporary forms of re-enchantment, Christopher Partridge similarly argues that popular culture is a powerful 'sacralizing' force, since it has a 'shaping effect on Western plausibility structures'.[22] The argument may be pressed further though.

The return of the Gothic, the mysterious and the magical also seems to be a reflection, in some refracted sense, of changes in what people actually believe, or at least are prepared to countenance as possible. For another central feature of postmodern re-enchantment is of course a return of the religious. Drummond Bone has even gone so far as to claim that: 'Postmodernism is *not* a secular hypothesis, but rather an ideology verging on a theology.'[23] Obviously, the religious is returning differently – in terms of its kaleidoscopic manifestations but also in terms of the epistemological posture it elicits and the role that it plays in people's lives – as what it seems we are witnessing in the twenty-first century is the emergence of a range of alternative spiritualties (or what Partridge collectively refers to as 'occulture'),[24] alongside the resurgence of an increasingly militant fundamentalism.[25] This is not to say that the process of secularization has come to an end. Instead, to quote Partridge again, what we appear to be witnessing in the West is 'a confluence of secularization and sacralization'.[26] This confluence is especially apparent – and hard to disentangle – in the 'camp' tonalities of popular forms, in which it is possible to discern a twinkling of kitsch in the sublime as well as a glimmer of sublimity in the kitsch, whose delight in 'artefacts that exorcise [...] the referential' is a legacy of the exalted frivolity of the Baroque.[27] Nevertheless, some may still prefer to see the kitsch 're-enchantment of the real' and the return of the religious as a 'special effect' as a continuation by alternative means of the process of disenchantment.[28]

The postmodern re-enchantment of the West differs in other important ways from the pre-modern enchantment to which it is compared, perhaps most conspicuously in the role played by science and technology. In particular, whereas during the period of modernity, the scientific gaze was held responsible for 'unweaving the rainbow' and 'emptying the haunted air', it now also uncovers mysteries and wonders – such as dark matter and black holes – which not so long ago would have seemed like the stuff of Gothic fiction. The extraordinary beauty in the creation sequence of Terrance Malick's *Tree of Life*, for example – which seems to be a conscious allusion to the surreal journey 'beyond the infinite' in *2001: A Space Odyssey* – is presented as a 'scientific' narrative, though formally it appears to be a work of extravagant fantasy. Thus, thanks to science, nature is becoming evangelical again. Likewise, technology – in its digital, cybernetic and biomedical forms – which would seem to be the embodiment of instrumental rationality and hence something that helps to *eliminate* a sense of mystery in the world – has in fact radically complicated what we call nature and what it means to be human, which has led to a dissolution of the 'ontological hygiene' that underwrote modernity's exemplary conceptions of the real.[29] In the process, technology has opened up a new form of transcendence or 'technochantment' – which includes a 'technologization of the ineffable' and a conception of cyberspace as a species of *sacred* space[30] – such that it has, in the words of Graham Ward, become 'the bearer of messianic possibilities'.[31]

We should note, however, that the contemporary re-enchantment of the real is marked by a kind of retreat as well as an advance. This is because its openness to the mysterious is predicated on the waning sovereignty of that well-known chimera 'pure reason' and a corollary consciousness that we lack a transcendental vantage, outside of interpretation, from which we can objectively and conclusively determine the ultimate nature of that which is. The characteristic postmodern gesture thus advertises itself as provisional, relative, subjective and contingent – typically articulated by way of an arch foregrounding of its own constitutive performance – all of which in turn bespeak a hermeneutic or epistemological weakening, described by Gianni Vattimo as '*pensiero debole*' and by John Caputo as 'spectral hermeneutics'.[32] The historical significance of this may be broadly indicated as follows.

According to Gavin Hyman, the 'role and position of the human subject in relation to reality' during the period of modernity was fundamentally *nominative* (in that 'the self becomes the *subject* that applies the disciplines of reason and science to the world, which is thereby conceived to be the *object* of that activity'), which may be contrasted with the pre-modern model, in which 'human beings understood themselves as existing in an *accusative* mode' (since they 'and the wider reality of which they were a part were created by God and were therefore, in a sense, *objects* of God's creative activity').[33] If this is the case, how could we characterize a postmodern comportment towards reality? In terms of Hyman's heuristic model, it might be suggested that what we are witnessing in the postmodern reaction to the Enlightenment project is not a return to an 'accusative' mode – though as we have seen it involves a subversion of the subject's dominion and a re-opening of mystery – but rather the advent of a *subjunctive* posture. What I mean by this is a posture that retains the subject position of modernity's characteristic stance but radically differs in the *mood* of its comportment, in accordance with what we might refer to as its 'self-deprecating' epistemology. This would reflect a sense of the 'irreality' of its positings

or a reticence with respect to its ability to refer.[34] It would announce
a relinquishing of any pretension to constitute a metanarrative and a
concomitant acknowledgement of its own discursive or 'narrativized'
status. It would also advertise a retreat from the definitive and betoken
a certain playfulness or lightness of tone – in forsaking the indicative for
an 'as if' posture – which is typically associated with postmodern art.[35]
Crucially, however, while the subjunctive posture is more sceptical and
less serious – in a way that *contrasts* with the securities of the pre-modern
period – it is thereby less fettered by predetermined notions of the
possible or thinkable and is more free in its imaginative exploration of
the real. It thus undergirds what Keats refers to as a mode of 'being
in uncertainties, Mysteries, doubts'[36] and – in a manner that *converges*
with pre-modern epistemology – permits us to entertain the possibility
of that which is 'scandalous to reason'.[37] In other words, a sceptical
weakening of its claims leads to a widening of its fiduciary horizons.
In this sense, the subjunctive posture of the postmodern gesture may
be said to open the way for a 'post-nihilistic' form of faith. (This helps
to explain the prevalence of theological formulations – such as God
'without being' or the God who 'may be' – that have a wink to the
nihilist in the midst of their confession.)[38]

We have thus come upon the paradox at the heart of postmodern
re-enchantment – namely, that it is *scepticism* that dilates the parameters
of the possible and underwrites the contemporary hospitality towards
the spectral. Indeed, for Levinas, scepticism is itself a kind of ghost,
since it returns after its refutation and can never be finally laid to rest:
'Le scepticisme est le réfutable, mais aussi *le revenant*.'[39] Yet this is a
very particular type of scepticism. It isn't a 'one-sided' Enlightenment
scepticism that questions everything with the exception of the enterprise
of questioning.[40] It is rather a form of what Hegel referred to as
'self-perficient' scepticism – that is, a reflexive or 'self-consummating'
scepticism, which conditions the possibility of its own escape. As Simon
Jarvis explains:

> Hegel described his own thinking as a highway of despair. By this he
> meant not that it ended in despair but that it had to pass through it.
> His thinking involved 'self-perficient scepticism'. [...] It would defeat
> scepticism, not by clinging to illusions, but by pushing sceptical claims as
> far as they would go.[41]

Such scepticism therefore undermines, even as it carries to its logical
conclusion, the Enlightenment project of 'radical doubt', and thus opens
the way for a new kind of non-pejorative credulity or what Paul Ricoeur

has called a 'second naiveté'.[42] The implications of this for the present study are helpfully summarized by Colin Davis: 'skepticism might look as if it asks us to reject the belief in ghosts, but in fact it asks us to be willing to suspend *all* our beliefs, including the belief that ghosts do *not* exist.'[43]

If the foregoing sketch of postmodern re-enchantment helps to explain one aspect of the current volume's enterprise – namely, a scholarly concern not only with Derridean spectres but also with what Mary Shelley describes as 'the true old-fashioned, foretelling, flitting, gliding ghost'[44] – the question remains: what has this got to do with Romanticism in general and Byron in particular?

II

As Jane Stabler observes in her introduction to the Palgrave Advances volume on Byron, the 'study of Romantic poetry now seems increasingly dominated by the realm of the material'.[45] According to the early modern scholar David Hawkes, this is part of an even larger pattern; he writes: 'The vast majority of today's literary theorists, like the overwhelming majority of Western intellectuals as a whole, share a methodological commitment to materialism. In fact this commitment is often so deep as to be unconscious.'[46] In the first instance, then, it is important to take note of the re-enchantment of the West and its accompanying hospitality towards the immaterial, since it poses a challenge to the currently dominant materialist consensus in Romantic studies. This largely unconscious critical consensus is manifestly the product of complex cultural and ideological factors, which it isn't possible to investigate here.[47] Nevertheless, it may be worth highlighting how the immaterial came to be quarantined and discredited in a field where once the spiritual, the ideal and the transcendent were central.

There appear to be three interrelated ways in which the immaterial has been excluded or distorted by the current critical orthodoxy. Most obviously, the advent of cultural materialism, which led to a 'shifting' of 'our angles of vision', began as a counter-hegemonic corrective that sought to recover 'neglected historical figures and events'[48] and so perhaps inevitably turned away from certain phenomena. Thus, for example, in his materialist reading of Byron's dramas, Daniel P. Watkins talks of the 'social relevance' and 'class significance' of the plays' protagonists, while showing little interest in the fact that many of these are angels, witches, spirits and demons.[49] Over time, however, what began as a corrective redirection of attention appears to have developed into a programmatic incuriosity about the immaterial as such.[50] Secondly, and somewhat more surreptitiously, the realm of the immaterial has been excluded from recent critical discussion by means of a prevenient interpretive move, which takes for granted – as a matter of dogmatically held faith – that any attempt to transcend the material is a species of illusion, projection or escapism. The most prominent example of this kind of exclusionary manoeuvre is to be found in Jerome McGann's *The Romantic Ideology* (1983), which purports to speak of an ultimate, objective, unmediated reality in categorically asserting that any intimations of transcendence are the 'grand illusion' of Romantic ideology.[51] The influence of this critique has been so pervasive that David Fuller is able to claim that 'the scholarship and interpretation of Romanticism is dominated by McGann-inspired representations'.[52] And yet, for all its salutary suspicion of the transcendent gesture – which highlights the Romantics' own anxieties about their not always wholly candid aspirations – we should not lose sight of the uninterrogated presumption of the project, which proceeds as though it were able to determine by way of self-certifying assertion the conditions of possibility for all reality.[53] (It might also be noted that in seeking to outlaw the possibility of transcendence in Romantic writing on the basis of its own historically specific cultural assumptions, McGann's project succumbs to a form of 'presentism', and so is in a sense curiously dependent on the very procedures it seeks to prohibit.) In the third place, it should be borne in mind that the current materialist ideological consensus grew out of a reaction to canonical construals of Romanticism, which is to say 'pre-critical' readings of the period, such as Abrams's *Natural Supernaturalism* (1971), which preceded the poststructuralist revolution in literary theory. What such materialist criticism therefore rejects is an outdated and unreconstructed model of 'transcendentalizing' Romanticism. What it hasn't overcome – and what it is now reciprocally challenged by – is the profound and widespread rethinking of the immaterial, which is *itself* a product of the poststructuralist revolution.[54] It is, then, partly on account of this reconception of materialism's others, which challenges the prevailing critical consensus, that postmodern enchantment is of importance to Romantic studies.

It is furthermore of interest because it pointedly gives the lie to Thomas Love Peacock's notorious but widely accepted assessment of Romanticism's historical significance. In the text that provoked the 'sacred rage' of Shelley[55] – and his *Defence of Poetry* (1821) – Peacock writes of the Romantic poet:

While the historian and the philosopher are advancing in, and accelerating, the progress of knowledge, the poet is wallowing in the rubbish of departed ignorance, and raking up the ashes of dead savages to find gewgaws and rattles for the grown babies of the age. [...] He lives in the days that are past. His ideas, thoughts, feelings, associations, are all with barbarous manners, obsolete customs, and exploded superstitions. The march of his intellect is like that of a crab, backward. The brighter the light diffused around him by the progress of reason, the thicker is the darkness of antiquated barbarism, in which he buries himself like a mole, to throw up the barren hillocks of his Cimmerian labours.[56]

For Peacock, who takes for granted an equation of progress with Enlightenment rationalism ('the march of the intellect' and the 'progress of reason'), Romantic poetry is a retrograde move, since it carries us back into the darkness of 'departed ignorance' and 'exploded superstitions'. But in view of the contemporary re-enchantment of the West, which calls into question this simplistic equation and challenges the ideals of the Enlightenment project – which Peacock assumes are self-evident and timelessly established – the counter-Enlightenment tendencies of the Romantic poets cease to seem like a sort of regression and instead appear to be an inchoate movement in the direction of knowledge and a prescient exploration of postmodern concerns. In other words, from a contemporary 're-enchanted' perspective, the Romantics' 'superstitious' imaginings appear to be *beneficent* cracks in the system.[57] It should be emphasized that this is not to suggest a wholesale opposition to the Enlightenment project.[58] It is, however, more modestly to observe that the counter-Enlightenment venture of the Romantics is at least to some extent vindicated by the contemporary re-enchantment of the real. Yet this modest concession has far-reaching ramifications, for it means that the enchantments of Romantic writing – which have in recent decades been routinely patronized, as a result of the dominance, now apparently waning, of materialist, secular presuppositions – should not be dismissed *a priori* as a form of escapism or illusion, on the basis of an Enlightenment scepticism that presumes to know better. It also suggests that the Romantic venture may, in spite of its historical distance, be of much more relevance to current philosophical and theological debates than has hitherto been assumed.[59]

The contemporary re-enchantment of the real is additionally important as it prompts us to rethink T.E. Hulme's frequently rehearsed description of Romanticism as 'spilt religion'.[60] This is owing to the fact that his interpretation presupposes, prior to the 'incontinence' of the Romantic period, that there is a narrowly circumscribed sphere of sacrality, which he takes to be an exemplary religious environment. Yet, as David Brown amongst others has pointed out, this radical circumscription of the sacred – absolutized by Hulme to a normative condition – is the product of very particular theological and ideological circumstances and was itself a retreat from, or draining away of, a sense of sacrality that *flooded* the cosmos and was *of its nature* an 'uncontained' presence.[61] The contemporary return, in a different form, of a more diffused sacrality therefore troubles the assumed normativity of Hulme's paradigm of containment, which in turn suggests an alternative reading of Romanticism's 'spillage'. To be more precise, in view of the contemporary diffusion of the sacred, rather than an illicit spillage of what was and ought lawfully to be narrowly confined, the Romantic sacralization of nature may be seen as a *recovery* of what had been lost or the unshackling of an artificial curtailment of the divine, and the benighted inauguration of a counter-movement that had to wait for postmodernism to be brought to fruition.

How, then, does this relate to Byron in particular? Why is his poetry, of all the Romantics, especially relevant to debates about postmodern enchantment? And why, conversely, might the re-enchantment narrative be a fruitful context in which to reconsider his work?

III

The materialist bias in Romantic studies has become especially entrenched in writing on Byron, who is typically celebrated as a carnivalizing voice with a 'scorn for "metaphysics"'[62] and who was famously excluded from Abrams's 'supernaturalist' reading of Romanticism 'because in his greatest work he speaks with an ironic counter-voice and deliberately opens a satirical perspective on the vatic stance of his Romantic contemporaries'.[63] This image of Byron as the debunking nemesis of vatic Romanticism was reinforced and given a Marxist twist by McGann's *Romantic Ideology*, which championed a proto-Nietzschean Byron, who exposed the period's escapist 'false consciousness' and brought critics and poets alike down to earth. This pattern of 'hallow[ing] in order to desecrate'[64] parallels Anne Mellor's influential model of Romantic irony – according to which the poet's writing exhibits an ontology of chaos in circularly exposing the illusion that it fosters[65] – and is repeated with different emphases in Bakhtinian readings, which privilege the tendency in Byron's poetry to tip 'the reverenced life of the spirit [...] into a realm habited by the desires, needs and functions of the corporeal'.[66] While all these readings have in different ways helped to identify the significance of prominent tendencies in Byron's work, the emerging picture of the poet as a radical materialist, whose writing is prized as an immanent critique of Romantic aspiration, is seriously skewed. For Byron is also a poet of the immaterial.

His early verse, for example, is filled with spirits, seraphs, sylphs and shades, while in his major poetry spectral entities play an even more fully realized and integral role (one thinks, for instance, of the ghost of Francesca in *The Siege of Corinth*, the phantom of Astarte and the spirits in *Manfred*, the apostrophized presences in *Childe Harold's Pilgrimage*, the otherworldly cast of *Cain* or *Heaven and Earth*, the inhabitants of 'neutral space' in *The Vision of Judgment*, the body-swopping spirit of Arnold in *The Deformed Transformed* and the ghost of the Black Friar at the end of *Don Juan*). Such spectral entities tend to be passed over as poetic conventions, imaginative conveniences or synecdochic ciphers of psychological states, which aren't of any real interest in themselves and pose no ontological or epistemological challenges to a seamlessly materialist vision of reality.[67] And while Byron is championed as a fearless sceptic, who claimed 'I deny nothing, but doubt everything',[68] his adventurous curiosity about the limits of the *material* – which is equally a product of his daring scepticism – is less frequently examined. The present collection of essays by contrast considers the significance of Byron's ghosts – their status, their mode of being, their provenance and their function – from a variety of perspectives and seeks to correct the skewed impression of a poet who professed a 'partiality for *Spirit*'.[69]

There is another reason, aside from the attention it gives to the ghostly, why Byron's work is of particular relevance to debates about postmodern enchantment, which has to do with its philosophical outlook or characteristic stance towards reality.[70] Broadly speaking, this seems to be informed by two apparently antithetical tendencies. On the one hand, as we have noted, Byron was a sceptic;[71] the consequence of which is that he is 'of no party' (*DJ*, IX, 26) and arrives at no answer to life's ultimate questions. As he writes in *Don Juan*:

> My tendency is to philosophize
>   On most things, from a tyrant to a tree;
> But still the spouseless Virgin *Knowledge* flies.
>   What are we? and whence came we? what shall be
> Our *ultimate* existence? what's our present?
> Are questions answerless, and yet incessant. (VI, 63)

His scepticism is not, however, without limit or interruption, in spite of these 'incessant' and 'answerless' questions. Indeed, as a number of recent critics have observed, Byron's scepticism has a paradoxical aspect, in that it reflexively subverts itself and gives way to something other than scepticism ('I doubt if doubt itself be doubting', he writes in *Don Juan*, IX, 17).[72] This 'something' is worth pondering further, since it points us towards the second feature of the poet's characteristic stance.

Byron's self-suspending scepticism – which he appears to discover in attempting to make sense of his own multiplicity – anticipates the 'self-consummating' scepticism of postmodernism, which, as we have seen, conditions the possibility of its own escape and opens the way for a 'post-nihilistic' form of faith.[73] We might therefore expect to find in Byron's verse, too, the emergence of something like a 'second-order' or 'post-sceptical' naiveté, since if one doubts everything – as Byron does – this would obviously have to include doubt itself, and so would ultimately lead to a suspension of doubt or a recognition that, on the basis of scepticism alone, one cannot *rule out* the claims of faith. This negatively constituted openness – which is predicated on, even as it is qualified by, a comprehensive doubt – is evinced in Byron's pronouncement to Hodgson: 'I deny nothing, but doubt everything' and reaffirmed in *Don Juan*: 'He who doubts all things, nothing can deny' (XV, 88). And it is precisely this kind of suspension of scepticism that we find Byron accepting, in relation to ghosts, in his most sceptical poem:

> I merely mean to say what Johnson said,
>   That in the course of some six thousand years,
> All nations have believed that from the dead
>   A visitant at intervals appears;
> And what is strangest upon this strange head,
>   Is, that whatever bar the reason rears
> 'Gainst such belief, there's something stronger still
> In its behalf, let those deny who will. (*DJ*, XVI, 7)[74]

According to Shelley, who is unlikely to exaggerate the significance of something he hated so vehemently, it is this openness to something stronger than reason that makes Byron religious *in spite of* his scepticism:

> Moore [...] seems to deprecate *my* influence on [Byron's] mind on the subject of religion, & to attribute the tone assumed in Cain to my suggestions [...] Pray assure him that I have not the smallest influence over Lord Byron, in this particular; if I had I certainly should employ it to eradicate from his great mind the delusions of Christianity, which in spite of his reason, seem perpetually to recur, & to lay [sic] in ambush for the hours of sickness & distress.[75]

While here at least Shelley deplores the renunciation of reason as a swerve away from reality, it seems that for Byron, by contrast, reason may *obscure* our perception of that which is. We should notice, however, that while Byron is prepared to countenance a reality beyond the purview of reason, what he defends isn't an uncritical or unthinking credulity, since in both cases the poet's suspicions persist but are transcended by 'something stronger still'. One is reminded of his choice of epigraph for *Manfred* ('There are more things in heaven and earth, Horatio, / Than are dreamt of in your philosophy'),[76] except that in *Don Juan* both perspectives – Horatio's sceptical rationalism and Hamlet's openness to that which exceeds it – are paradoxically contained within the same subjectivity. And it is this conjunction of scepticism and metaphysical openness – the insignia of which is the posture of wonder – that I suggest constitutes the poet's characteristic stance towards reality. For while Byron liked to advertise the ennui by which he was also genuinely tormented, his poetry is filled with moments of suddenly unobstructed and dilated attention, when scepticism gives way to awestruck stasis, as he gazes in raw amazement at 'this unriddled wonder, / The World' (*DJ*, XI, 3). The importance of these moments of wonder in Byron's verse has been emphasized by Bernard Beatty:

> When Byron looks at the familiar and everyday world, he does so with 'The difficult air of the mountain's top' still in his being. He enters more fully into that familiar world in his poetry and in his life than most of us, but retains always that sense of oddity, precariousness, blankness, danger and wonder that marks the one who stands 'with naked head' buffeted by 'contending tempests' on 'The loftiest peaks'. [...] A main reason for reading and needing poetry is that it can recall us to a proper sense of amazement at the world; [...] Byron had this sense of astonishment at things acutely and he writes directly out of it.[77]

We can see this sense of astonishment or radical wonder in those moments when the poet suddenly stands still and says 'lo!' (as he does, for example, in contemplation of the Velino waterfall or on entering St Peter's)[78] and then gestures towards some heart-astounding facet of the world – or the even more heart-astounding fact that there is a world at all. Indeed, it's perhaps not too much of an exaggeration to suggest that if *Childe Harold's Pilgrimage* could be said to have a 'plot', it is structured as a series of such 'lo!' moments – the supreme instance of which is the radiant adagio that is the vision of Venice, on which the curtain of Canto IV is lifted. This sense of wonder – which is memorably described by G.K. Chesterton as the capacity to see things 'in a kind of sunlight of surprise'[79] – is incipiently signalled in the apostrophic effusions that ladder the fabric of Byron's narrative verse ('And as for Love – Oh Love! – We will proceed')[80] and is also apparent in his 'effervescent' syntax, which excitedly treads water in its accretive descriptions (one thinks, for instance, of the lines in *The Giaour* describing the 'loveliness in death' of Greece, which stave off their main clause with a proliferation of intoxicated impressions).[81]

The historical process of disenchantment outlined above manifestly correlates with a waning of this kind of wonder, which for Plato and Aristotle (and, in an elegiac key, for Kierkegaard, Heidegger and Wittgenstein as well) is the foundational disposition of philosophy but which during the course of the Enlightenment period came to be displaced by doubt.[82] Thus Carlyle's Teufelsdröckh, for example, laments that by the early nineteenth century, 'the reign of wonder is done, and God's world all disembellished and prosaic'.[83] It is therefore no surprise to discover a countervailing prestige accorded to wonder in Romantic writing. (The posture is exemplarily staged in the sestet of Keats's 'On First Looking into Chapman's Homer', which concludes with a moment, at once 'silent' and 'wild', of sublimely widened vision.)[84] Indeed, according to Tony Tanner, the attitude of existential wonder – in which the beholder looks at things as if they have never been looked at before – is 'one of the crucial romantic preferences'.[85] However, such moments of wonder in Byron's verse have been eclipsed or domesticated in recent years by a focus on the poet as congenital ironist and debunker of illusions, looking on from a position of quasi-transcendence at a clockwork cycle of creation and destruction. Such readings are of course intended to honour the poet as the least deceived, but in doing so they situate him safely on the far side of the uncanny and perplexing rift in the everyday that is the space of radical wonder.[86] And yet, for all his arch impassibility, Byron's poetry is engendered and distended by an openness to wonder, which is marked by a willingness to write out of something presently unfolding that he *doesn't* control and *cannot* fathom. It is this adventurous openness to the adventitiousness of things that underlies the experience of radical wonder.

This posture of wonder, in which the poet shows us and invites us to share in the perilous moment of astonishing experience, is the very opposite of the arch manipulation of self-conscious fictions to which recent criticism has reduced the poet. And while we are, as a result, no longer presented with a poet who couldn't really think or who thought like a child, what we have lost in the process is a sense of the irruptive disturbance of unmastered moments, in which the tables are turned and the rug is pulled from beneath the *ironist's* feet.[87] In other words, what is involved in such moments is a shift in the subject's relation to reality, from a 'nominative' to an 'accusative' stance – or from a relation of mastery to a posture of uncovetous receptivity – in which we can see a convergence back towards a pre-modern sense of enchantment and an anticipation of the 'self-deprecating' epistemology of postmodernism.

Stephen Cheeke has written perceptively about the adventitiousness of place in Byron's poetry in a way that comes close to this experience of radical wonder; *Childe Harold*, he avers,

> appears to be written not merely by an English nobleman travelling on the continent, but also by a sequence of places, or rather a sequence of geo-historical spots with pre-existing narratives, spots that in some way speak for themselves. Looking at it this way round Byron might be seen as a brilliantly individual amanuensis to whom the European landscape is dictating its histories.[88]

This is a fine observation, to which I would only wish to add that it isn't just their histories that such spots dictate. Rather, they speak to us about being itself – attesting to the astonishing fact there is an 'is' – and in doing so speak of something else as well. As Manfred explains, what he has also learned from nature is 'the language of another world' (III, iv, 7). To paraphrase a well-known Lacanian axiom: there is something in it more than itself.

The focus on scepticism, by Hoagwood and others, has to some degree countered this overemphasis on the impassable knowingness of Byron. However, this also tames the interrogative strangeness involved in the experience of radical wonder. For instead of a ceaseless shuttling in a paralysis of perpetual movement – to which the model of 'outside-less' scepticism condemns the poet – what we encounter in Byron's verse is a tarrying with or dwelling in wonder, as an epiphanic clearing *in the midst of* scepticism. That is to say, the Pyrrhonian 'sea of speculation'[89] is punctured by moments in which the everyday world startles us as something miraculous and is suddenly unveiled as 'a wide realm of wild reality';[90] moments in which the sceptic is silenced in contemplative assent to the given – even if, as in the case of the ghostly, this givenness exceeds the claims of reason; moments, in Manfred's astonished formulation, of '[i]nexplicable stillness' (III, i, 7), in which scepticism dilates into more profound wonder and reason yields to 'something stronger still'. Byron is rightly celebrated as a virtuoso of scepticism, but he is also a poet of radical wonder, which he evinces, preserves and helps to awaken in others. It is on account of this receptivity to wonder

– this openness to the mysterious that paradoxically has scepticism as the condition of its possibility – that Byron's imaginative reflections on the spectral may contribute to and be illuminated by the postmodern re-enchantment of the real.

IV

The essays in this collection are not governed by a single critical approach or sense of what is meant by the ghostly. On the contrary, it is one of the aims of the volume to highlight the diverse forms of spectrality that feature in Byron's verse. Some of these are more conventional – such as spirits, demons, the ghost of the Black Friar or the afterlife of the poet – though there are also essays on spectral violence, figures of 'half-aliveness' and flirtatious conjuring of fugitive presences. The opening chapter, by Bernard Beatty, 'Determining Unknown Modes of Being: A Map of Byron's Ghosts and Spirits', offers a much-needed overview of the nature, function, authority and significance of spectral entities in Byron's verse. While ghosts and spirits are frequently seen as 'bit-part' characters, peripheral to the poet's thinking or are univocally glossed as an insignia of indeterminacy, Beatty shows that Byron thought with discriminating precision about 'beings of the mind', heavenly and infernal spirits, 'palpable presences from the realm of the dead' and religious or eroticized resurrections, and reveals that an examination of such spectral presences tells us 'a great deal about Byron that could not be uncovered in any other way'. The poet's fascination with spirits and ghosts is helpfully contrasted with other Romantic writers' depictions of extra-material presences and opens the way for a luminous discussion on 'the radical incongruities and transferences between spirit and matter' that preoccupy Byron and invite diverse aesthetic and theological inquiries.

The second chapter, by Gavin Hopps, 'Shades of Being: Byron and the Trespassing of Ontology', preserves the general focus of Beatty's essay, but concentrates on a less conspicuous form of 'ontological trespassing' – namely, the advent of that which 'neither is nor is not', to which Derrida ascribes the logic of spectrality. The chapter focuses on three such 'shades of being' in particular: ghostly presences that flicker uncannily between being and not being; a numinous 'excess' in nature 'that is radically other than and yet paradoxically part of that which communicates it'; and an 'ec-centric' mode of being, in which human nature is 'elevated beyond itself'. In highlighting the prevalence of these shades of being – whose appearance the poet seeks to preserve by means of a 'syndetic fidgeting', the fashioning of 'linguistic icons' and other catachrestic strategies – the essay reveals a more extensive and coherent metaphysical vision than is customarily attributed to Byron, and argues that 'purely materialist readings [...] are inadequate to the poet's vision of art, nature and human being'.

In Chapter 3, 'Byron and the Noonday Demons', Mary Hurst continues the exploration of theological undercurrents in Byron's verse, but turns to the subject of infernal ghosts and focuses on the condition of melancholic boredom traditionally known as *acedia*. As Hurst argues, while we have come to see the dull violence of *ennui* – to which so many of Byron's figures are prone – as a wholly secular psychological state, it is in fact a silhouette of 'the Greek and Scholastic theological notion of *acedia*, which has been loosely translated from the term that describes a spiritual condition of the Desert Fathers, understood as "the noonday demon"'. Moreover, as Hurst reveals in an illuminating new reading of *Childe Harold's Pilgrimage*, 'the spiritual origins of *acedia* provide us with a vocabulary that foreshadows aspects of Byron and his poetry, which secular terms such as melancholy and *ennui* do not'. Thus, she concludes, if we probe Byron's descriptions of boredom and *ennui*, 'we cannot progress very far without the spiritual vocabulary of demons'.

One of the obvious problems with ghosts is that they won't go away, but they are also problematic as they don't fully arrive either. Dale Townshend's chapter, 'Conjuration and Exorcism: Byron's Spectral Rhetoric', explores this dual elusiveness in the 'oppositional but complementary gestures' of 'ghostly invitation and expulsion' that are elaborated across Byron's poetry. Opening his discussion with reference to a hitherto unexamined tract, *Spiritual Interview with Lord Byron* (1880), and drawing on recent theoretical writing by Derrida and de Man on the signature and epitaphs, Townshend examines the spectral efficiency of the poet's name and traces the shift in Byron's conceptualization of fame 'from a positive ghostly entity that is actively pursued and invoked to a negative phantasm that is to be wholeheartedly rejected or exorcised'. In the course of which, Townshend draws attention to the way that Romanticism offers itself – even as it is preoccupied with ghosts of its own – 'as an antidote to Gothic excess', while highlighting Byron's more complex desire on the one hand to exploit what Wordsworth described as 'this degrading thirst after outrageous stimulation' and on the other to 'present the Gothic vogue for ghosts in a somewhat more positive light'. This positive polarity is elaborated in Townshend's conclusion, which turns to Derrida's *Specters of Marx* and relates its advocacy of 'an ethics of ghostliness' to the defiant elusiveness of Byron's ghosts, in which the ineradicable alterity of the other is preserved.

Chapter 5, 'Byron avec Sade: Material and Spectral Violence in *Childe Harold's Pilgrimage* Canto IV', by Piya Pal-Lapinski, extends the ethical focus of the preceding chapter but leaves aside the positive polarity of the spectre and concentrates instead on a 'phantasmatic, symbolic violence' that exceeds material force. Pal-Lapinski looks at the way Sade's obsession with a pure corporeal violence is transformed in *Childe Harold* IV into a specifically Byronic discourse of violence, in which the material violence of history and spectral violence of the sign converge. In order to theorize such forms of violence, Pal-Lapinski puts the poem into dialogue with Walter Benjamin's 'Critique of Violence', Derrida's 'Violence and Metaphysics' and Agamben's work on 'bare life' – a form of existence which is at once 'spectral' in its dissolution of legal and political existence but 'material' in its association with sovereign power and juridical violence. Against this theoretical background, the chapter ponders the following questions: how does a 'spectral' Byronic violence both encompass and move beyond its Sadean counterpart? How does it distinguish itself from the ferocious distillation of the 'pure' materiality of violence in Sade? The chapter concludes with a consideration of architectural spaces in the Palazzo Ducale – as the symbolic centre of material and spectral violence in the poem – and the way that these spaces conflate the violence of war, politics and torture.

In Chapter 6, ''Twixt Life and Death': *Childe Harold's Pilgrimage, Don Juan* and the Sublime', Philip Shaw keeps questions of violence and nihilism in view, while reconsidering Romantic discourses on the sublime, in light of Žižek's neo-Lacanian account, according to which, the truth revealed by the sublime is 'nothing less than the ultimate nullity of being'. Beginning with their origins in the sceptical tradition, Shaw tests the relevance of such nihilistic interpretations for Byron's poetry, deftly interweaving philosophical exposition with close readings of *Childe Harold's Pilgrimage* and *Don Juan*. As Shaw contends, although 'Byron appears to share Žižek's suspicion of the transcendental aspirations of the sublime, his particular critique is directed not against transcendentalism *per se* but rather against the ambitions of the sublime to take the place of religion.' Indeed, what Shaw uncovers over the course of his investigation of *Don Juan* is 'a faith founded paradoxically on doubt', which prompts him to argue that 'for Byron the encounter with the sublime leads not to the triumph of Reason nor to its nihilistic voiding but results, rather, in the opening out of consciousness to the haunting of the divine'.

In her chapter 'Byron, Ann Radcliffe and the Religious Implications of the Explained Supernatural', Alison Milbank has her sights relatedly set on 'the complex nature of the poet's attitude to the transcendent' and concurs with Shaw that Byron 'turns scepticism into a religious value'. However, while arguing that *Don Juan* effects a 're-enchantment of the material' and attempts to 'keep awake the possibility of the transcendent', she seeks to 'mediate between the Christian idealism of Bernard Beatty's interpretation [...] and those, like Jerome McGann, who uphold Byron's ultimate scepticism'. Beginning with the poet's 'damned and brooding heroes', Milbank outlines the Gothic novel's debt to Byron, who is on the one hand aligned with 'Walpole and Matthew Lewis's Whiggish and "masculine" Gothic' and yet is also on the other hand aligned to 'the stance and the particular discourse of what might be called the "female" Gothic of Radcliffe', on account of the narrator's 'pensive melancholy', which is the 'shared moral discourse of the society of the virtuous in Radcliffe's fiction'. After an ingenious rereading of the 'explained' supernatural – according to which all phenomena are returned to the 'natural' order retroactively 'shadowed with the supernatural' – Milbank turns to the ghost scenes of *Don Juan* and the theological importance of the poem's 'mediatory women'. On the basis of this twofold model of 'benign mediation', she is then able to argue that Byron traces a numinous middle path between 'idealism and a dead materialism'.

Peter Graham's chapter, 'The Haunting of *Don Juan*', offers an alternative reading of the English Cantos' erotic spectral escapades and identifies a number of other ways in which the poem is haunted. These include the protagonist's status as an intertextual revenant; the poet's unstable blending of memory and imagination; the poem's depictions of 'the spirit-flesh amalgam that for [Byron] constitutes humanity'; and the semi-personified Platonic presences, such as Love and Philosophy, that appear throughout the poem. The major part of the chapter, though, is given over to a sparkling close reading of the Black Friar narrative. According to Graham, the ghost story of Canto XVI is 'a narratological hybrid', which draws upon the conventions of the Gothic supernatural tale but also upon the civilized comedy of manners, and in this way 'scramble[s] the signals that, unmixed, would indicate how readers should appraise the details'. Helpfully contrasting Byron's narrative with Jane Austen's parodic blending of conventions in *Northanger Abbey*, Graham draws an epistemological moral from the tale of the Black Friar, which, he argues, 'encourages the reader to discard rigid preconceptions and to cultivate an open-minded, self-doubting attitude that's receptive to all possibilities yet also sceptical about them'. For Graham, it is thus a virtue as well as a matter of exquisite skill that Byron 'leave[s] the thing a problem'.

Susan Wolfson has recently drawn attention to 'the intimate relation of ghostliness and gossip in the Byronic register' and has spoken of the 'vast social text of speculation and opinion' that surrounded the poet as 'the elusive ghost of another Byronic text'.[91] Corin Throsby's chapter, 'Being neither Here nor There: Byron and the Art of Flirtation', turns away from the 'old-fashioned' ghosts of *Don Juan* and focuses instead on such 'social' or 'non-Gothic' forms of spectrality, which she identifies as a species of flirtation. As Throsby explains, for Byron – who was a consummate flirt – this typically involves a gesture in which 'disclosure and veiling' coincide, which gives rise to a peculiarly fugitive presence that seems to allure the more it eludes our grasp. Such 'flirtatious' gestures, Throsby contends, are a feature of Byron's poetic style as well as an extra-textual habit, for the poet teasingly engenders 'apparitional forms' by including in his work 'just enough biographical information [...] to encourage [his readers] to believe that his characters are a thinly disguised version of himself'. Focusing in detail on *The Giaour*, the chapter examines the poem's alluringly elusive narrative, with its shadowy characters and 'curtain of asterisks', and the equally teasing circumstances of its gradual dissemination. As Paul West once observed, there is something 'radioactive' about Byron, whose presence somehow lives beyond itself, flickering uncannily in forms not his. *The Giaour*, as Throsby's discussion skilfully reveals, is teeming with such 'radioactive' presences, which testify to the erotic charge of the ghostly.

The Afterword, by Peter Allender, 'Blowing on a Dead Man's Embers: Byron's Biographical Ghosts', discusses the ways in which literary biographies attempt to 'bring the dead to life', with varying degrees of sympathy and animosity. Noting the dramatic alteration in assessments of Byron's significance – from George Eliot's account of his 'melancholy heroism' and his 'high and sympathetic purpose' to Phyllis Grosskurth's description of him as the bored and helpless protagonist in 'a black comic opera' – Allender reflects on what has been gained and lost in the spate of recent biographies of the poet. After a brief discussion of Ian Hamilton's chapter on Byron in *Keepers of the Flame* and Jerome McGann's portrait of the poet in *Byron and Romanticism*, the chapter focuses on Kay Redfield Jamison's *Touched with Fire: Manic Depressive Illness and the Artistic Temperament*, Grosskurth's *Byron: The Flawed Angel*, Benita Eisler's *Byron: Child of Passion, Fool of Fame* and Fiona MacCarthy's *Byron: Life and Legend* – the author of which claimed that the poet's ghost was 'operating a posthumous vendetta' aimed at preventing her from finishing the biography. These various attempts at keeping Byron's flame alight prompt insightful comments on the poet's theatricality and notorious mobility; the peculiar way in which he was, like many of his heroes, 'haunted by his own thoughts and moods'; and the 'deeply redemptive spirit [he brought] to the problems of despair, ennui, uncertainty and disillusionment'. In spite of the apparently insatiable appeal of such studies, however, Allender concludes that 'Byron's spirit eludes conventional chronological biography' – that uncanny genre that aspires to clairvoyance – and argues instead that his 'flame burns clearest in his own writing'.

In this, Allender speaks for all the contributors and corroborates the poet's 'unearthly' claim: 'Not in the air shall these my words disperse, / Though I be ashes'; for 'there is that within me which shall tire / Torture and Time, and breathe when I expire'.[92]

Notes

1 See Derrida, 'The Ghost Dance: An Interview with Jacques Derrida', trans. Jean-Luc Svoboda, in *Public*, 2 (1989); *Specters of Marx: The State of the Debt, the Work of Mourning, and the New International*, trans. Peggy Kamuf (New York, NY: Routledge, 1994); and 'Marx c'est quelqu'un', in *Marx en Jeu*, eds. Jacques Derrida, Marc Guillaume and Jean-Pierre Vincent (Paris: Descartes & Cie, 1997).

2 *Specters of Marx*, p. 225, n. 3.

3 Ibid., pp. 11–12.

4 Peter Buse and Andrew Stott, eds., *Ghosts: Deconstruction, Psychoanalysis, History* (Basingstoke: Macmillan Press, 1999), p. 10.

5 For a discussion of the divergent sources of 'hauntology' and the differing readings of the spectral to which they give rise, see Colin Davis, 'État Présent: Hauntology, Spectres and Phantoms', in *French Studies*, 59:3 (2005).

6 Jacques Lacan, *The Ethics of Psychoanalysis, 1959–1960*, trans. Dennis Porter (New York, NY: W.W. Norton, 1992), p. 270ff.; Nicolas Abraham and Maria Torok, *The Shell and the Kernel*, vol. 1: *Renewals of Psychoanalysis*, trans. Nicholas T. Rand (Chicago, IL: Chicago University Press, 1994); Slavoj Žižek, *Violence* (London: Profile Books, 2008), p. 129; Michel Foucault, *Aesthetics, Method and Epistemology*, vol. 2, in *The Essential Works of Michel Foucault, 1954–1984*, ed. James D. Faubion, trans. Robert Hurley (Harmondsworth: Penguin, 1998), p. 106; Emmanuel Levinas, *Otherwise than Being or Beyond Essence*, trans. Alphonso Lingis (Pittsburgh, PN: Duquesne University Press, 1998); Hélèna Cixous, 'Fiction and Its Phantoms: A Reading of Freud's *Das Unheimlich* ("The Uncanny")', in *New Literary History*, 7:3 (1976), p. 548; Vilashini Cooppan, *Worlds Within: National Narratives and Global Connections in Postcolonial Writing* (Stanford, CA: Stanford University Press, 2009), p. xvii; Judith Butler, *Bodies that Matter: On the Discursive Limits of 'Sex'* (London: Routledge, 1993); Carla Freccero, *Queer / Early / Modern* (Durham, NC: Duke University Press, 2006). For period studies on the subject of

spectrality, see *Romanticism and the Legacies of Jacques Derrida*, ed. David L. Clark, Special Issue of *Studies in Romanticism*, 46:2 (2007); Julian Wolfreys, *Victorian Hauntings: Spectrality, Gothic, the Uncanny and Literature* (Basingstoke: Palgrave, 2002); and Jean-Michel Rabaté, *The Ghosts of Modernity* (Florida, FL: University Press of Florida, 1996).

7 *Introduction to Criticism at the 21st Century*, ed. Julian Wolfreys (Edinburgh: Edinburgh University Press, 2002).

8 Gil Germain speaks of the 'spiritization' of humanity that results from the 'disincarnating power of technology' and 'our progressive release from the claims of the body' – that is, 'from the demands placed on us as creatures of spatiotemporal reality'. Germain, *Spirits in the Material World: The Challenge of Technology* (Maryland: Lexington Books, 2009), pp. xxii, xv.

9 Batchen, 'Spectres of Cyberspace', in *The Visual Culture Reader*, ed. Nicholas Mirzoeff (London: Routledge, 1998), p. 237. Emphasis in the original unless otherwise stated.

10 Jameson, 'Marx's Purloined Letter', in *Ghostly Demarcations: A Symposium on Jacques Derrida's Specters of Marx*, ed. Michael Sprinker (New York, NY: Verso, 1999), p. 39.

11 Luckhurst, 'The Contemporary London Gothic and the Limits of the "Spectral Turn"', in *Textual Practice*, 16:3 (2002), p. 536.

12 Derrida, 'The Rhetoric of Drugs', in *Points ... Interviews, 1974–1994*, trans. Peggy Kamuf et al. (Stanford, CA: Stanford University Press, 1995), p. 238.

13 *Kerygma and Myth: A Theological Debate*, with contributions by Rudolf Bultmann, Ernst Lohmeyer, Julius Schniewind, Friedrich Schumann, Helmut Thielicke and Austin Farrer, trans. Reginald H. Fuller (London: SPCK, 1954), p. 20.

14 See, for example, Zygmunt Bauman, *Intimations of Postmodernism* (London: Routledge, 1992); Graham Ward, *Cities of God* (London: Routledge, 2000); and *Theology and Contemporary Critical Theory* (Basingstoke: Macmillan, 2000); Charles Taylor, *A Secular Age* (Cambridge, MA: Harvard University Press, 2007); and Patrick Sherry, 'Disenchantment, Re-Enchantment, and Enchantment', in *Modern Theology*, 25:3 (2009).

15 Weber, *The Protestant Ethic and the Spirit of Capitalism*, trans. Talcott Parsons (London: Unwin Hyman, 1989).

16 Schiller speaks of '*Die entgötterte Natur*' (168) and doesn't in fact refer to '*Entzauberung*' in the poem.

17 The disenchantment involved in the scientific method is famously described by Keats in *Lamia* (1819): 'There was an awful rainbow once in heaven: / We know her woof, her texture; she is given / In the dull catalogue of common things. / Philosophy will clip an Angel's wings, / Conquer all mysteries by rule and line, / Empty the haunted air, and gnomed mine – / Unweave a rainbow, as it erewhile made / The tender-person'd Lamia melt into a shade' (II, 231–38).

18 The role played by the Reformation in Weber's disenchantment thesis has been qualified and questioned by more recent studies. Scholars such as Robert W. Scribner, for example, have argued that things weren't in fact as black and white as Weber's narrative suggests. This is partly because Protestantism exchanged a pre-modern 'enchanted' cosmos for a 'moralized universe' – which continued to acknowledge divine involvement in terrestrial affairs – and had its own forms of 'covert evangelical sacramentalism'; partly because Catholicism was *also* engaged in

a policing of superstitious practices, and thus itself contributed to the process of 'desacralization'; and partly because there was a heretofore unnoticed discrepancy between the revolutionary pronouncements of doctrinal Protestantism and the 'untidiness of the phenomenon as it was put into practice'. Scribner, *Religion and Culture in Germany (1400–1800)*, ed. Lyndal Roper (Leiden: Brill, 2001), pp. 357, 289, 363.

19 Byron's relevance to the contemporary re-enchantment of the West is nicely illustrated by his cameo role in Susanna Clarke's bestselling fantasy novel *Jonathan Strange and Mr Norrell* (London: Bloomsbury, 2004), in which the poet is described as 'the one person in all the city [Venice] who treated the appearance of Eternal Night as a sort of entertainment' (p. 820).

20 See, especially, Gaiman's *Sandman* series (DC Comics, 1989–1996) and his novel *American Gods* (2001), in which the old gods of ancient mythology are engaged in battle with the new gods of Media, Technology, Transport *et al.*

21 Graham, *Representations of the Post/Human: Monsters, Aliens and Others in Popular Culture* (Manchester: Manchester University Press, 2002), p. 26.

22 Partridge, *The Re-Enchantment of the West*, vol. 1: *Alternative Spiritualities, Sacralization, Popular Culture and Occulture* (London: T&T Clark, 2004), pp. 119, 126, 123.

23 Bone, 'A Sense of Endings: Some Romantic and Postmodern Comparisons', in *Romanticism and Postmodernism*, ed. Edward Larrissy (Cambridge: Cambridge University Press, 1999), p. 83.

24 Partridge, *The Re-Enchantment of the West*, passim.

25 David Brown's reconception and cultural extension of the sacramental – which argues for the religious potential of marginalised or excluded areas of human experience – represents a more 'traditional' theological attempt to recover lost forms of enchantment. This might loosely be distinguished from 'postmodern' models of re-enchantment, in which there is more of an emphasis on the emergence of alternative forms of spirituality. See, in particular, Brown, *God and Enchantment of Place: Reclaiming Human Experience* (Oxford: Oxford University Press, 2004).

26 Partridge, *The Re-Enchantment of the West*, p. 4.

27 The quotation is from Michel de Certeau, *The Mystic Fable*, vol. 1: *The Sixteenth and Seventeenth Centuries*, trans. Michael B. Smith (Chicago, IL: University of Chicago Press, 1992), p. 41. I am indebted for this point to Graham Ward's 'Transcendence and Representation', in *Transcendence: Philosophy, Literature, and Theology Approach the Beyond*, ed. Regina Schwartz (London: Routledge, 2004).

28 For a balanced evaluation of the theological significance of postmodern enchantment, see Graham Ward's discussion of *Romeo and Juliet* in *True Religion* (Oxford: Blackwell, 2002), Chapter 1. For a consideration of 'fully secular' strategies for re-enchantment, see *The Re-Enchantment of the World: Secular Magic in a Rational Age*, eds. Joshua Landy and Michael Saler (Stanford, CA: Stanford University Press, 2009).

29 Graham, *Representations of the Post/Human*, p. 11.

30 Ibid., p. 9.

31 *True Religion*, p. 129. For a discriminating untangling of the taken-for-granted connection between religion and transcendence, which highlights the formative involvement of cultural, political and gendered contexts, see Graham, *Representations of the Post/Human*, Chapter 7.

32 See Vattimo, *Nihilism and Emancipation* (New York, NY: Columbia University Press, 2004); and Caputo, 'Spectral Hermeneutics: On the Weakness of God and the Theology of the Event', in *After the Death of God*, eds. John D. Caputo and Gianni Vattimo (New York, NY: Columbia University Press, 2007).

33 Hyman, *A Short History of Atheism* (London: I.B. Tauris & Co., 2010), p. xvii.

34 The subjunctive encompasses the hypothetical, the conditional, the dubitative and the optative as well as counterfactual states, so while it is set over against what are known as 'realis moods', it isn't absolutely shut off from reality.

35 An extreme example of this would be the fiction of Christine Brooke-Rose, who has a novel – *Between* – in which the copula 'to be' does not appear, and another – *Amalgamemnon* – in which all verbs appear in 'non-realizing' forms, and who has herself written a work of criticism entitled *A Rhetoric of the Unreal* (1981).

36 Keats, Letter to George and Tom Keats, 21, 27 (?) December 1817, in *LJK*, p. 193.

37 George Steiner, *Real Presences* (Chicago, IL: University of Chicago Press, 1989), p. 226.

38 See Jean-Luc Marion, *God Without Being: Hors Texte*, trans. Thomas A. Carlson (Chicago, IL: University of Chicago Press, 1991); and Richard Kearney, *The God Who May Be: A Hermeneutics of Religion* (Bloomington, IN: Indiana University Press, 2001).

39 Levinas, *Autrement qu'être ou au-dela' de l'essence* (The Hague: Martinus Nijhoff, 1974), p. 261.

40 Kierkegaard criticizes the 'one-sided' anxiety of modern scepticism – that is, its fear of believing on insufficient evidence – and notes that what this fails to take account of is the obverse risk or opportunity cost – namely, the forfeiture of a possible good that may be entailed by trust. As he writes in *Works of Love*: 'We can be deceived by believing what is untrue, but we certainly are also deceived by not believing what is true.' See Kierkegaard, *Works of Love*, trans. Howard V. and Edna H. Hong (Princeton, NJ: Princeton University Press, 1995), p. 5.

41 Jarvis, *Wordsworth's Philosophical Song* (Cambridge: Cambridge University Press, 2007), p. 147.

42 Ricoeur, *The Symbolism of Evil*, trans. Emerson Buchanan (Boston, MA: Beacon Press, 1967), p. 351.

43 Davis, 'The Skeptical Ghost: Alejandro Amenábar's *The Others* and the Return of the Dead', in *Popular Ghosts: The Haunted Spaces of Everyday Life*, eds. María del Pilar Blanco and Esther Peeren (New York, NY: Continuum, 2010), p. 67.

44 Mary Shelley, 'On Ghosts', in *SWMS*, 2, p. 143.

45 *Palgrave Advances in Byron Studies*, ed. Jane Stabler (Basingstoke: Palgrave Macmillan, 2007), p. 5.

46 Hawkes, 'Against Materialism in Literary Theory', in *The Return of Theory in Early Modern English Studies: Tarrying with the Subjunctive*, eds. Paul Cefalu and Bryan Reynolds (Basingstoke: Palgrave Macmillan, 2011), p. 237.

47 For an illuminating discussion of 'the aporetic philosophical problems hardwired into New Historicism and its organizing respect for alterity, its desire to "speak with the dead"', see Ken Jackson and Arthur F. Marotti, 'The Turn to the Religious in Early Modern English Studies', in *Criticism*, 46:1 (2004).

48 'Introduction', *An Oxford Companion to the Romantic Age: British Culture 1776–1832*, ed. Iain McCalman (Oxford: Oxford University Press, 1999), p. 2.

49 Watkins, *A Materialist Critique of English Romantic Drama* (Florida, FL: University Press of Florida, 1993), pp. 178, 151.

50 For a positive assessment of the corrective advances made by cultural materialism, see Alex Benchimol, 'Remaking the Romantic Period: Cultural Materialism, Cultural Studies and the Radical Public Sphere', in *Textual Practice*, 19:1 (2005).

51 McGann, *The Romantic Ideology: A Critical Investigation* (Chicago, IL: University of Chicago Press, 1983), p. 131.

52 Fuller, 'Keats and Anti-Romantic Ideology', in *The Challenge of Keats: Bicentenary Essays 1795–1995*, ed. Allan C. Christensen et al., *Studies in Literature*, 28 (Amsterdam: Rodopi, 2000), p. 10.

53 McGann's materialist polemic prompted the following riposte from Fuller: 'I like to fancy Jerome McGann regaling a mystic of any of the world's great religions with his argument that the idea that consciousness can set you free from material contingencies, and that poetry (say, the Upanishads) can administer to that freedom, is an illusion invented in the West in the late eighteenth century and now sustained by the universities of the capitalist world. [...] Being a milder character than I am, this mystic might reflect agreeably that the world is indeed full of illusions; and then, if he were feeling a little acid that day, that some illusions are more extraordinary than others.' Ibid.

54 Jackson and Marotti make a similar point: 'Most practitioners of early modern studies remain blithely unconcerned or unaware that deconstructive thought still wrestles with the aporia of self/other relations and has undergone its own explicit and complex turn to religion as a result. While the "linguistic" turn in philosophy provided by Derrida in the 1970s and 1980s had a profound impact on early modern studies, the "religious" turn of Derrida in the 1990s has gone largely unnoticed and, for us, consequently, alterity remains undertheorized. We have been, in brief, cafeteria critics of alterity.' ('The Turn to Religion in Early Modern English Studies', p. 178.)

55 Letter to Thomas Love Peacock, 15 February 1820, in *LPBS*, vol. II, p. 261.

56 Peacock, *Memoirs of Shelley and Other Essays and Reviews*, ed. Howard Mills (London: Rupert Hart-Davis, 1970), pp. 128–29.

57 Michel de Certeau, *The Practice of Everyday Life*, trans. S. Rendall (Berkeley, CA: University of California Press, 1999), p. 106.

58 For a judicious critique of the blanket rejection of Enlightenment values in certain recent accounts of postmodernism, see John Cottingham, *The Spiritual Dimension: Religion, Philosophy and Human Value* (Cambridge: Cambridge University Press, 2005), Chapter 6.

59 For an exploration of this contemporary relevance, see *Philosophical Romanticism*, ed. Nikolas Kompridis (London: Routledge, 2006).

60 Hulme, 'Romanticism and Classicism', in *Speculations*, ed. Herbert Read (London: Routledge, 1936), p. 118.

61 The story is of course much more complicated than this, not least because the advent of monotheism – which underwrote the pre-modern sense of enchantment – was itself originally a form of *dis*-enchantment, in that a polytheistic immanent sacrality came to be displaced by a more transcendent sense of the divine. This is the burden of 'Die Götter Griechenlandes', in which Schiller laments: '*Einen* zu bereichern, unter allen, / Mußte diese Götterwelt vergehn' (155–56).

62 Harold Bloom, *The Visionary Company: A Reading of English Romantic Poetry* (New York, NY: Cornell University Press, 1961), p. 262.

63 M.H. Abrams, *Natural Supernaturalism: Tradition and Revolution in Romantic Literature* (New York, NY: W.W. Norton, 1971), p. 13.

64 William Hazlitt, *The Spirit of the Age: or, Contemporary Portraits*, in *CWWH*, vol. XI, p. 75.

65 Mellor, *English Romantic Irony* (Cambridge, MA: Harvard University Press, 1980).

66 Philip Martin, 'Reading *Don Juan* with Bakhtin', in *Don Juan: Theory in Practice*, ed. Nigel Wood (Buckingham: Open University Press, 1993), p. 112.

67 See, for example, C.C. Barfoot, 'Hauntings 2: Byron's Phantoms', in *Centennial Hauntings: Pope, Byron and Eliot in the Year 88*, eds. C.C. Barfoot and Theo D'Haen (Amsterdam: Rodopi, 1990).

68 Letter to Francis Hodgson, 4 December 1811, *BLJ*, II, p. 136.

69 'Detached Thoughts', 98, *BLJ*, IX, p. 46.

70 Emily Bernhard Jackson surely overstates the case in claiming that Byron had a 'well thought-out and fully articulated philosophy of knowledge' (*The Development of Byron's Philosophy of Knowledge: Certain in Uncertainty* (Basingstoke: Palgrave Macmillan, 2010), p. 2). I would agree, however, that his poetry possesses a philosophical dimension – even in its *anti*-philosophical gestures – and that it is possible to discern recurrent tendencies in the poet's posture towards reality.

71 This has been argued at length, with different emphases and according to divergent conceptions of scepticism, by Edward Wayne Marjarum, *Byron as Skeptic and Believer* (New York, NY: Russell & Russell, 1962); Terence Allan Hoagwood, *Byron's Dialectic: Skepticism and the Critique of Culture* (Toronto: Bucknell University Press, 1993); and Emily Bernhard Jackson, *The Development of Byron's Philosophy of Knowledge*.

72 See Bernard Beatty, *Byron's 'Don Juan'* (Kent: Croon Helm, 1985); David J. Leigh, S.J., '*Infelix Culpa*: Poetry and the Skeptic's Faith in *Don Juan*', in *Keats-Shelley Journal*, 28 (1979); and the essays in the present volume by Philip Shaw and Alison Milbank. See also Hoxie Fairchild, who favours a divergent reading but who speaks of the 'sceptical road to Rome' (*Religious Trends in English Poetry*, vol. III: 1780–1830 (New York, NY: Columbia University Press, 1949), p. 438).

73 T.S. Eliot made a similar point in a sermon preached in Magdalene College Chapel, Cambridge, in 1948: 'One may become a Christian partly by pursuing scepticism to the utmost limit' (cited in *Inventions of the March Hare: Poems 1909–1917*, ed. Christopher Ricks (New York, NY: Harvest Books, 1998), p. 214).

74 Byron, as we know, was profoundly superstitious and repeatedly spoke of Newstead as haunted and of a 'strange fatality which seemed to hang over his existence' (Marjarum, *Byron as Skeptic and Believer*, p. 18). See also Arthur Palmer Hudson, 'The "Superstitious" Lord Byron', in *Studies in Philology*, 63:5 (1966).

75 Letter to Horace Smith, 11 April 1822, in *LPBS*, vol. II, p. 412.

76 According to Susan Wolfson, Byron's epigraph converts this adage into an ontology ('Byron's Ghosting Authority', in *ELH*, 76:3 (2009), p. 770).

77 Beatty, *'Don Juan' and Other Poems* (Harmondsworth: Penguin, 1987), pp. 21, 65.

78 *CHP*, IV, 71ff., 153ff.

79 'Wonder and the Wooden Post', in *The Coloured Lands* (London: Sheed and Ward, 1938), p. 157.

80 *DJ*, XV, 5.

81 *The Giaour*, 68ff.

82 For a panoramic account of the demise of wonder, see Hans Urs von Balthasar, *The Glory of the Lord*, vol. 4: *The Realm of Metaphysics in Antiquity*, trans. Brian McNeil et al. (Edinburgh: T&T Clark, 1991); and vol. 5: *The Realm of Metaphysics in the Modern Age*, trans. Oliver Davies et al. (Edinburgh: T&T Clark, 1991). For a discussion of the philosophical nature of wonder, see Josef Pieper, 'The Philosophical Act', in *Leisure: The Basis of Culture*, trans. Alexander Dru (New York, NY: Pantheon, 1952).

83 Carlyle, *Sartor Resartus* (Oxford: Oxford University Press, 1987), p. 54.

84 In the original manuscript version, Keats describes Cortez as staring at the Pacific with 'wond'ring eyes', which is subsequently changed to 'eagle eyes'.

85 Tanner, *The Reign of Wonder: Naivety and Reality in American Literature* (Cambridge: Cambridge University Press, 1965), p. 5.

86 Mary-Jane Rubenstein, *Strange Wonder: The Closure of Metaphysics and the Opening of Awe* (New York, NY: Columbia University Press, 2008), p. 10. As Rubenstein points out, wonder is not limited to positive or uplifting experiences and still less is it reducible to the sugarcoated conception of contemporary usage, but it is 'inherently ambivalent', and encompasses 'marvel and dread, amazement and terror' (p. 10).

87 What I am suggesting is that the 'permanent parabasis' of Romantic irony, which posits a perpetual dialectic of illusion and the disruption of illusion, is in Byron's poetry suspended or *wounded* by the opening of wonder, which constitutes a kind of 'meta' disruption, since the radically aporetic character of such moments dissipates the superordinate vantage that would be required to take their measure and identify such oscillations *as* a dialectic.

88 Cheeke, *Byron and Place: History, Translation, Nostalgia* (Basingstoke: Palgrave Macmillan, 2003), p. 41.

89 *DJ*, IX, 18.

90 'The Dream', 4.

91 Wolfson, 'Byron's Ghosting Authority', pp. 780, 773.

92 *CHP*, IV, 134, 137.

CHAPTER ONE

Determining Unknown Modes of Being: A Map of Byron's Ghosts and Spirits

Bernard Beatty

It is fashionable, still, to press the case for discontinuities and indeterminacies of all kinds. Byron himself, with some plausibility, is often hailed as a harbinger of this view of all worlds and all words as shifting, merging, non-concluding. Ghosts and spirits, in this view of things, would most naturally be seen as liminal, the shadows and spectral traces through which language-bearing animals make their indeterminate way.[1] It is certainly true that where Byron most explicitly talks about the business of ghosts – in cantos XV and XVI of *Don Juan* – a liminal context is immediately set up: ghosts are associated with 'the horizon's verge' (XV, 99), 'the limits of the coast' (XVI, 4) and with waterfalls and shade (XVI, 15).

Perhaps we may end up here, but it would not be a good place to begin, for Byron thought through categories, outlines and analogies as well as through processes and mergings. He dissolves but he also seeks out the contours of genres. Unlike Keats, he does not crowd intensities into a blurred but fecund centre; rather, he discriminates carefully between differing modes of being, even when they interact and change places. He thinks that some vast, apparently indefinable things can be mapped but others, more at hand, cannot. Ruined Rome, for instance, cannot be mapped according to Byron but, on the other hand, 'The ocean hath his chart, the stars their map' (*CHP*, IV, 81). I think that Byron's variegated poetry is more amenable to mapping than ruined Rome. So it is both helpful and possible to try and establish a basic map or chart of Byron's habitual practices in representing ghosts and spirits, which will presume that distinctions exist as well as connections and that the two basic habits of mind assist one another.

For instance, Byron seems customarily to make a distinction between ghosts and spirits.[2] Ghosts have been alive and are now dead. Spirits do not know death at all, for they live in some other sphere than mortals altogether, though some mortals claim to be essentially spirits. Fictions or 'beings of the mind', as Byron calls them, are more like ghosts than spirits and are sometimes indistinguishable from them. This works the other way round, too: ghosts and the realm of the dead in general are fictions. That does not mean that they are not 'true' or 'real' in any sense, but that they would not be realized without some act of making. Byron says 'I can repeople with the past' (*CHP*, IV, 19), and he does not distinguish between doing so with historical or non-historical presences. Either way, they are an available but non-manifest 'people' who need to be summoned into existence. This makes the writer sometimes analogous to the magician or necromancer, who can summon up the dead within a prescribed circle of incantation, as Manfred does. Byron does this, for example, when he stands in the Coliseum at night ('in this magic circle raise the dead', *CHP*, IV, 144), and we see a long-dead gladiator die again. The gladiator is based on a statue, a work of art,[3] so Byron's repeopling of the past repeats and participates in a past act of representation. Both statue and past seek life in our life. In the same way, the Venice of *Childe Harold's Pilgrimage* is crowded with formed fictional presences – 'Shylock and the Moor, / And Pierre' (IV, 4) – who mingle with the 'mighty shadows' and 'dim forms' of 'her dead Doges [...] declin'd to dust' (IV, 4, 15). Furthermore, the device that Byron uses is the rhetorical trope of 'visio' ('I see before me the Gladiator lie', IV, 140), in which the classical understanding of mimesis – a virtual copy of a possible or actual existent – is difficult to disentangle from a conception of the artist as prophetically realising the hitherto unrepresentable. This repeats therefore the cross-over between the realm of the fictional and the realm of the dead, the 'made' or fabricated and the world of shadows – 'this protracted dream' (IV, 185) – which was mentioned earlier and is so important in *Childe Harold's Pilgrimage*, especially Canto IV.

What else should be on our basic map? We can make a broad distinction of another kind between ghosts and spirits. It is not absolute, but it usually works. Ghosts have nothing to do with morality (other than reminding us of our mortality). They are simply summoned or palpable presences from the realm of death. Spirits, on the other hand, imply a moral order that cannot be evaded. The most obvious examples are *The Vision of Judgment* and *Heaven and Earth*. In the former, spirits are either 'a goodly work', like Michael (30) or, like Satan, who has

'Eternal wrath on his immortal face' (24), but the distinction between good and bad spirits, both of whom require obedience, is implied everywhere. Stanza 53 of *The Vision of Judgment* tells us that the ghosts of the dead theoretically come from hell – unless they are saints, like Peter – but once they are assembled in the law court of neutral space, we forget this. At the end of the poem, the devils return to hell, but the ghosts return to 'their own dominions', whose whereabouts, we are pointedly told, is 'undecided' (103). The change mirrors the reader's final attitude towards them. Ghosts bring indecisive presences.

In a similar way, the point of the trial is to establish the guilt of the ghost of George III for his political shortcomings, but he is allowed to creep into heaven at the end; all who see him as a present ghost are inclined to pity for the blind and powerless old man (68). *The Vision of Judgment* is undoubtedly what Byron would call an 'ethical' poem, but although the ghosts (in effect, Wilkes and 'Junius') participate in the trial, they do not have any special moral power or force as ghosts. Indeed, Satan rebukes Wilkes for acting exactly as he did in life (72). Two obvious exceptions to this rule are the ghost of Francesca in *The Siege of Corinth* (an important and special case, which we shall need to look at) and the ghosts in Sardanapalus's dream. Both of these imply a moral order and wish to affect characters in non-spectral reality. The ghost of Astarte hovers on the edge of this but does not quite cross over. Nevertheless, the distinction between the moral order of spirits and the amoral world of ghosts is a real – that is to say – working one.

The distinction between ghosts and spirits seems to be bound up with another, more surprising, emphasis. Ghosts imply mortality and demonstrate the impossibility of resurrection. In the first version of *Childe Harold's Pilgrimage* I and II, Byron goes out of his way to agree with the Sadduccees, who denied both the existence of spirits (angels) and the resurrection of the body.[4] When he comes to rewrite these stanzas in order to secure publication, he says only that there might be '[a] land of souls beyond that sable shore, / To shame the doctrine of the Sadducee' (II, 8). Yet Byron knew better than most that the Sadducees were not concerned with the Greek idea of the immortality of the soul, but with the inter-testamental notion of the resurrection of the body; and the emphasis of his lines ('souls' [...] 'shore') is on some ghostly after-presence that is not much more vital than Sheol and Hades. Commentators have pored over these lines in order to find out Byron's viewpoint on such matters. I would prefer to emphasise that *Childe Harold's Pilgrimage* as a poem could not tolerate the idea of resurrection. It emphasises 'the grass / Which now beneath them, but above shall grow' over the dead of Waterloo, who were once 'living valour [...] burning with high hope' (III, 27), just as we see the newly dead of Thrasimene hurtling into the crack made by an earthquake (IV, 63). It is true that Byron says that the Earth 'bore them to Eternity' (IV, 64), but the eternity here is that of the sunset meeting point 'Where the Day joins the past Eternity' (IV, 27). That is an exact, though unusual, placing and coinage. The dead are not in an eternity apart from time – an eternity to which the transformed body might be resurrected or the timeless soul enter – but a 'past Eternity' which preserves their past identity and moment of dying for ever. They are ghosts in this sense – shadowy but unobliterated past presences that haunt the places where they lived and died, still fashioning the shapes and utterances of those who are aware of them. These are Manfred's 'dead, but sceptred sovereigns, who still rule / Our spirits from their urns' (III, iv, 40–41), though they remain in their urns or under marble slabs or grass and trees, which, unlike them, will 'revive / With fruits and fertile promise' each spring (*CHP*, III, 30).

We can put some further distinct places on the map. Some of Byron's ghosts talk, although most are silent or merge invisibly with the rhetoric and spectral authority of the poet. Some ghosts announce themselves or can be discerned in quiet attentiveness; others have to be summoned in some way. Byron is intermittently interested in armies of ghosts and the ghosts of armies and, once, peoples the battlements of Rome with a row of phantoms, who 'flit along the eternal city's rampart, / And stretch their glorious, gory, shadowy hands' (*The Deformed Transformed*, I, ii, 192–93), like Gray's 'griesly band' of avenging ghosts around Snowdon in 'The Bard' (45). However, there is enough on our map now to give us a broad sense of Byron's spirit topography.[5]

What we notice at first is the sheer number of ghosts and spirits in Byron's oeuvre. Ghosts figure little in his lyrics, but if we scan the thirty major poems and translations, 50 per cent of them contain some kind of significant mention of ghosts or spirits, and in over half of this half the presence of, or reference to, ghosts and spirits is a crucial feature.[6] If we simply take the eight dramas, for instance, 50 per cent depend upon spirits as major characters and 50 per cent do not.

I suppose that if we compare this incidence of supernatural figures with the spirit-laden poetry of, say, Blake, Southey or Shelley, it will not seem that surprising. Yet Byron gives a far more historically and realistically grounded version of life than Blake, Southey or Shelley, so we should be surprised, perhaps, by the high incidence of spectres and spirits in his poetry, which are in any case far more differentiated and vivid than theirs. Secondly, Byron is much more concerned with the status and mode of being of ghosts and spirits – both ontological and fictional – than his contemporaries. A book on spirits in Southey, for example, would not tell you much about him, but the present volume reveals a great deal about Byron that could not be uncovered in any other way.

The business of resurrection is a case in point. Francesca, in *The Siege of Corinth*, is Byron's most realized ghost and the only one, apart from Wilkes and 'Junius', to talk at any length. Her entrance is choreographed skilfully within a traditional set. Alp stands by a ruined temple, much as the poet stands in front of the ruined Parthenon in Canto II of *Childe Harold's Pilgrimage*. Like the poet in stanza X, Alp then sits down to meditate 'at a pillar's base'. The posture reminds us of the schoolboy Byron lying on the Peachy Stone in Harrow churchyard, which is reminiscent, most distantly, of Jacob lying down with his head upon a stone before his vision (Genesis 28: 10–22) and, more recently, of eighteenth-century poets or clergymen meditating in churchyards, of which William Sotheby's 'Nettley Abbey. Midnight' is a contemporary example (1790):

> Upon the mossy stone, I lie reclined,
> And to a visionary world resigned
> Call the pale spectres forth from the forgotten tombs. (18–20)[7]

The poet of *Childe Harold's Pilgrimage*, too, sits by a 'massy stone', though the ghosts of the poem are not much more than meditated presences until Canto IV. They are slightly more than this in Sotheby's poem – they are the ghosts of long-dead monks, who threaten revenge on the heirs of the usurping family that drove them out at the time of the Reformation, just like the Black Friar in Norman Abbey. But Francesca is far more than this. She even has, uniquely for Byron's ghosts, apart from *The Vision of Judgment*, a degree of substantiality. She can put her hand onto Alp's, whence 'shot a chillness to his heart' (552). Admittedly, this same hand is literally 'transparent' (516), but it can be felt. Doubtless, this detail comes from familiar figures such as Margaret's ghost in David Mallet's well-known ballad of that title, whose lily hand is 'clay-cold'.[8] Yet Byron does not put this detail in for the sake of intertextuality. It is part of a delicate tapestry of hand movements at this stage in the poem. When Alp sees her, '[h]is trembling hands refused to sign / The cross he deem'd no more divine' (493–94); she raises her hand on high (515), speaks to him and he replies. In return, dramatically, '[u]pon his hand she laid her own', which 'thrilled to the bone' (549–50). This has an unmistakeable erotic charge, but also testifies to Byron's fascination with the direct mingling of the living and dead. In Sardanapalus's dream, the most dreadful moment is when he directly encounters the dead Nimrod: 'then – then / The hunter laid his hand on mine' (IV, i, 142–43). This is the point where the ghosts in his dream have 'lost a part of death to come to me, / And I the half of life to sit by them' (126–27). Alp sits in the same terrifying propinquity. But the detail (ten lines are devoted to it) has further force. Francesca lays her dead hand on his with a mixture of affection and menace. He cannot release her hold (555). We are, I think, to presume that he is still holding her hand while she delivers her second speech to him. The point of this speech is to influence Alp to renounce his apostasy and accept a mixture of mercy and judgment, and it ends with an ultimatum, which Alp refuses. Francesca, in this way, acts like a ghost in Senecan or Renaissance drama, who represents both revenge and warning. However, she remains a phantom, despite her palpable hands. We see her as this because of what precedes this stage-set dialogue.

Alp walks towards the walls of enemy Corinth. He leads an enchanted life here, mysteriously saved from enemy fire. Similarly, although this is not directly stated, he moves unconsciously towards the city where Francesca lived and the community from which he sprang. It is not surprising that Francesca in return moves towards him. Nevertheless, what he encounters beneath the walls of Corinth is the exact opposite of these spiritual emphases. In one of the most celebrated passages in the poem, Alp sees dogs tearing the flesh and bones of the dead, who have been killed in earlier stages of the siege. Byron directs our horrified attention especially to the skull from which the flesh has been peeled like a fig:

> And their white tusks crunched o'er the whiter skull,
> As it slipped through their jaws, when their edge grew dull [...].
> (415–16)

We move immediately from this scene into a scene where 'a temple in ruin stands' (450) and thence, via Alp reclining 'at a pillar's base' (462), to the appearance of Francesca.

This sequence is curiously like that of *Childe Harold's Pilgrimage*. There, the ruins of the Parthenon temple are juxtaposed with the skull of some forgotten hero (II, 1–6). The poet asks disdainfully of the skull: 'Is that a temple where a God may dwell?' (II, 5). The implication is that there are no gods in the temple and no inhabiting spirit in the flesh. There is an irrevocable gap between flesh and spirit. The spirits of the past may haunt Greece still – that is one thing – but neither soul nor spirit can transfigure the world of matter. That is why this passage leads directly in its original version to the pro-Sadducee stanza. The effect in *The Siege of Corinth* is not quite the same as this, for Francesca is almost palpable, but the effect of seeing this gliding ghost with transparent hands immediately after the description of dogs tearing a head to pieces is to render belief in any resurrection impossible. This effect is repeated more strikingly and enigmatically at the end of the poem, when Minotti ignites the explosion that transforms living bodies to unresurrectable substance:

> Many a tall and goodly man,
> Scorched and shrivelled to a span,
> When he fell to earth again
> Like a cinder strewed the plain [...]. (987–90)

Byron carefully links this scene with the earlier one by telling us that the explosion causes the wild dogs to flee and leave 'the unburied dead' (1015). We should link both of these accounts to the vivid description of Alp's death.

Importantly, this occurs at the exact moment when he learns that Francesca has died. Her father says that he does not weep 'for her spirit's flight' (817). We might imagine that the poet would want to make something out of Alp's sudden realization that, earlier on, he had been talking to a ghost (uniquely, in Byron's work, here someone encounters a ghost without realising it), but Byron puts in an 'already with the slain' (821), which suggests that he has no time to register the fact. Instead, and in opposition to Minotti's vocabulary of 'spirit's flight', Byron insists on the experience of death as something wholly contained and material:

> The sharp shot dashed Alp to the ground;
> Ere an eye could view the wound
> That crashed through the brain of the infidel,
> Round he spun, and down he fell [...]. (830–33)

We are told that his trunk is still palpitating and blood is oozing from his mouth, though there is no throb in his pulse. The phrase 'no more to rise' applies to him and to the 'goodly man' who is now in cinders. Indeed, the hurling of the living Corinthians into the air from whence they descend in fragments or ashes is a ghastly parody of St Paul's words addressed to earlier Corinthians, who doubted the resurrection: 'we will all be changed – in a flash, in the twinkling of an eye, at the last trumpet. For the trumpet will sound, the dead will be raised imperishable, and we will be changed' (1 Corinthians 15: 51–52). The ghost of Francesca needs this opposing frame of irreducible materiality in order to establish her merely spectral presence. She confirms rather than contradicts it. There is, however, one detail that does contradict it.

Just before the explosion, Byron describes the church in which the gunpowder has been stored. On the altar is still the chalice used at the morning Mass, which is deliberately presented in a believer's terms:

> That morn it held the holy wine,
> Converted by Christ to his blood so divine,
> [...]
> Still a few drops within it lay [...]. (957–58, 961)

This patently resurrected living blood, in opposition to the death-announcing blood oozing from Alp's corpse, is blown up with the rest. We may wonder why Byron goes out of his way momentarily to suggest this third possibility of miraculous resurrection, alongside spectral existence and absolute materiality. He carefully seeks out the explicit formulas of transubstantiation ('wine converted [...] to [...] blood'), rather than some vague Zwinglian symbolism. In doing so, he clearly seeks out a different kind of spirit/matter juxtaposition than that of the earlier canine carnival over the dead (a horrible play on words) with the appearance of a ghost in this equally immediate juxtaposition of transubstantiated indestructible matter and mere matter that is destroyed and recycled endlessly and without point.

For Byron, matter is normally the antithesis to spirit. Byron is a thorough-going dualist for most of the time. This position fits his habitual sense that the world cannot be fully represented by any single version of it and his dislike of any unitary system of thinking in philosophy, politics or poetry. Matter and spirit seem to destroy the absolute authority of each other. Nevertheless, although matter is the antithesis to spirit, Byron is also intrigued by the idea that an absolute concentration on materiality flips into something else. This is a different kind of dualism altogether. The most explicit evidence for this is in his letter to Moore (8 March 1822):

> I am really a great admirer of tangible religion [...] What with incense, pictures, statues, confession, absolution, – there is something sensible to grasp at. Besides it leaves no possibility of doubt; for those who swallow their Deity, really and truly, in transubstantiation, can hardly find anything else otherwise than easy of digestion.
> I am afraid that this may sound flippant, but I don't mean it to be so;

only my turn of mind is so given to taking things in the absurd point of view, that it breaks out in spite of everything every now and then.[9]

In the seven years that separate this letter from the transubstantiation reference in *The Siege of Corinth*, Byron was as much concerned with resurrected matter as with ghosts or spirits but, in the first instance, this has more to do with eros than Christianity. The very first instance occurs in *Mazeppa*. The celebrated description of the protagonist's lapse into unconsciousness tied to a dead horse reads much as Alp's experience of death:

> An icy sickness curdling o'er
> My heart, and sparks that cross'd my brain –
> A gasp, a throb, a start of pain,
> A sigh, and nothing more. (792–95)

The unremittingness of 'nothing more' reminds us of Alp's 'no more to rise'. But in *Mazeppa* of course, the next line (across a section's blank gap) says 'something more' and 'will rise again':

> I woke – where was I? – Do I see
> A human face look down on me?

We find the same pattern in *Don Juan*, where shipwrecked Juan reaches the shore alongside a corpse who had died 'two days before, and now had found / An unknown barren beach for burial ground' (II, 109). Juan experiences the ending that Alp and Mazeppa experience ('his dizzy brain spun fast, / And down he sunk', II, 110), but Juan, unlike Alp and the unresurrected two-day corpse beside him, wakes, much as Mazeppa does, to a pretty female face that summons him to a new life. Torquil, in *The Island*, has the same experience, but remains conscious throughout the change. Torquil asks if Neuha has

> brought me here to die?
> Is this a place of safety, or a grave,
> And yon huge rock the tombstone of the wave? (IV, 54–56)

The vocabulary here recalls the most elaborate of Byron's ghost settings – the extraordinarily choreographed conclusion to *The Bride of Abydos*, where the stone pillar that acts as a tombstone for Zuleika (the pillar and tombstone are the usual precursors of spectral presence in Byron, as we have already seen) is suddenly moved miraculously towards the shore line, half in and half out of the water. This is the spot where Selim was shot, just as Alp was, without any space of time for him to register it, in an instant's change. Yet there is a ghostly afterlife for Selim that

Alp cannot have, for there, by night, 'a ghastly turban'd head' reclines upon the tombstone (II, 725–26) in some dreadful parody of the sleeping Jacob or the meditative Harrow schoolboy.

Torquil, led by Neuha, fears that he has been brought to a similar conjunction as Selim (slaughtered while his gaze is momentarily distracted by Zuleika), though of course he is resurrected to new life in the womb of the rock that only appears to be a tombstone. Strikingly, the pursuing sailors assume that he has become a ghost – 'The vanish'd phantom of a seaman's dream' (IV, 82) – but what would they know about it?

Once again, Byron is at pains to stress the materiality of this wholly new unconditioned life beyond the apparent tombstone. Neuha has carefully brought kindling for a new fire and piled up food, including a turtle-shell, 'which bore / A banquet in the flesh it covered o'er' (IV, 171–72). This is the exact opposite of the 'carnival' of human flesh that the dogs enjoy under the walls of Corinth. The insistence on physical detail, which is contrasted with the change of Fletcher Christian's body into basic matter ('His body crushed into one gory mass', IV, 342) and with the ghosts of the sailor's imaginings, reminds us of the New Testament insistence that the resurrected Jesus, whatever He is, is definitely not a ghost, for He eats some cooked fish on the sea shore (John 21: 12–13). However, the resurrection beyond death into new life for Mazeppa, Juan and Torquil is of course accomplished by the nurturing body of a woman, not by the unseen operations of the Holy Spirit. What is important – and we need to mark this on our map – is that an insistence on resurrection cancels out the possibility of ghostly appearance, just as an insistence on ghostly presence cancels out the possibility of resurrection.

Except, of course, for *The Vision of Judgment*. Earlier, we were principally concerned with the distinction between moral or immoral spirits and amoral ghosts, though we did not ask if they were resurrected or not. We first see George III as 'an old man / With an old soul' (181–82). Like Francesca, he is sitting, but whereas her immateriality is suggested by the solid 'pillar's base' on which she sits, George's materiality (man as well as soul) is stressed by his being seated 'on a cloud' (184). Byron clearly wants to get the maximum fun out of placing material beings in the immateriality of 'neutral space'. St Peter, when we first encounter him, is falling asleep (122), has knocked Louis XVI's head out of his hand with the keys of heaven (152) and, with the same keys, knocks Southey down to Derwentwater (827). The assembled ghosts are all wearing clothes that belong to the various

times in which they lived: 'For all the fashions of the flesh stick long
/ By people in the next world' (524–25). We do not see these ghosts
as transformed by resurrection, though we do see them as embodied
in some strangely possible yet impossible location. They do not deny
resurrection, but place it in a comic setting. Since we are wholly in their
world, we do not see them as pressing in upon ours but rather as like
us, only somewhere else. Unlike the material 'resurrections' of Mazeppa,
Juan and Torquil, this existence on the other side of the experience of
death does not depend on women. *The Vision of Judgment* is the only
major poem of Byron's not to have any women in it all.[10] This other
dimension is Byron's experimental comic construct, if you will, where
the comedy has no connection at all with eros, but it is just as much
realized as a canto in Dante's *Purgatorio* or the space through which
his Cain travels. It is an authentic vision. We have no doubts that we
are before heaven's gate. But everything in this realm of pure space and
ethical judgment is material.

Byron goes out of his way, for instance, to materialize his angels.
They stop their ears in order not to hear Southey's poem, which also
sets the Archangel Michael's teeth on edge (824). Angelic wings are
material, too, for the recording angel has stripped both of his to make
quill pens for his 'black bureau' (20), and 'The devil Asmodeus' has
sprained his left wing in carrying Southey to the assembly (681–82). At
one point, the entire cast give 'an universal cough', which 'Convulsed
the skies' (737). We laugh at the delicate sustaining of this simple joke,
but the joke that entertains us is made up of those radical incongruities
and transferences between spirit and matter which preoccupy the author
of *Don Juan*, for:

> words are things, and a small drop of ink,
>   Falling like dew, upon a thought, produces
> That which makes thousands, perhaps millions, think […].
>   (III, 88)

The ghost appearances in the final cantos of *Don Juan* are a *tour de
force* made out of an almost relentlessly inventive dissolution of these
incongruities and transferences. C.C. Barfoot, in one of the few articles
directly focused on this subject, asserts that

> the walking spirit, the ghost in *Don Juan* is really a smoke-screen, like so
> much else in the poem, a decoy, a distraction from what is really going on
> … For in *Don Juan*, Byron in the *Persona* of the narrator is really hunting
> and haunting himself.[11]

Read in context, this is by no means as silly as it sounds, yet it is still surely wrong. It assumes that the narrator is still the main object of attention as he was in cantos IX to XII. But the 'story of a ghost' (XVI, 4) signals the return of narrative incident to the poem after a long gap. Truth, here, is navigating 'o'er fiction', Byron argues (XV, 88), and 'fiction' means 'making' or 'repeopling'; it is not the same as the factual, but it is not necessarily opposed to truth. We have a compulsion to believe that 'from the dead / A visitant at intervals appears' (XVI, 7), and this compulsion, stronger than reason (XVI, 7), is associated with a general will to believe or take on trust both religious truths and repeopling fictions. Byron has not so deftly or explicitly drawn our attention to this beforehand. Only in *The Lament of Tasso* has Byron ever expressed any interest in whether ghosts are real or not. Tasso wonders whether the 'strange demon' that vexes him is real or whether it is caused by the 'decline' of his mind in captivity (189–94). Elsewhere, Lucifer is as real as Cain; Arimanes is as real as the chamois hunter; the dying gladiator is as real as Napoleon or the spirit of Cecilia Metella. The question does not arise. Here, it is pushed centre stage, both by the elaborate introduction at the end of Canto XV to the two ghost stories in the next canto and by Byron's deliberate use of stock Gothic horror motifs in his 'story of a ghost'. These constitute a different choreography from the tombstone meditation or act of necromantic or rhetorical summoning that has preceded ghost appearances hitherto.

Some of the ingredients are the same. We are aware of 'the mystery by midnight caused' (XVI, 15) and of an adjacent wooded landscape with the noise of water, etc. But we are now in a Gothic gallery with pictures, as we might be in a novel by Ann Radcliffe. One detail, in particular, probably owes something to her.

In Chapter IV of Volume IV of *The Mysteries of Udolpho*, Emily gazes at the picture of a dead Marchioness,[12] who looks both 'blooming' and 'melancholy', but whose face just before her actual death in the same room twenty years ago is recalled by her servant, Dorothée.[13] In an adjacent large saloon is a tapestry. Emily imagines that she sees a phantom there. The furnishings of this scene are burlesqued in Chapter 20 of *Northanger Abbey*. Byron doubtless recycles such details when he associates the deathly look of Francesca with 'the figures on arras, that gloomily glare / Stirred by the breath of the wintry air' (575–76).

The machinery that is presented straightforwardly in *The Siege of Corinth* is ironized in the ghost appearances of *Don Juan*. We are supposed to recognize his deliberate use of familiar stage props as straight out of Gothic horror stock. At the same time, Byron is not simply burlesquing the cult of ghost stories, as Jane Austen certainly is. Just as Byron knows that scepticism can outwit scepticism, so he can use irony to undercut itself. There is not much that is ironical, however, in Byron's wording of his equivalent to Mrs Radcliffe's portrait:

> And the pale smile of Beauties in the grave,
>   The charm of other days, in starlight gleams
> Glimmer on high; their buried locks still wave
>   Along the canvas; their eyes glance like dreams
> On ours, or spars within some dusky cave,
>   But death is imaged in their shadowy beams.
> A picture is the past; even ere its frame
> Be gilt, who sate hath ceased to be the same. (XVI, 19)

The couplet aphorism makes good sense but, like the final couplet of a Shakespeare sonnet, it does not necessarily sum up the stanza. The Radcliffean ingredients are all present, but what she associates and yet separates – the pictured face and recollection of the dying woman's face – Byron wondrously binds together. It is not the pale smile of Beauties of former days that glimmer on high but those of Beauties in the grave. We could rationalise it, like the final couplet. They were once alive, beautiful and smiling, but now they are dead, yet the smile of their living selves is still active in the portrait, so that we receive the past in the present tense and vice versa. However, that is not what 'the pale smile of Beauties in the graves' first suggests. The smiling activity in the picture is not that of the once living but of the now dead. That this is the main meaning is confirmed by the even more grotesque reference to hair whose 'buried locks still wave / Along the canvas'. Byron often astonishes me and I think this sequence is astonishing. The hair that we see is active and alive, for the locks 'wave'. The first reference that the *OED* gives to waves in hair is in *Our Mutual Friend*.[14] Byron anticipates the later usage by attributing the activity of waves to the wave-like appearance of the hair. But this attractive, living and moving hair is 'buried locks'. The hair in the pictures is of present under-earth corpses, rather than of past above-earth women. Even odder is the insisted upon materiality of 'canvas'. The hair is not so much within the painting as on top of the canvas. The buried hair is displaced into another material conjunction. The eyes, on the other hand, simply image death 'in their shadowy beams'.

When we look at a religious icon, the presumption is that we are looking through the eyes – 'windows of heaven' – into an eternity that also looks at us directly. That is the point of icons. In the portraits in

Norman Abbey, you look through the eyes directly into an immediate, not a past, death. The materiality of buried locks and canvas is, as it were, the agency of this non-material survival, which mimics but is the antithesis of resurrection.

It is obvious at once, of course, to those who know the poem, that this shocking reversal – which gets under our metaphysical skin as Radcliffe and Lewis and Maturin do not – is also an exact reversal of the Black Friar's transformation. His 'straggling curl showed he had been fair-haired' (XVI, 121), but before we or Juan have time to absorb this, the cold ghost is transformed in an instant into the 'glowing bust' of Fitz-Fulke. A resurrection of a different kind and yet of the same kind. It is equally in exact and balancing opposition to the face of a present beauty in the Abbey, Aurora Raby, who, like the women in the portrait, smiles (a 'quiet smile of contemplation', XVI, 93) and whose bright eyes Juan recalls immediately before the first ghost walk (XVI, 12). Her eyes 'sadly shone' like those in the portrait of the Marchioness in *The Mysteries of Udolpho*, but they shine 'as seraphs' shine' (XV, 45). Again, we should note the oddity that the apostrophe alerts us to. Her eyes do not shine as bright as the brightness of seraphs, but as the bright eyes of seraphs do.

There are, it seems, eyes 'in death', as Marino Faliero insists (III, i, 94), and they stare down at us from the walls of Norman Abbey or as the 'bright eye' of the first ghost does, who looks directly at Juan (XVI, 21). There are the eyes of the living, too, which glow with all life's force nowhere more memorably than in the dying Haidée:

> Glazed o'er her eyes – the beautiful, the black –
> Oh! to possess such lustre – and then lack! (IV, 69)

And there are eyes like those of Aurora, which are like those of the seraphs that can never, ever, lack lustre. Juan is situated between the blue eyes of Fitz-Fulke, which glared 'rather variably for stony death' (XVI, 121), but which will nevertheless, in due time – like the 'black, bright, downcast, yet espiegle eye' (XVI, 65) of the unmarried mother – turn into the death-imaging 'shadowy beams' of 'Beauties in the grave', and the seraphic eyes of Aurora, which glance lightly across to Juan (XVI, 92) from time to time but also behold infinite space (XVI, 48). G. Wilson Knight, sixty years since, rightly saw Byron's peculiar genius in the lines on the death of Medora:

> Oh! o'er the eye death most exerts his might,
> And hurls the spirit from her throne of light! (*The Corsair*, III, 611–12)[15]

Eyes in Byron's verse are, so to speak, sites where death, life and immortality contend but also merge.

Juan is situated, too, between the two ghost appearances, and we should firmly grasp the nettle that the narrator sets up for us at the end of Canto XV. Is the ghost real?

The question seems as *passé* as whether Lady Macbeth did or did not have children. Should we not be discussing strategies of fictional representation or the alleged decline of religious belief in the late eighteenth century and the resultant rise in ghost stories? We would doubtless keep excellent company if we did so, but we might forfeit Byron's, for he most certainly invites us to ask this question as readers and human beings in, assuredly, the deftest of ways. The controversy over the Cock-Lane ghost, for instance, was very much bound up with the authority of Dr Johnson. Charles Churchill's four canto poem on the subject – *The Ghost* (1762) – ridicules Johnson and ghosts in general. Byron takes a detail from the poem and reuses it for both appearances of his ghost(s). Churchill writes:

> Hark! Something creeps about the house!
> Is it a spirit, or a mouse?
> Hark! Something scratches round the room!
> A cat, a rat, a stubb'd birch-broom. (*The Ghost*, II, 303–06)[16]

Byron uses the mouse for the first appearance ('A supernatural agent – or a mouse,' XVI, 20) and the cat for the second appearance ('Ye powers! it is the – the – the – Pooh! the cat', XVI, 112). But Churchill, unlike Byron, has not the smallest interest in ghosts and expects his readers to take their satirical stand in the reason which Byron specifically relativizes:

> whatever bar the reason rears
> 'Gainst such belief, there's something stronger still
> In its behalf, let those deny who will. (XVI, 7)

I think that the first ghost is a real ghost and the second is obviously that of Fitz-Fulke. Is it possible to be certain on this matter? Of course not. But we can say that it is highly probable given the clear clues in the text – and interpretation, which is a form of rational belief, has its home in probabilities rather than certainties or indeterminacies.

Here are some arguments. In any ghost story, the evidence of a commonsensical person, like Lord Henry Amundeville or Horatio, is always to be preferred to that of an impressionable person, like Hamlet or Catharine Morland. But Lord Henry has seen the ghost and takes its reality for granted (XVI, 38). Why should we doubt him? Secondly, if the first ghost is Fitz-Fulke – and if not a real ghost it must be her – she has no motivation for manufacturing this appearance. What does she gain by it? True, she is a prankster, but her pranks are part of her erotic adventurousness, and the first haunting seems to have no such purpose, for the ghost does what ghosts do – walk up and down in a long gallery and disappear through a wall – whereas the second ghost does not do what ghosts do at all, for it rather noisily opens the door of Juan's bedroom ('a most infernal creak', XVI, 116) and allows itself/herself to be discovered. This is what sexual predators do. If she had planned the second assignation before the first, the first would hinder rather than help the second, for everyone would be on the lookout for ghosts. Finally, the hard look that Fitz-Fulke gives to Juan (XVI, 31) when she sees that he is pale after seeing the first ghost and her attentive presence at the ballad of the Black Friar are best explained by a sudden realization that she has the means of getting into Juan's bedroom the coming night, which she then proceeds to do. Why else would the poet put this detail in? This section of the poem delights in its own rediscovered comic-narrative inventiveness, of which Fitz-Fulke is the indispensable lowest common denominator. Byron shows us the birth of a comic idea which will serve the interests of eros and of the narrative.

Byron has left enough clues for us to be undecided at first as to whether the ghost is real, then decide at the unmasking of Fitz-Fulke that both ghost appearances are now explained, and then he invites us to backtrack and notice the differences between the two appearances. It is not supposed to be crystal clear, but the presumption must be both that ghosts can be real in fiction and fact, and to the exposure of human credulity in believing in them while at the same time treating them as a literary genre, like the ghost stories that Byron and the Shelleys read at Geneva, which is both satirized and utilized. It would be absurd, I suggest, to think that Byron simply intends the whole episode to burlesque any possibility of non-material existence. And he certainly wishes us to make distinctions between the two ghost appearances.

The amount of space taken up by the ghost appearances as such, even if we add in the stanzas about their reality, is small. However, I don't think that we can say, here or elsewhere in Byron's verse, that they are 'a distraction from what is really going on'.

This phrase prompts me to a more general summary of my argument. What is really going on in Canto IV of *Childe Harold's Pilgrimage* is the realization of dead and fictional presences, which press in knowingly and enlarge pilgrim, poet and reader. In *The Siege of Corinth*, a dead presence intervenes in the narrative for narrative purposes, but also as a foil both to the absoluteness of the deaths of Alp and those caught up in the explosion, and to the idea of transubstantiated matter. In the eroticized resurrections of Mazeppa, Juan and Torquil, we envisage a glowing transformation of the trapped and exhausted body that seems to escape death, rather than live within some blurred territory of spirit. In *The Vision of Judgment*, this resurrection is 'realistic' in every sense and thus rendered ridiculous, but also so tangible as to blur (in quite a different way) our sense of the borderline between body and spirit. In *Manfred*, Byron shows us a man who obeys Nietzsche's aesthetic imperative 'to live surrounded by hosts of spirits',[17] but who yet has to die without difficulty. In Norman Abbey, Byron shows us a world that, unlike that of *Childe Harold's Pilgrimage*, is wholly cut off from history and spirit presences and which lives in the bored cultivation of time. Nevertheless, what is excluded mysteriously exerts its authority in the house. Here, as in *The Siege of Corinth* and *The Island*, though with much greater elaboration, he juxtaposes different modes of living, transcendent, and dead being. He brings the great echoing masculine spaces of *Childe Harold's Pilgrimage* directly into the feminine social world of *Don Juan* and criss-crosses them, so that Aurora knows infinite space, and the dead male ghost within all dark, serious, histories turns into a joke pleasingly embodied in a woman who is looking forward to raising a young man's dormant body from the dead. Juan, bullied by Adeline, attracted to Aurora's transcendence, fearful and altered by the ghost's first appearance, awakened again from his sexual hibernation since Catharine the Great by another ghost, who, in an instant, becomes attractive flesh, is himself the fleshly counterpart to the narrator's wholly mental existence, but now seems to know more about the spirit than the narrator does. Hence, his fleshly arousal by ghost and woman combined leaves him 'wan and worn, with eyes that hardly brooked / The light' (XVII, 14). We cannot get past this masterly interim ending.

Perhaps I was wrong and the liminal is where we should both have started and ended up. But whereas Wordsworth – no one better – can stay loyal to the workings of his brain 'with a dim and undetermined sense / Of unknown modes of being' (1805, *The Prelude* I, 419–20), Byron, I would argue, who admired the precision in unknown modes of being that marks *The Ancient Mariner* and *Christabel*, does something rather different. He has an uncanny ability to determine the sense of 'unknown modes of being' when they are brought into much greater contact with familiar reality than Coleridge can muster. I have concentrated here on his ability to determine and distinguish modes of spirits, ghosts, fictions and the dead and his ability to watch the play of their interactions. There is nothing else quite like it in Romantic literature.

Notes

1 Aristotle said that he saw human beings as animals differentiated by logos. This is usually translated via Latin as 'rational animals' but I would prefer the translation given.
2 Sometimes, of course, he will use both terms indiscriminately. He is not a philosopher. But there is an evident pattern of distinction.
3 It does not matter that it is not actually a gladiator.
4 See *CPW*, II, p. 46 for the omitted stanza.
5 The map is pretty basic. Other entities that could be included, such as demons, are considered by Mary Hurst in Chapter 3 and other forms of spectrality are discussed by Gavin Hopps in the following chapter.
6 *Childe Harold's Pilgrimage, Don Juan, The Curse of Minerva, The Bride of Abydos, The Siege of Corinth, Manfred, Cain, Heaven and Earth, The Vision of Judgment.*
7 *The New Oxford Book of Eighteenth-Century Verse*, ed. Roger Lonsdale (Oxford: Oxford University Press, 1987), p. 769.
8 Ibid., p. 159.
9 *BLJ*, IX, p. 122
10 There aren't many women in most of the satirical poems of course – *English Bards, Hints from Horace* or *The Age of Bronze*. However, the absence of them in *The Vision* is still striking.
11 C.C. Barfoot, 'Hauntings 2: Byron's Phantoms', p. 169.
12 Ann Radcliffe, *The Mysteries of Udolpho*, ed. Bonamy Dobrée (London: Oxford University Press, 1966), p. 533.
13 Ibid., p. 535.
14 Dickens, *Our Mutual Friend* (1864–5; Oxford: Oxford University Press, 1989), p. 41: 'Bella ... employed both her hands in giving her hair an additional wave.'
15 G. Wilson Knight, *Poets of Action* (London: Methuen, 1967), p. 185.
16 *The Poetical Works of Charles Churchill with Memoir etc by the Rev. George Gilfillan* (Edinburgh: James Nichol, 1855), p. 237.
17 Friedrich Nietzsche, *The Birth of Tragedy*, trans. Francis Golffing (New York, NY: Doubleday, 1956), p. 55.

CHAPTER TWO

Shades of Being: Byron and the Trespassing of Ontology

Gavin Hopps

Byron was fascinated by the in-between, and his gaze was often drawn to bits of reality that the fabric of language doesn't quite cover: 'And then his former movements would redouble / With something between carelessness and trouble' (*The Island*, III, 4, 115–16). This sense that there are bits of reality that incorrigibly slip between the cracks of language is signalled by those features of the poet's manner – such as his lack of polish, his indifference to grammar, the 'forwardness' or 'galloping nature' of his rhetoric[1] – which create the impression of language *in pursuit of* something. It is also apparent in his notorious tolerance of self-contradiction: 'But if a writer should be quite consistent, / How could he possibly show things existent?' (*DJ*, XV, 87). There are, however, certain bits of reality in particular that give language the slip, since they stray outside or play between our either/or ontological categories. This kind of 'ontological trespassing' has been brought into focus by the work of Jacques Derrida, who has identified the in-between as a form of spectrality and proposed an alternative 'hauntological' grammar to describe its shadowy comings and goings.[2] This alternative economy of the spectral is helpfully summarized by Mary-Jane Rubenstein:

> In *Specters of Marx*, Derrida reminds us that classical ontology is constituted dialectically, drawing the boundaries of is-ness itself by drawing definitive distinctions between being and non-being, presence and absence, me and you, the living and the dead, here and there, now and then, etc. Looking to unsettle the monadic understanding of identity that emerges from the mutual exclusion of these pairs [...] Derrida locates in the pseudo-logic of haunting a certain anteriority to, and perpetual exceeding of, the onto-logic of binary opposition. Something that haunts me unsettles all the

self-identical products of ontology, because a ghost – whether it be mine or another's – neither is nor is not, is neither simply present nor simply absent, neither me nor someone entirely different from me, neither living nor properly dead, neither fully here nor fully there [...].[3.]

In this chapter, without tying myself too tightly to Derrida's particular conception of such 'unhomely' phenomena, I want to highlight these 'shades of being' that make language stammer in Byron's verse and consider what is at stake in his recurrent exploratory meditations on the spectral. I shall focus on three forms of trespassing in particular: (1) ghostly presences or spectral figures that affect the speaker in spite of their apparent absence or non-existence; (2) a numinous 'excess' in the natural order or the sense that nature 'gives more than it has'; and (3) an 'ec-centric' mode of being in which human nature is elevated beyond itself. It is my hope that reconceiving the poet's treatment of immanence and transcendence in terms of spectrality will allow us to gain a better purchase on Byron's 'sacramental' vision of nature[4] – which has proved problematic for both religious and materialistic readings alike – and may also help us to see certain features of his syntactic 'dis-ease' in a more positive light.

I

It is perhaps fitting to begin with the Muse:

> Oh, thou! in Hellas deem'd of heav'nly birth,
> Muse! form'd or fabled at the minstrel's will!
> Since sham'd full oft by later lyres on earth,
> Mine dares not call thee from thy sacred hill:
> Yet there I've wander'd by thy vaunted rill;
> Yes! sigh'd o'er Delphi's long-deserted shrine,
> Where, save that feeble fountain, all is still;
> Nor mote my shell awake the weary Nine
> To grace so plain a tale – this lowly lay of mine. (*CHP*, I, 1)

The Muse of *Childe Harold* is a quintessential spectral entity, who affects the speaker in spite of her apparent non-existence. Indeed, the opening stanza of the poem proper is perfectly poised between reverence and levity, credulity and scepticism; for if the stress that falls on 'deem'd' implies an opening of distance or incipient disavowal, it occurs within an invocation which – as a peculiarly 'preposterous' gesture – is both prompted by, and conjures the presence of, that to which it calls.[5] Similarly, the 'or' of the postposed modification ('form'd or fabled at the minstrel's will') holds the two opposing options equally unforeclosed, as does the wonderfully ambiguous 'all is still', which allows a faint adverbial sense of things subsisting alongside the dominant sense of dereliction. The speaker's behaviour thus suggests that it is possible to be haunted by what we do not or do not *think* we believe in. This complicated sense of what it means to believe – which suggests that reason isn't the sole or sovereign arbiter – is rendered more explicit in *Don Juan*:

> All nations have believed that from the dead
> A visitant at intervals appears;
> And what is strangest upon this strange head,
> Is, that whatever bar the reason rears
> 'Gainst such belief, there's something stronger still
> In its behalf, let those deny who will. (XVI, 7)

It is worth noticing in passing how the poet's ironic manner in the invocation covertly safeguards, even as it makes light of, the gesture, since it enables the preservation of a religious comportment largely abandoned by his more straight-faced contemporaries. What's more, the poet's defence of credulity against the suspicions of reason in the stanza from *Don Juan* suggests that here, too, in the act of calling out, the impulse to acknowledge a transcendent other may be 'stronger still' than whatever 'bar' reason rears against it. Hence, somewhat surprisingly, instead of the poet's scepticism undermining his reverence, it seems that the devotion he makes light of may subvert his scepticism.[6]

The curiously alluring spectrality of the Muse is exhibited later in the canto as well:

> Oh, thou Parnassus! whom I now survey,
> Not in the phrensy of a dreamer's eye,
> Not in the fabled landscape of a lay,
> But soaring snow-clad through thy native sky,   615
> In the wild pomp of mountain majesty!
> What marvel if I thus essay to sing?
> The humblest of thy pilgrims passing by
> Would gladly woo thine Echoes with his string,
> Though from thy heights no more one Muse will wave
>   her wing. [...]   620

> Shall I unmov'd behold the hallow'd scene,
> Which others rave of, though they know it not?
> Though here no more Apollo haunts his grot,
> And thou, the Muses' seat, art now their grave,   635
> Some gentle Spirit still pervades the spot,

Sighs in the gale, keeps silence in the cave,
And glides with glassy foot o'er yon melodious Wave.
        (I, 60, 62)

This suddenly irrupting apostrophic passage is relevant to our discussion
for a number of reasons. First of all, it presents itself as a stepping outside
of fiction within a work of fiction, leaving aside his 'strain' and 'the
fabled landscape of a lay' for what purports to be an authorial gaze and
a temporality coextensive with the moment of speaking. We are thus
within a strange 'parergonal' space, at once both within and without
the poem.[7] The utterance itself evinces a similarly 'in-between' character,
as the passage is at once a moment of silence and an irrepressible act
of address ('What marvel if I thus essay to sing?'). Furthermore, there
is a kind of flickering with respect to the addressee, which is formally
Parnassus, though this is of course a metonymy for the Muse (who is
also a plurality), whom the speaker therefore in a sense simultaneously
turns towards and away from in the act of address. Most intriguingly
of all, though, the stanzas once again exhibit an 'oxymoronic' sense of
reality in the speaker's comportment towards the Muse. The stigmata
of this oxymoronic comportment are the correlative uses of 'though'
in lines 619 and 634, which illustrate the poet's peculiarly adversative
syntax – that is, his fidgeting habit of 'yet' and 'but'.[8] In the first
case, the 'though' clause follows and sets itself against a description of
irresistible affectivity, introducing a counter-statement about the place's
dereliction. However, in the second case, the 'though' clause introduces
a statement of desertion, which is then overturned by a description of
presence. What's odder still is that the second qualified assertion of
presence functions *itself* as a kind of 'although' clause, countermanding
or qualifying the preceding disavowal. What are we to make of this?

In his illuminating discussion of these stanzas in *Byron and Place*,
Stephen Cheeke speaks of 'secular pilgrimage', 'the sacred spot' and
'the sacred and secular meaning of place'.[9] While Cheeke's discussion is
sensitively alert to the poet's frequently overlooked reverence – perceptively pointing towards 'an etiquette of lowered voices in holy places,
of a respectful hush or awe-struck silence as if a spot consecrated by
events of historical significance becomes a kind of church'[10] – I wish
to suggest that the either/or, secular/sacred distinction upon which it
is based is an inadequate framework for describing Byron's response
to the nature of things. As a way of evading the distortions of this
oppositional distinction, it may be helpful to invoke Giorgio Agamben's
recent reconception of the profane.

As Agamben observes in his brilliant short essay 'In Praise of Profanation', while '"to consecrate" (*sacrare*) was the term that indicated the removal of things from the sphere of human law' and '"to profane" meant, conversely, to return them to the free use of men',[11] the latter is not exactly the opposite of the former. This is because 'these operations [...] must every time reckon with something like a residue of profanity in every consecrated thing and a remnant of sacredness in every profaned object'.[12] This residual continuity between the sacred and the profane is explained by Agamben by means of an analogy with play, which, he argues, 'frees and distracts humanity from the sphere of the sacred without simply abolishing it'.[13] This conception of the profane as that which is separated from, but bears within it, 'a remnant of sacredness' is, I suggest, more helpful than an exclusively oppositional notion of the secular for thinking about the 'oxymoronic' spaces and ontological trespasses of Byron's pilgrimage.[14]

If, then, we return to the poet's stanzas on Parnassus with this model of felicitous impurity in mind, Byron's gainsaying of his own assertions seems less contradictory or incoherent. Indeed, from such a perspective, the speaker's shuttling between positions ceases to seem like confusion and instead appears to be a 'catachrestic' strategy or attempt to speak about that which evades the conventional categories of speech. In other words, it is *reality* that flickers with evanescent presences, and the speaker's apparent self-contradiction is an accurate description of its instability. Let us consider some more examples.

The Muse is not the only figure in *Childe Harold's Pilgrimage* whose mode of appearing cannot be quarantined by the customary ontological categories of presence and absence or life and death. These distinctions are also transgressed by darkened moments of I-Thou relation – moments in which a sense of relational presence floods without obliterating an awareness of the other's absence:

> There, thou! – whose love and life together fled,
> Have left me here to love and live in vain –
> Twin'd with my heart, and can I deem thee dead,
> When busy Memory flashes on my brain? (II, 9)

> Thou too art gone, thou lov'd and lovely one!
> Whom youth and youth's affection bound to me;
> Who did for me what none beside have done,
> Nor shrank from one albeit unworthy thee.
> What is my being? thou hast ceas'd to be! (II, 95)

These moments of relation with the deceased (John Edleston) have a tragic or elegiac quality. They are pervaded by a sense of separation, which carries them away from Martin Buber's conception of the I-Thou encounter, in which the call is spoken 'with the whole being' and the presence of the other 'fills the heavens'.[15] However, if the speaker's sense of relation is sundered, so is his sense of separation. For while on the one hand the act of calling out conjures up or corroborates the ghostly presence of the absent other, it is on the other hand an *affective* presence that is sufficient to raise troubling ontological questions which unsettle the speaker's construal of the real ('can I deem thee dead [...]?' 'What is my being?'). The way the speaker is affected by the metaphysical implications of apostrophe therefore seems to carry such moments of relation equally away from what Jonathan Culler and others encourage us to read as a purely metapoetic gesture.[16] Hence, what we are faced with in *Childe Harold's Pilgrimage* are figures of 'half-aliveness'; that is, apostrophic presences that appear to belong neither to the realm of the living nor the dead, which make claims on the speaker that he can neither entirely refuse nor accept.[17] Agamben's writing on the 'third space' of fetishistic relation – whose subjects 'apparently belong neither to the internal and subjective nor to the external and objective spheres'[18] – may help us to characterize the poet's comportment towards such trespassing presences. Speaking of the child's ambiguous disavowal of reality in Freud's account of fetishistic fixation, he writes:

> In the conflict between the perception of reality, which urges him to renounce his phantasm, and between the perception of reality, which urges him to deny his perception, the child does neither one nor the other; or, rather, he does both simultaneously, reaching one of those compromises that are possible only under the rule of the laws of the unconscious.[19]

One might wish to dispute the final assertion – that such compromises are possible 'only under the rule of the laws of the unconscious' – and point towards a conscious religious equivalent, according to which the claims of apparently divergent realities are simultaneously accepted. Nevertheless, the identification of an in-between space with its own ontological protocol, in which the subject on the one hand 'disavows the evidence of his perception' and on the other 'recognizes its reality', may be a useful way of describing the haunted apostrophic spaces of *Childe Harold*.[20]

Such moments of relation and the spaces that they open up are doubly uncanny, for neither the speaker nor the addressee is as it were 'at home'. Rather, the former 'gets carried away' from the present by the sense of relation that '[b]ursts from [his] heart' (I, 91), while the act of apostrophe 'restores to time and physicality that which cannot be seen, and exteriorizes that which is contained within ideality'.[21] What's more, as Paul de Man famously observed in his reading of Wordsworth's *Essays upon Epitaphs*, the space of apostrophic relation involves an uncanny chiastic exchange of animism, since the act of addressing 'an absent, deceased or voiceless entity [...] posits the possibility of the latter's reply and confers upon it the power of speech', which in turn according to the symmetrical structure of the trope, 'implies [...] that the living are struck dumb, frozen in their own death'.[22] This uncanny etiquette of ontological exchange – and the in-between zone of being it opens up – is precisely described by Byron in Sardanapalus's vision of a 'legion of the dead':

> all turn'd upon me,
> And stared, but neither ate nor drank, but stared,
> Till I grew stone, as they seem'd half to be,
> Yet breathing stone, for I felt life in them,
> And life in me: there was a horrid kind
> Of sympathy between us, as if they
> Had lost a part of death to come to me,
> And I the half of life to sit by them.
> We were in an existence all apart
> From heaven or earth [...]. (*Sardanapalus*, IV, i, 120–29)

Such crossings over into 'an existence all apart / From heaven or earth' are not uncommon in Byron's poetry. In *The Prisoner of Chillon*, for example, Bonnivard undergoes the following experience of insentience:

> First came the loss of light, and air,
> And then of darkness too:
> I had no thought, no feeling – none –
> Among the stones I stood a stone,
> And was, scarce conscious what I wist,
> As shrubless crags within the mist;
> For all was blank, and bleak, and grey,
> It was not night – it was not day [...]
> But vacancy absorbing space,
> And fixedness – without a place;
> There were no stars – no earth – no time –
> No check – no change – no good – no crime –
> But silence, and a stirless breath
> Which neither was of life nor death;
> A sea of stagnant idleness,
> Blind, boundless, mute, and motionless! (IX)

Here again we find a loss of animism ('Among the stones I stood a stone') and the opening up of 'an existence all apart', where it 'was not night' and 'was not day', which is outside darkness as well as light, in which the difference between internal and external spheres is collapsed, and where the only registered phenomenon is a spectral antithesis of inspiration – the description of which deprives it of the sole characteristic that manifests its being: 'a stirless breath / Which neither was of life nor death'. (As a seething dehiscence in the fabric of reality – which somehow retains its unruffled appearance – this otherworldly 'stirless breath' would seem to be a paradigmatic example of the ghostly.) There is also in the final lines of this stanza a sense of the subject's dissolution or 'deterritorialization' into the vacancy it contemplates, as the characteristics 'blind' and 'mute' seem to have migrated outside the subject, suggesting an effacement of selfhood and a radically uncanny 'not-being-at-home'.

We encounter comparable experiences of suspended animation or a mode of hovering 'between two worlds' in the extended description of 'loveliness in death, / That parts not quite with parting breath' in *The Giaour* (68–102); in Mazeppa's dark trance, in which 'he who dies / Can die no more than [Mazeppa] died' (XIII, 539–68); in Juan's swoon after surviving the shipwreck, in which 'earth was gone [...] / And Time had nothing more of night nor day' (*DJ*, II, 111); and in the tragic slow-motion passing of Haidée, who recalls Juan's 'spirits back from death', but lies for days herself '[l]ike one life could not hold, nor death destroy' (*DJ*, IV, 59–69). But since the general point should be clear, I want to turn from the becoming-inanimate of human beings to an ontological trespassing in the other direction – that is, the becoming-animate or self-exceeding character of the natural world.[23]

II

In *Creative Intuition in Art and Poetry* (1953), Jacques Maritain offers a fascinating account of artistic practice and its privileged ability to disclose certain dimensions of reality. According to Maritain's 'ontological' account of poesis, which is based on a Thomistic understanding of engraced nature, art discloses a 'surplus in things [...] that belongs to reality itself'.[24] As Maritain puts it: 'things are not only what they are' and 'give more than they have'.[25] Byron of course has come to be known as an anti-Romantic debunking materialist, who rejects the Wordsworthian vision of a benevolently self-exceeding nature.[26] But Byron cares little for systems and consistency – which applies to negative perspectives as well – and we find, recurring throughout his poetry, vivid and sustained depictions of a sacramental or engraced nature, in which things 'give more than they have'.[27] One of the most powerful examples of this occurs in *Childe Harold*:

> Clear, placid Leman! thy contrasted lake,
> With the wild world I dwelt in, is a thing
> Which warns me, with its stillness, to forsake
> Earth's troubled waters for a purer spring.
> This quiet sail is as a noiseless wing
> To waft me from distraction; once I loved
> Torn ocean's roar, but thy soft murmuring
> Sounds sweet as if a sister's voice reproved,
> That I with stern delights should e'er have been so moved.
>
> It is the hush of night, and all between
> Thy margin and the mountains, dusk, yet clear,
> Mellowed and mingling, yet distinctly seen [...]
> There breathes a living fragrance from the shore,
> Of flowers yet fresh with childhood; on the ear
> Drops the light drip of the suspended oar,
> Or chirps the grasshopper one good-night carol more; [...]
>
> There seems a floating whisper on the hill,
> But that is fancy, for the starlight dews   820
> All silently their tears of love instil,
> Weeping themselves away, till they infuse
> Deep into Nature's breast the spirit of her hues.
>
> Ye stars! which are the poetry of heaven!
> If in your bright leaves we would read the fate
> Of men and empires, – 'tis to be forgiven,
> That in our aspirations to be great,
> Our destinies o'erleap their mortal state,
> And claim a kindred with you; for ye are
> A beauty and a mystery, and create
> In us such love and reverence from afar,
> That fortune, fame, power, life, have named themselves a star.
>   (III, 85–88)

The passage begins with an act of address, which in Byron frequently elicits or is elicited by a shift into a more metaphysical vision. This address is accompanied by a personifying comparison ('thy soft murmuring / Sounds sweet as if a Sister's voice reproved') that along with the apostrophe lightly suggests a sense of presence or personhood that haunts the material realm. Such personifying tendencies are of course a poetic device, which need not carry any metaphysical implications. In light of the subsequent stanzas, however – which culminate in an explicitly metaphysical vision – they appear to be an 'iconic' attempt to represent a stirring sense that things may paradoxically be more than they are. What I mean by this is that what is conventionally known as 'pathetic fallacy' may in some cases turn out to be neither pathetic nor fallacious; for if the poet's animistic description of nature represents an attempt to signify a sense of presence or personhood that exceeds and yet is mediated by means of the material – which, against the 'bar' of reason, the poem posits as a considered possibility – then such descriptions will cease to be a passionate 'poetic' confusion and may instead be seen as a literary fashioning of 'icons', which endeavour by means of non-naturalistic figurations to gesture towards that which is beyond representation. Such an 'excessive' vision of nature, which necessitates an 'iconic' swerve away from realism in order to depict things as they 'are', is described by Ruskin himself, a few chapters after his more well-known account of pathetic fallacy. The discussion is worth quoting at length, as it tends to be mistakenly assumed that Ruskin considered *all* intimations of presence or personhood in the natural order to be a fallacious projection:

> we see in this [scriptural view of nature] that the instinct which leads us thus to attribute life to the lowest forms of organic nature, does not necessarily spring from faithlessness, nor the deducing a moral out of them from an irregular and languid conscientiousness. In this, as in almost all things connected with moral discipline, the same results may follow from contrary causes; and as there are a good and evil contentment, a good and evil discontent, a good and evil care, fear, ambition, and so on, there are also good and evil forms of this sympathy with nature, and disposition to moralize over it. In general, active men, of strong sense and stern principle, do not care to see anything in a leaf, but vegetable tissue [...] hence there is a strong presumption, when first we perceive a tendency in any one to regard trees as living, and enunciate moral aphorisms over every pebble they stumble against, that such tendency proceeds from a morbid temperament [...]. But when the active life is nobly fulfilled, and the mind is then raised beyond it into clear and calm beholding of the world around us, the same tendency again manifests itself in the most sacred way: the simplest forms of nature are strangely animated by the sense of the Divine presence; the trees and flowers seem all, in a sort, children of God; and we ourselves, their fellows, made out of the same dust, and greater than they only in having a greater portion of the Divine power exerted on our frame, and all

the common uses and palpably visible forms of things, become subordinate in our minds to their inner glory, to the mysterious voices in which they talk to us about God [...].[28]

Ruskin thus offers us *two* explanations of aesthetic depictions of 'excessive' presence or 'good and evil forms of [...] sympathy with nature'.[29] And while the latter (associated with pathetic fallacy) has almost entirely eclipsed the former – and encouraged a misreading of Romantic moments of vision – what we find in Ruskin's aesthetic theory is the foundation of a positive theological mandate, according to which 'the artist *does* set out to change the world, but – if we can manage the paradox – to change it into itself'.[30] In other words, in representing things in nature as 'not only what they are' and as giving 'more than they have', the artist may paradoxically, from a theological point of view, be offering a truthful depiction of reality.[31]

Returning to Byron, we can see that this sense of a 'strangely animated' landscape is carried over into stanza 86, where we find an image of difference-in-unity – in which all things are mingled and yet remain distinct – and where the use of an 'existential' *there* construction ('There breathes a living fragrance') uncannily dilates the subject position, so that it is unclear whether the fragrance itself is breathing or if it is the 'breath' of something else – and if so, what this 'something else' might be, and in what sense in any case this fragrance is 'living'.[32] Similarly, in stanza 87 – which employs another 'existential' construction ('There seems a floating whisper on the hill') – we find an effect without material cause, which is rendered more uncanny by the use of the term 'seems'.[33] This is followed by a characteristic Byronic syndetic shuffle, in which the poet turns on his utterance and then turns on his turning (ll. 820–23). The 'but' clause appears to disavow the preceding sense of an inhabited landscape, yet the explanation that is given in the illative clause ('for the starlight dews / All silently their tears of love instil') radically narrows the scope of the disavowal and in fact *reaffirms* the anterior sense of an animated landscape with a personifying image or 'icon' of its own. We thus have an even more carefully delineated representation of a world in which things 'give more than they have'. Moreover, the speaker's apparent disavowal ('But that is fancy') suggests that he is aware – and wants us to know that he is aware – and yet proceeds *in spite of* the dismissive reading of such intimations. What Byron says in *Don Juan* about ghosts would therefore seem to apply to pathetic fallacy, too: 'Whatever bar the reason rears / 'Gainst such belief, there's something stronger still / In its behalf'.

Part of what makes the poet's vision of engraced nature so compelling is its gradual harmonizing evolution, which anticipates the 'piecemeal' epiphany of St Peter's (IV, 155–58) and suggestively awakens a transcendent dimension in a variety of elements, involving a range of senses, on the way to its climactic apprehension of 'the great whole' (IV, 157). The final sensory and perspectival shift prior to this dilated vision involves the stars (III, 87), which are in Byron frequently associated with transcendence.[34] Here, in the description of them as 'the poetry of heaven', the stars are presented as a synecdoche of the 'speaking' universe, which is explicitly described as such in *Manfred*:

> The stars are forth, the moon above the tops
> Of the snow-shining mountains. – Beautiful!
> I linger yet with Nature, for the night
> Hath been to me a more familiar face
> Than that of man; and in her starry shade
> Of dim and solitary loveliness,
> I learn'd the language of another world. (III, iv, 1–7)

The description of the stars as 'the poetry of heaven' is also, however, a subtle *mise en abyme*, for while the line in one sense may simply mean that the stars are the beautiful forms of the sky, it also means – especially in view of the succeeding lines about their 'textual' aspect – that the stars are finite signifiers of an immaterial reality, which is precisely what the poem itself is doing at this point – namely, attempting to signify by means of the finite a sense of that which indwells and yet immaterially exceeds it.

The dilated vision in which the passage culminates draws together the separately registered intimations – with respect to the lake, the stars and the air – that things may beneficently exceed themselves and renders the theological character of this 'excess' explicit:

> All heaven and earth are still – though not in sleep,
> But breathless, as we grow when feeling most;
> And silent, as we stand in thoughts too deep: –
> All heaven and earth are still: From the high host
> Of stars, to the lull'd lake and mountain-coast,
> All is concentered in a life intense,
> Where not a beam, nor air, nor leaf is lost,
> But hath a part of being, and a sense
> Of that which is of all Creator and defence.
>
> Then stirs the feeling infinite, so felt
> In solitude, where we are *least* alone;

A truth, which through our being then doth melt
And purifies from self: it is a tone,
The soul and source of music, which makes known
Eternal harmony, and sheds a charm,
Like to the fabled Cytherea's zone,
Binding all things with beauty; – 'twould disarm
The spectre Death, had he substantial power to harm. (89–90)

At the centre of the poem's sacramental vision is a sense of repose, which widens out from 'the hush of night' and 'the lulled lake' to encompass 'All heaven and earth', which are brought into continuity by their coordinated stillness. (The sacramental widening of the poet's gaze is reflected in miniature in the zero article use of 'heaven', which subtly dilates the sky and the vision of that which is beyond it.) According to Ruskin, the beauty of nature is intrinsically revelatory, since we find 'the signature of God upon His works' and 'the inevitable stamp of his image on what He creates'.[35] Yet for Ruskin the aspect of nature that is most suggestive of the divine is repose. He writes:

> As opposed to passion, change, fullness, or laborious exertion, Repose is the especial and separating characteristic of the eternal mind and power. [...] the rest of things in which there is vitality or capability of motion actual or imagined; and with respect to these the expression of repose is greater in proportion to the amount and sublimity of the action which is not taking place, as well as to the intensity of the negation of it.[36]

It is this sense of cosmic repose, which bespeaks an unexerted vitality, and hovers between the potential and actual, that we find in *Childe Harold* Canto III. However, there is in Byron's description of nature an additional *transitive* sense of repose, which carries it further in a theological direction, since in Byron's vision, all things repose in the being of God (stanza 89). In order to establish the significance of this second kind of repose, it may be helpful to compare it to a parallel moment of vision in repose in the poem to which Byron's metaphysics is customarily attributed:

Nor less, I trust,
To them I may have owed another gift,
Of aspect more sublime; that blessed mood
In which the burthen of the mystery,
In which the heavy and the weary weight
Of all this unintelligible world,
Is lightened: – that serene and blessed mood,
In which the affections gently lead us on, –

Until, the breath of this corporeal frame
And even the motion of our human blood
Almost suspended, we are laid asleep
In body, and become a living soul:
While with an eye made quiet by the power
Of harmony, and the deep power of joy,
We see into the life of things.

('Lines Composed a Few Miles above Tintern Abbey', 36–50)

Wordsworth's moment of suspended animation is a perfect example of Ruskinian repose, which 'demands for its expression the implied capability of its opposite'.[37] It is a moment of vision in which the eye is 'made quiet' or in a sense stops seeing; it is a suspension of motion in which we are simultaneously 'led on'; and it is a mental lightening that is laden with significance, in which heightened vitality coincides with dormition. The moment of repose in 'Tintern Abbey' is also, obviously, a moment of revelation or spiritual vision, and hence is in sympathy, too, with the natural theology of Ruskin's account. In both of these respects – in the paradoxical involvement and suspension of vitality and the religious significance of the accompanying vision – Wordsworth's moment of epiphanic repose may be seen as a model for Byron's in *Childe Harold*. However, it is at this point that the differences begin to emerge.

According to most commentators on Canto III, the differences tend to be in Wordsworth's favour, whose model of 'supernatural naturalism' is imperfectly imitated, if not spoilt, by Byron, who is typically viewed as more worldly, rhetorical, ironic and pessimistic – where the 'more' in each case is seen as a lack.[38] I think that Byron is, undoubtedly, all of these things, though whether or not this constitutes a pejorative assessment is open to debate. What is seldom noticed in such comparisons, however, is that Byron is also *more orthodox* in his religious envisioning of nature.[39] And this takes us back to the second sense of repose.

Byron's sacramental vision of nature exhibits a 'participatory' conception of the created order. That is to say, he envisions a universe in which created entities are real and distinct from, and yet owe their being to, a divine reality in which they participate.[40] This contrasts with pantheism, in which both the reality and distinctiveness of the created realm is more or less effaced by the greater reality of the divine, to which they give way but by which they are subsumed. Thus, the Platonic-Thomistic notion of participation preserves the transcendence as well as the immanence of the divine – which may be mediated by, in spite of its radical otherness from, the created order – whereas in pantheism, divine transcendence is lost in the identification of the universe with God, just as created phenomena are turned into a kind of shadow reality in the drift towards Idealism. If we return with this in mind to our two sacramental descriptions of nature, we can see, firstly, that there is little sense of divine transcendence in Wordsworth's vision, as whatever it is to which nature gives way is viewed as an immanent life or presence, which 'dwells', 'rolls through' or is 'interfused' in things and appears to have no existence apart from them.[41] Secondly, this indwelling 'surplus' that is mediated by the natural world never rises above an immanent anonymity, as the poet scrupulously keeps to a language of vagueness ('something', 'life', 'spirit', 'presence'), which is rendered all the more uncertain by the multiplicity of the poet's attempts at naming it and the synonymic fallout of these 'raid[s] on the articulate'.[42] Hence, for all the poem's emphasis on vision, what we are presented with is a rather opaque epiphany.[43] Finally, we can also see a melting away of the material realm in Wordsworth's use of 'things' – in which created phenomena are undifferentiatedly left aside as a sort of by-product or husk – and a concomitant Idealist drift in the use of 'forms', in which, as Brian Barbour points out, 'the universal is abstracted from the particular'.[44]

In Byron's moment of vision, by contrast, the poet's intimations of immanence are accompanied by a more orthodox preservation of divine transcendence:

> All is concentered in a life intense,
> Where not a beam, nor air, nor leaf is lost,
> But hath a part of being, and a sense
> Of that which is of all Creator and defence.

All creation, for Byron, participates in and is indwelt by but is nonetheless distinguished from its Creator, who is infinite, all-loving and stronger than death. Secondly, and again in contrast to Wordsworth's anonymous epiphany, Byron's sense of an immanent 'life intense' is explicitly identified with a personal Creator God, who inspires worship, as opposed to contemplation (III, 91). Furthermore, Byron's theological vision does not let go of or vitiate the reality of created phenomena, as we saw in 'Tintern Abbey'. Rather, all things participate and are thus preserved – in all their distinctiveness and beyond their extinction – in the being of God.[45] Finally, it should not escape our attention that the vision culminates with a reference to the 'spectre Death' (III, 90), which involves a startling inversion of our quotidian conceptions; for ordinarily of course it is death that takes life from things – or things from life – whereas in Byron's description life as it were is taken from Death – which, in being reduced to a spectre, lacks 'substantial power to harm'. This Pauline gesture, in which death is robbed of its sting, reinforces the sense that there is a providential 'indifference to ontic difference' in the all-sustaining life of the divine and emphasizes the scriptural underpinning of Byron's sacramental vision.[46] Wordsworth also of course alludes to Scripture in 'Tintern Abbey'; yet the reference to Genesis 2: 7 ('we are laid asleep / In body and become a living soul') writes God out of the event in its passive formulation and 'subtly deifies the One Life' in the process.[47] The difference that I am trying to establish between the two poets' moments of sacred perception may be summed up in terms of the historical shift – in which the Romantics were instrumental – from the transcendent to the sublime.

As John Milbank has convincingly argued, it is possible to trace throughout the period of modernity not only a prizing apart of the sublime and the beautiful but also a more insidious substitution of sublimity for transcendence.[48] This process, which is already underway in seventeenth-century classicist interpretations of Longinus, by Boileau and others, and is most emphatically encouraged in the eighteenth century by Burke and Kant, involves 'a new thinking of the transcendent as the absolutely unknowable void, upon whose brink we finite beings must dizzily hover, as opposed to an older notion of a supra-hierarchical summit which we may gradually hope to scale'.[49] In the process, and as a result of parallel tendencies in Protestant theology, the divine comes to be construed as 'abstract will without transcendental goodness, truth and beauty':

> Where once the sublime God was *also* beautiful, also regarded as the eminent infinite reality of every mode of harmonious proportion and value, modernity and postmodernity tend strictly to *substitute* sublimity for transcendence. This means that all that persists of transcendence is sheer unknowability or its quality of non-representability and non-depictability.[50]

Now, while it is precisely this shift from a transcendent Creator in analogical continuity with creation to a radically unknowable and unnameable sublimity that I am contending is apparent in the poetry of Wordsworth – and, as Milbank argues, in Romanticism more generally – I also wish to suggest that in this respect Byron is '*anti*-Romantic'. This is because while in Wordsworth's moment of mystical vision we find the hallmarks of sublime experience – an overthrow of the conscious subject ('we are laid asleep'), a pleasing displeasure ('A presence that disturbs me with the joy / Of elevated thoughts') and a consistent emphasis on anonymity – in Byron's supposedly 'Wordsworthian' vision we find a knowable, nameable, transcendent God, who is identified with the good, the beautiful and the true.[51] This is even more apparent later on in *Childe Harold*, where the poet offers us a parallel account of epiphanic vision, although this time in relation to art rather than nature:

> But thou, of temples old, or altars new,
> Standest alone – with nothing like to thee –
> Worthiest of God, the holy and the true,
> Since Zion's desolation, when that He
> Forsook his former city, what could be,
> Of earthly structures, in his honour piled,
> Of a sublimer aspect? Majesty,
> Power, Glory, Strength, and Beauty, all are aisled
> In this eternal ark of worship undefiled.
>
> Enter: its grandeur overwhelms thee not;
> And why? it is not lessened; but thy mind,
> Expanded by the genius of the spot,
> Has grown colossal, and can only find
> A fit abode wherein appear enshrined
> Thy hopes of immortality; and thou
> Shalt one day, if found worthy, so defined,
> See thy God face to face, as thou dost now
> His Holy of Holies, nor be blasted by his brow. (IV, 154–55)

Here we find a subject that exceeds itself ('we thus dilate / Our spirits to the size of that they contemplate') which is nonetheless in possession of itself ('its grandeur overwhelms thee not'). We also find an orthodox balancing of immanence and transcendence in the moment of mediated vision, which is exquisitely conveyed by the enjambment of stanza 155, in which the line-break after 'as thou dost now' allows a momentary sense of seeing God 'face to face' within the created order, while the utterance as a whole reverently defers such vision until the eschaton. The enjambment in this way precisely represents in the spectral status of its textual conjuring an intimation of divine presence. Finally, we can see in Byron's description something akin to the gradual scaling of a 'supra-hierarchical summit' by way of the created order that Milbank associates with the transcendent encounter. Indeed, the poet appears to be consciously *opposing* his vision of the transcendent to the fashionable 'Romantic' experience of the sublime, which his critics would have us believe that he is copying. At the climax of the vision, he enjoins us to 'pause and be enlightened':

> there is more
> In such a survey than the sating gaze
> Of wonder pleased, or awe which would adore
> The worship of the place, or the mere praise
> Of art and its great masters, who could raise
> What former time, nor skill, nor thought could plan;
> The fountain of sublimity displays
> Its depth, and thence may draw the mind of man
> Its golden sands, and learn what great conceptions can. (IV, 159)

Byron disdainfully sets a range of purely 'aesthetic' responses as well as a modern experience of the sublime – which spends itself in anonymous awe – over against a traditional theological conception of the transcendent, in which the sublime is unsundered from and is itself an aspect of the beautiful, which exerts a kind of 'erotic' lure that carries us beyond itself towards its 'depth' and a mystery that exceeds us and yet disclosively arrives.

If this contrastive reading is substantively correct, it suggests a modification of the dominant conception of Byron's anti-Romanticism; for while this is conventionally seen as a matter of irony, nihilism and a worldliness or materialism that contrasts with the visionary supernaturalism of Wordsworth and Coleridge, the foregoing comparison of moments of vision in *Childe Harold's Pilgrimage* with those on which it is allegedly based – which exhibit a drift away from a knowable, nameable transcendence towards the 'white radiance' of an anonymous sublime – suggests that Byron's anti-Romanticism may in part, paradoxically in spite of his scepticism, be a matter of his more orthodox religious inclinations.[52]

I have devoted a disproportionate amount of attention to a sense of the sacramental in Byron's verse, as this is one of the most contentious subjects in contemporary discussions of the poet. What is important for the argument of this chapter, however, is more simply the emergence of another kind of spectrality – namely, an immanence or numinous 'excess' at the heart of nature, such that things transcend themselves in being themselves and are paradoxically 'not only what they are'. Instead, by virtue of their participatory possession of that which is beyond them, created phenomena have an immaterial dimension, which is a constitutive part of what they are and enables them to 'give more than they have'. It is this uncanny sense of an 'is' without a subject or a presence that is manifested by something other than itself, which eludes our dialectically constituted ontological categories, that Byron's animistic imaginings and agitated syntax attempt to keep track of,

and which a logic of spectrality may help us apprehend. Parallel to
such spectral 'excesses' in nature, we also encounter in Byron's verse
a becoming-animate of man-made objects, as seen for example in the
extended description of the Apollo Belvedere, which 'breathes the flame
with which 'twas wrought' and exhibits a kind of Platonic contagion
in its mediation of divine inspiration, where 'each conception was a
heavenly guest' (IV, 162–63). However, since the preceding discussion
referred to the art of St Peter's and the way in which it sacramentally
'gives more than it has', I shall focus instead on one final category of
the in-between – namely, a form of ontological 'ec-centricity' in which
human being is lifted beyond itself.[53]

III

Byron's poetry appears to recognize three interrelated ways in which
human nature may be raised above itself: (1) as a result of our engraced
condition; (2) in moments of ecstatic communion; and (3) in living
'ec-centrically'. In spite of the continuities that blur these distinctions,
it will be helpful to consider them one at a time.[54]

In *Heaven and Earth*, a 'Mystery' based on Genesis 6, Aholibamah
– a descendent of Cain – calls out to one of the angels and says:

> There is a ray
> In me, which, though forbidden yet to shine,
> I feel was lighted at thy God's and thine.
> It may be hidden long: death and decay
> Our mother Eve bequeath'd us [...]. (I, i, 103–07)

This suggestively condensed description of human nature exhibits a
number of intriguing theological complexities. In the first place, instead
of a timeless and self-sufficient conception of human being, we are
presented with a 'narrativized' relational ontology, which involves a past
('was lighted', 'bequeath'd') and an implied future ('yet') that extend
beyond this-worldly existence. Secondly, on account of these constitutive
ontological continuities, human nature is said to have within it that
which exceeds it ('There is a ray / In me [...] I feel was lighted at thy
God's and thine'). However, thirdly, this light is 'hidden' and 'forbidden
yet to shine', as a consequence of a countervailing event ('death and
decay / Our mother Eve bequeath'd us') – namely, original sin. Human
nature is thus, in its created state, opened up to that which is beyond
it, though in a paradoxical manner; for, on this account, it 'is not only
what it is', and yet this 'excess' at the heart of its 'is' has a spectral

character, since it subsists in some sense 'without being'. What are we to make of this?

However puzzling it may appear to assert that, as ourselves, we are more than ourselves, and that this 'more' has a proleptic character, it does in fact correspond to a traditional theological understanding of the relationship between grace and nature. This has been summarily described by Hans Urs von Balthasar as 'the paradox of the spiritual creature that is ordained beyond itself by the innermost reality of its nature to a goal that is unreachable for it and that can only be given as a gift of grace.'[55] How relevant is the theological anthropology of *Heaven and Earth* to Byron's work more generally?

While the poet is famous for his dark and brooding heroes, who typically harbour some unnamed guilt and are tormented by their imprisoning interiority, there is also in his work a recurring and corroborating sense that man exceeds his material nature – that we have a 'mixed essence', described by Manfred as '[h]alf dust, half deity' (I, ii, 40), and that 'this clay' contains, without being able to contain, a 'spark immortal' or '[r]ay of him who form'd the whole'.[56] As Byron writes in 'Prometheus': 'Man is part divine, / A troubled stream from a pure source' (47–48). This does not, we should note, do away with the darkness; in fact, if anything, it *increases* the torment and sense of imprisonment.[57] It does, however, pointedly call into question materialist readings that deny the existence of any intimation in Byron's verse that the natural order – including human nature – communicates and participates in that which is beyond it. Perhaps the most illuminating reflections on this paradoxical state of being are to be found in *Childe Harold's Pilgrimage* Canto IV:

> Our life is a false nature – 'tis not in
> The harmony of things, – this hard decree,
> This uneradicable taint of sin,
> This boundless upas, this all-blasting tree,
> Whose root is earth, whose leaves and branches be
> The skies which rain their plagues on men like dew –
> Disease, death, bondage – all the woes we see –
> And worse, the woes we see not – which throb through
> The immedicable soul, with heart-aches ever new.
>
> Yet let us ponder boldly – 'tis a base
> Abandonment of reason to resign
> Our right of thought – our last and only place
> Of refuge; this, at least, shall still be mine:
> Though from our birth the faculty divine

Is chain'd and tortured – cabin'd, cribb'd, confined,
And bred in darkness, lest the truth should shine
Too brightly on the unprepared mind,
The beam pours in, for time and skill will couch the blind.
  (126–27)

To modern ears, there is doubtless something quite shocking about the extremity and inescapability of Byron's dark vision of human nature. The upas tree – a popular symbol in the nineteenth century of the deadliest poison – is in Byron's vision 'boundless' and 'all-blasting', whose root is the earth and whose branches are the sky. We are a long way here from Nature as a nurse or guide. Indeed, in Byron's image – in which plagues of disease and death fall 'like dew' – life itself becomes a form of destruction. (The poet seems to be syntactically mired and unable to get beyond the sentence's subject, which clogs its own progression in a spawning of synonyms – this, this, this, this – in a way that reinforces a sense of the proliferating blight it describes.) What is perhaps most shocking of all, though, is the fact that, for Byron, this is not a matter of contingent misery – the natural shocks to which flesh is heir. Instead, it is a matter of sin – 'uneradicable' and 'immedicable' sin – which is a constitutive feature of our fallen nature. As a result of such sin, according to Byron, we are not ourselves ('Our life is a false nature') and we are innately disfigured. Furthermore, as he affirms with extraordinary force, there is no hope of removing this 'taint', which, he implies, is divinely willed ('this hard decree'). And yet there is a 'yet'.

We have within us – which is also a constitutive part of our nature – a 'faculty divine'. And though it is 'chain'd and tortured – cabin'd, cribb'd, confined', this makes possible our reception of the 'beam' of 'truth'. At this point two paradoxes come into view, which are a key part of Byron's account of human nature. The first is bought about by the insistence on the one hand that our fallen nature is 'immedicable' on account of an 'uneradicable' taint, while also asserting on the other hand that we bear within us the efficacious imprint of the divine. The second paradox concerns the causal relationship between 'the faculty divine' and the 'beam' of 'truth', both of which appear to occupy the subject position, as a result of the curiously chiastic syntax of stanza 127 – in the course of which our incapacity becomes a kind of protection ('lest the truth should shine / Too brightly on the unprepared mind'). How do these two paradoxes tie in with the emerging account of human nature?

In the first case, the poet seems to be saying, we are blind and imprisoned, as a result of sin – which distorts even as it constitutes our nature – from which on the basis of our natural capacities there is emphatically no possibility of escape. (Byron would seem to be influenced here by the Calvinist doctrine of 'total depravity'.) And yet, while escape is impossible for us, as a result of the self-revelation of the divine – whose 'beam pours in' – we are lifted beyond our incapacities, without this elevation compromising our fallen status. In other words, what is given in divine revelation is the capacity to receive that revelation. However, this is immediately complicated by the second paradox, which seems to affirm – in spite of its gratuity – that this is not an extrinsic imposition that is alien to our nature. Rather, what Byron's description of 'the faculty divine' and the cooperative causality that it shares with the 'beam' of 'truth' suggests is that the human capacity to receive revelation is paradoxically ours and yet supernaturally given. (The argument is subtly conducted by the syntax, which appears to establish a relationship of identity between the 'faculty divine' that is within us from birth and the 'beam' of 'truth' that pours in from without.) In short, what we are given, as part of our nature, is 'a dynamic prescience of grace',[58] which lures us towards and furnishes us with the capability to receive that grace. Byron's description of human nature as paradoxically both fallen beneath and elevated above itself therefore makes sense from a theological perspective. This is how the matter is explained by de Lubac: human nature, he writes, has an 'unstable ontological constitution',

> which makes it at once something greater and something less than itself. [...] Hence that kind of dislocation, that mysterious lameness, due not merely to sin, but primarily and more fundamentally to being a creature made out of nothing which, astoundingly, touches God. [...] By the fact of being created, man is the 'companion in slavery' of all nature; but at the same time, because he is an image – 'in quantum est ad imaginem Dei' – he is 'capable of beatific knowledge' and has, as Origen said, 'the precept of liberty' implanted deep within him.[59]

This 'mysterious lameness' – which lies at the tormented centre of *Manfred* – that comes of our 'unstable ontological constitution' helps us to understand the second way in which human nature is elevated beyond itself. For this 'faculty divine' or 'precept of liberty', which is innate to us and yet gratuitously given, is the source of man's ecstatic potential. In the words of *Childe Harold*'s narrator: 'there is a fire / And motion of the soul which will not dwell / In its own narrow being' (III, 42); or, as Manfred insists, 'though cooped in clay', human beings possess an 'ethereal essence' or 'Promethean spark', which is the 'lightning of

[our] being' (II, iv, 68; I, i, 154–57). Hence, for Byron, it seems that human beings are – at least potentially – self-transcending, in spite of our 'uneradicable' fallen nature, since the grace that lifts us beyond our capacities, and prepares us as it were for its own reception, paradoxically allows us to overcome without cancelling our radical separation. As Byron affirms in *The Giaour*, this self-transcendence is an 'antiphonal' response to the *extasis amoris* of the divine, which is simultaneously the condition of its possibility:

> Love indeed is light from heaven –
> A spark of that immortal fire
> With angels shar'd – by Alla given,
> To lift from earth our low desire.
> Devotion wafts the mind above,
> But Heaven itself descends in love;
> A feeling from the Godhead caught,
> To wean from self each sordid thought –
> A Ray of him who form'd the whole –
> A Glory circling round the soul! (1131–40)

In this sense, human nature, for Byron, also has a spectral dimension and 'gives more than it has'. This is because, as he repeatedly insists, we have within us, as part of our nature, that which is infinitely other than us – 'A spark of that immortal fire', 'A Ray of him who form'd the whole' – which means paradoxically that we 'are not only what we are' or that in being ourselves we are *more than* ourselves.

I have written elsewhere about this kind of self-transcendence,[60] so will confine myself here to a few general remarks. It should firstly be emphasized, against a recurrent assumption to the contrary, that the fleeting character of the ecstatic moment – described by Buber as the 'lightning and counter-lightning of encounter'[61] – is not an argument against its legitimacy.[62] Indeed, to hold that such experience cannot be sustained or that the 'momentary glimpse of Eden also precipitates its loss' is not an argument against its efficacy – it is part of the *religious* conception of such moments. As T.S. Eliot famously writes, without in any way impugning the validity of his visionary claims: 'human kind / Cannot bear much reality.'[63] Being creatures of a 'mixed essence' means that 'this clay will sink / Its spark immortal'; though it also means – since it must first take flight in order to sink – that this 'spark immortal' may escape its clay.[64]

There is another feature of the poet's ecstatic vision that warrants attention. In both *The Giaour* and *The Island*, Byron seems to distinguish between 'vertical' and 'horizontal' forms of ekstasis – that is, between the ecstasy of the devotee, whose 'soul is gone before his dust to heaven' (*The Island*, II, 14, 370–75), and the moment of ecstatic communion with nature or other created phenomena:

> How often we forget all time, when lone,
> Admiring Nature's universal throne,
> Her woods – her wilds – her waters – the intense
> Reply of hers to our intelligence!
> Live not the Stars and Mountains? Are the Waves
> Without a spirit? Are the dropping caves
> Without a feeling in their silent tears?
> No, no; – they woo and clasp us to their spheres,
> Dissolve this clog and clod of clay before
> Its hour, and merge our soul in the great shore. (II, 16, 382–91)[65]

As with most amorous entanglements, it's hard to say exactly who started it, since Nature's ecstatic address to us is described as a 'reply', and yet things in nature appear preveniently to be soliciting us. Further complications are brought into view by the use of the word 'woo' to describe the ecstatic solicitations of nature, as this is also how the poet describes the erotic lure of heaven, which incites a reciprocal ekstasis in man and 'woos us to its brink' (*CHP*, III, 14). This suggests that the distinction between 'vertical' and 'horizontal' ekstasis may not be absolute after all or that the difference is subsumed by a superordinate continuity within the divine – since in Eckhart's epigrammatical phrasing, 'Both grace and nature are his'[66] – which is precisely what one would expect from the 'participatory' ontology evinced in the poet's vision of nature. Either way, whoever started it and however grace and nature perichoretically intertwine, the poet's description of 'horizontal' ekstasis reveals an amorous interlacement of call and response – an 'excess' in us answering a 'more than it is' in nature – which is experienced as a two-way relationship, even if our 'answer' is the only evidence of the call that provoked it.[67]

This kind of reciprocal 'horizontal' ekstasis, of which we find corollaries in Denys and Augustine, is of particular interest to our present discussion because the poet's connection of our engraced condition to the self-exceeding character of nature points towards a much wider and more coherent metaphysical vision than is usually allowed in discussions of transcendence in Byron's verse.[68] This extended metaphysical vision is widened still further by the account of art in *Childe Harold* Canto IV, in which there is a clear parallel between what Ward Pafford describes as the 'living flame and cloddish substance' that constitutes the poet's conception of human nature and the 'miraculous blending of substance and spirit' in his 'ecstatic' conception of art.[69]

Of course, Byron isn't always convinced by – or interested in – moments of transcendent vision, and frequently delights in a materiality *un*apparelled in celestial light. However, he is recurrently prepared, in a more or less consistent and cogent fashion, to entertain it as a possibility. This means that purely materialist readings – which, as Chesterton observed, involve a more absolute veto (since 'the materialist is not allowed to admit into his spotless machine the slightest speck of spiritualism or miracle')[70] – are inadequate to the poet's vision of art, nature and human being.

Something else has come to light in our consideration of Byron's account of human nature, which he sees as radically disfigured by sin, to the extent that 'Our life is a false nature'. Why is this emphasis on sin so significant?

There is an uninvestigated tendency to view the poet's nagging sense of imprisonment in 'this clog and clod of clay' as a sign of a recalcitrant materialism that sets his work over against the religious.[71] And yet, as we saw in his discussion of original sin, that which impedes the poet's transcendental aspirations – the clay that sinks its 'spark immortal' – is *itself* conceived in religious terms. Moreover, if we compare Byron's thwarted, partial and unsustainable moments of 'nocturnal' ekstasis – in which 'the veil / Of heaven is *half* undrawn'[72] – with Wordsworth's descriptions of epiphanic vision, there appears to be a more orthodox reverence in the impediments of the former. This is because, in line with traditional theological accounts of the *visio dei*, Byron preserves a sense that, ahead of the eschaton, God 'dwells in unapproachable light' (1 Timothy, 6: 16), and so immediate vision of the divine essence is beyond the natural capacities of the finite mind. Such reverent reservations are rendered explicit in the stanzas on St Peter's quoted earlier (*CHP*, IV, 155). In this climactic moment of vision, as the mind is '[e]xpanded by the genius of the spot', we can see an orthodox religious reservation not only in the poet's moral proviso – 'if found worthy' – but also in his fidelity to the Old Testament teaching that we cannot look upon the face of God without being 'blasted by his brow'. We have thus arrived at a rather surprising conclusion, which may be summed up as follows. Byron is commonly assumed to be the most transgressive and irreligious of the Romantic poets; and yet in his account of human nature and related descriptions of visionary experience, we see him persistently and emphatically setting limits – limits that have a theological provenance and betoken an orthodox religious consciousness.[73]

In addition to the intrinsic 'excess' of our engraced nature and the self-transcendence of the ecstatic moment, there is finally a third possibility that comes to light in Byron's verse whereby human being may be elevated beyond itself. This is most conspicuously evident in the character of Aurora Raby, who is consistently described in terms of a paradoxical 'ec-centric' existence:

> she had something of sublime
> In eyes which sadly shone, as seraphs' shine.
> All youth – but with an aspect beyond time [...].
>
> Her spirit seem'd as seated on a throne
> Apart from the surrounding world [...].
>
> The worlds beyond this world's perplexing waste
> Had more of her existence, for in her
> There was a depth of feeling to embrace
> Thoughts, boundless, deep, but silent too as Space.
> (XV, 45; 47; XVI, 48)

Aurora's poised contemplative air contrasts starkly with the 'far-darting' lightning of Manfred's being or the 'fire / And motion' of *Childe Harold's Pilgrimage*, 'which will not dwell / In its own narrow being'. But once again, what we find in the former is a sort of ontological vagrancy – an 'ec-centric' dilation of her existence 'beyond Time' and 'beyond this world's perplexing waste' – which parallels, even as it radically differs from, the ecstatic ontology of the Byronic hero. Such ontological ec-centricity, which is a matter of existing 'outside the self' in a perpetual ecstasy of spiritual life, rather than the discrete ekstasis of momentary communion, corresponds to a traditional theological conception of rapture[74] and further widens the poet's metaphysical vision. This should be extended in another direction, too, as the 'proleptic' ontological vagrancy of Aurora – whose finitude reaches forwards into eternity – may be seen as the chiastic counterpart to the 'analeptic' ontology of the Virgin Mary, whose ascended splendour shines 'backwards' into finitude, as seen in the 'Ave Maria' of *Don Juan* and mediating icon in *The Siege of Corinth*.[75] To be sure, this kind of 'ec-centricity' is something of an exception in Byron's work (though, as Bernard Beatty has shown, Aurora's 'immortal consciousness' and her 'intimacy with unimaginable space' are shared, albeit with a different valency, by the Byronic hero).[76] However, the poet's creation of Aurora

Raby, whose spiritual 'ec-centricity' may well have been destined to transform the course of his greatest work, reveals – *whatever* he had in mind for Juan – that there are, for Byron, more possibilities in heaven and earth than are granted in a materialist reading of his work.

*

What I have attempted to illustrate in this chapter is Byron's abiding fascination with the spectral, which extends beyond the curtain-flapping kind of ghost to include 'unhomely' in-between phenomena that are irreducible to classical ontological categories. I have focused on three such 'shades of being' in particular: 'vagrant' presences that flicker uncannily between being and non-being; an in-dwelling 'excess' in nature that is radically other than and yet paradoxically part of that which communicates it; and a form of 'ec-centric' being, in which human nature is elevated beyond itself. In each case, it was suggested, we are confronted by a mode of appearing that we are unable to reach by saying that it 'is'.[77] In doing so, I have sought to counteract a prevalent tendency in Byron studies to dismiss the poet's descriptions of transcendence as anomalous moments, attributable to a temporary and 'purely literary' influence. More specifically, it was suggested that if we take cognizance of the 'shades of being' with which such moments are connected and which appear throughout the poet's work, a more pervasive and coherent metaphysical vision emerges to view, the significance of which is harder to dismiss.

This more pervasive metaphysical vision, as I have sought to show, is not always, or even usually, a matter of abstract speculation (this was of course the kind of metaphysics the poet scorned), yet neither is it limited to the depiction of otherworldly entities. Byron's interest in 'shades of being' is also made manifest through a range of 'catachrestic' strategies, by means of which the poet attempts to save the appearance of these ever-escaping bits of reality, whose ontological trespasses baffle the processes of representation. On the one hand, for example, attention was drawn to the adversative 'dis-ease' of Byron's syntax, which crosses itself out with concessive clauses and subverts itself in a torturous proliferation of collateral ramifications.[78] While this kind of syndetic fidgeting has been interpreted as a sign of 'confusion' or lack of 'precise comprehension',[79] it may equally be seen as an 'apophatic' tactic, which attempts to convey by way of an performative unsaying what was precisely apprehended but which cannot be depicted – namely, a presence that gives itself to be sensed without substance. In this way, as Flannery

O'Connor once observed, distortion may serve as an instrument of revelation.[80] On the other hand, it is possible to discern in the poet's depiction of a 'universe tingling with anthropomorphic life'[81] an iconic expedient or swerve into something between *mimesis* and *poesis*, since a 'making' is required in order to reflect what's actually there. Of course, such animistic figurations have come to be almost universally derided as instances of 'pathetic fallacy'. And yet, as we have seen, Ruskin himself endorses a truthful theological variant of such 'sympathy with nature'. For if the created order analogically participates in a divine beyond, as Byron ventures in *Childe Harold's Pilgrimage*, then it will 'give more than it has' or disclose that which is beyond it as part of its being. It will therefore be necessary – against the bar of reason – to depict things as radically other than they are in order to signify their self-exceeding nature. In other words, in 'going beyond' things and 'making them strange', we are paradoxically revealing them as they ultimately are.[82]

This isn't Byron's way of speaking of course. However, his attempts to depict the ineffable in *The Vision of Judgment* – in which 'the person of the Deity' is reverently 'withheld from sight'[83] – appear to bespeak a comparable intuition. In trying to describe the Archangel Michael, for example, he writes:

> He turned all colours – as a peacock's tail,
>   Or sunset streaming through a Gothic skylight
> In some old abbey, or a trout not stale,
>   Or distant lightning on the horizon *by* night,
> Or a fresh rainbow, or a grand review
> Of thirty regiments in red, green, and blue. (61)

While the stanza's proliferating string of comparisons clearly evinces a this-worldly delight in the variousness of things, it is at the same time an advertisement of its own referential inadequacy. And yet, as a result of this very deficiency – which stages the failure of referentiality as such – it brings into view an unenvisageable object.[84]

In delineating a 'more than' or a 'going beyond' in an attempt paradoxically to depict that which is, Byron's poetry involves what Rowan Williams refers to as a 'transcendental realism'.[85] That is because, as I have attempted to show, there are bits of reality that 'is' doesn't cover, but which may be evoked by a discourse of spectrality. To put this in the poet's own language: in preserving a vision that 'day's broad light can not remove' of 'half-wrought / Shapes that must undergo mortality', 'spectres whom no exorcism can bind', a created order 'impregnate with divinity' and the 'Eternal Spirit of the chainless mind',[86] Byron's poetry may indeed be described as an enchanted tale 'of all that is and something more'.[87]

Notes

1 Jerome McGann, *Byron and Romanticism* (Cambridge: Cambridge University Press, 2002), p. 164; Virginia Woolf, *A Writer's Diary*, ed. Leonard Woolf (New York, NY: Harcourt, 1953), p. 3.

2 See Introduction above, p. 23, n. 1.

3 Rubenstein, 'Of Ghosts and Angels: Derrida, Kushner, and the Impossibility of Forgiveness', in *JCRT*, 9:1 (2008), p. 86.

4 Following the practice of the contemporary theologian David Brown, I am using the term 'sacramental' in a deliberately loose but traditional sense to refer to a 'symbolic mediation of the divine in and through the material' (Brown, *God and Enchantment of Place*, p. 30).

5 In describing the act of invocation as 'preposterous', I am alluding to the way in which – as a call that appears to seek a subsequent response and simultaneously reveal an anterior sense of calling – it is a gesture that seems to 'come after' and 'precede'.

6 According to Emily Bernhard Jackson, we should read the poet's unsettling of his own perspective in the invocation as the announcement of a 'commitment to confusion' (*The Development of Byron's Philosophy of Knowledge*, p. 53). However, not all equivocation or epanorthosis is necessarily a sign of confusion. It might instead, I suggest, be an attempt to communicate a complex reality or what Vincent Newey refers to as a 'composite perception – not an "either … or" but an "and … and"' – which may defy the regulative constraints of logic but is faithful to the 'illogicality' of experience (Newey, 'Authoring the Self: *Childe Harold* III and IV', in *Byron and the Limits of Fiction*, eds. Bernard Beatty and Vincent Newey (Liverpool University Press, 1988), p. 165). In this particular case, I think the poet is inclined to revere the Muse and is embarrassed about his inclination, both of which he seeks to represent in the 'oxymoronic' tonalities of the invocation.

7 In *The Truth in Painting* (1978), Derrida speaks of the frame or 'parergon' as mischievously outside and yet part of the work. In Byron's poem, this stepping outside the narrative, within the narrative, is itself framed by the 'parergonal' notes, which open up a space that disconcerts the opposition between 'inside' and 'outside' the work of fiction.

8 Byron draws attention to this habit himself: 'and yet – and yet – always *yet* and *but*' (*BLJ*, IV, p. 77). Emphasis in the original unless otherwise stated.

9 Cheeke, *Byron and Place: History, Translation, Nostalgia*, pp. 46, 45.

10 Ibid., p. 52.

11 *Profanations*, trans. Jeff Fort (New York, NY: Zone Books, 2007), p. 73.

12 Ibid., p. 78.

13 Ibid., p. 76.

14 This spectral 'remnant of sacredness', which induces an oxymoronic comportment in the poet – that swings between and at times conjoins a posture of scepticism and reverence – is apparent in Byron's vision of Greece more generally, which he

describes as a 'Land of lost gods', but then a few stanzas later insists: 'Where'er we tread 'tis haunted, holy ground' (*CHP*, II, 85, 88).

15 Buber, *I and Thou*, trans. Ronald Gregor Smith (New York, NY: Charles Scribner's Sons, 1958), pp. 3, 8.

16 Culler, 'Apostrophe', in *The Pursuit of Signs: Semiotics, Literature, Deconstruction* (Ithaca, NY: Cornell University Press, 1981).

17 In a discussion of Wordsworth's poetic language, Barbara Johnson observes how the trope of personification engenders 'figures of half-aliveness' (*A World of Difference* (Baltimore, MD: Johns Hopkins, 1987), p. 97).

18 Agamben, *Stanzas: Word and Phantasm in Western Culture*, trans. Ronald L. Martinez (Minneapolis, MN: University of Minnesota Press, 1993), p. 59.

19 Ibid., p. 31.

20 It is unfortunately beyond the scope of this chapter to consider the work of William Desmond on the 'metaxological', which he identifies as a 'porous' realm of being or milieu of overdeterminacy – distinct from the univocal, equivocal and dialectical – in which the fugitive intermediations of sameness and difference have their being. See his trilogy: *Being and the Between* (1995); *Ethics and the Between* (2001); and *God and the Between* (2008).

21 Catherine Pickstock, *After Writing: On the Liturgical Consummation of Philosophy* (Oxford: Blackwell, 1998), p. 195.

22 De Man, *The Rhetoric of Romanticism* (New York, NY: Columbia University Press, 1984), p. 78.

23 Byron makes a connection himself between the suspended animation of the living subject and the 'borrowed' life of inanimate objects in his description of Haidée's distended death, whose in-between state of being is compared to artworks that 'give more than they have' (*DJ*, IV, 61). See also the description of Dudù, who is compared to 'Pygmalion's statue waking, / The Mortal and the Marble still at strife, / And timidly expanding into life' (*DJ*, VI, 43).

24 Maritain, *Creative Intuition in Art and Poetry* (New York, NY: Pantheon, 1953), p. 670. For a detailed discussion of the theological complexities I am passing over here, see John Milbank's essay 'Scholasticism, Modernism and Modernity' (*Modern Theology*, 22:4 (2006)). See also Rowan Williams, *Grace and Necessity: Reflections on Art and Love* (London: Continuum, 2005), which offers a meditation on the 'revelatory dimension of the imagination' on the basis of Maritain's principles (p. x).

25 *Creative Intuition in Art and Poetry*, p. 127.

26 See, for example, McGann, 'Byron and Wordsworth', in *Byron and Romanticism*, pp. 173–201.

27 On this point, I disagree with Peter Cochran, who is determined, in spite of the evidence, to present Byron's poetry as a thoroughly disenchanted sphere, devoid of sacramental intimations. Contrasting Byron's description of nature with that of Gerard Manley Hopkins, he writes: 'No matter how shéerly Byron plóds, *his* plough down sillion never shines.' ('Byron, Body and Soul', in *Byron and Women (and Men)*, ed. Peter Cochran (Newcastle upon Tyne: Cambridge Scholars Publishing, 2010), p. 201.) In what follows, I hope to show the illegitimacy of this 'never'.

28 *Modern Painters*, vol. III (London: George Allen, 1906), p. 324.

29 We find a parallel attempt to distinguish between 'fallacious' and 'legitimate' uses

of the imagination – that is, 'feignings' which are permissible or necessary – in
Ruskin's accounts of the ideal and the grotesque. See *Modern Painters*, III, chapters
IV, VI and VIII.

30 Williams, *Grace and Necessity*, p. 18.

31 In his illuminating study of Wordsworth's 'poetic thinking', Simon Jarvis teases
out a 'laudable' counterpart to the pejorative bestowal of moral meaning that is
pathetic fallacy (*Wordsworth's Philosophical Song*, p. 46).

32 Derrida discusses the uncanny rustling of existential constructions in relation to
Marx's 'es spukt' – which recalls Heidegger's 'es gibt' – in *Specters of Marx*, p. 216ff.

33 For Freud, an exemplary instance of the uncanny is engendered by 'doubts whether
an apparently animate being is really alive; or conversely, whether a lifeless object
might not in fact be animate'. See 'The "Uncanny"' (1919), in *The Standard
Edition of the Complete Works of Sigmund Freud*, vol. 17, trans. James Strachey
(Harmondsworth: Penguin, 1985), p. 226.

34 See, for example, *Manfred*: 'the stars / Shone through the rents of ruin' (III, iv,
13–14) and later on in *Childe Harold*: 'the stars twinkle through the loops of time'
(IV, 144).

35 *Modern Painters*, vol. II (London: George Allen, 1906), pp. 39, 94. It is this strand
of natural theology in Ruskin's work that underwrites his counter-conception of
a revelatory poesis or 'epiphanic' variant of pathetic fallacy.

36 Ibid., p. 70.

37 Ibid., p. 72.

38 See, for example, Earnest J. Lovell, *Byron: The Record of a Quest* (Hamden,
CT: Archon Books, 1966), and Philip W. Martin, *Byron: A Poet before His
Public* (Cambridge: Cambridge University Press, 1982). Alan Rawes is a welcome
exception, who draws attention to the 'idealism' and sense of 'benediction'
in cantos III and IV, but argues that Byron was in fact 'distracted from [his
own idealism] by the very importation of Wordsworthian ideas' (*Byron's Poetic
Experimentation: Childe Harold, The Tales, and the Quest for Comedy* (Aldershot:
Ashgate, 2000), p. 117). For an insightful reconsideration of the debate, see Philip
Shaw, 'Wordsworth and Byron', in *The Byron Journal*, 31 (2003).

39 From a philosophical point of view, Christianity – the religious tradition in which
both Byron and Wordsworth were brought up – is customarily seen as exhibiting
a reconciled conjunction of transcendence and immanence. It is therefore in terms
of preservation of this 'Christian' conjunction that I am defining the religious
orthodoxy of the two poets. For a contextualizing discussion of this matter, see
David Brown, 'The Sacramental in Modern European Thought', in *The Oxford
Handbook of Theology and Modern European Thought*, eds. Nicholas Adams, George
Pattison and Graham Ward (Oxford: Oxford University Press, 2012).

40 This understanding of 'a transcendental Deity, sovereign, manifested in his works,
but not identified with them' is, according to Marjarum, 'Byron's most characteristic conception of the Divine' (*Byron as Skeptic and Believer*, p. 65).

41 A degree of separation is implied in the description of 'something far more deeply
interfused' (94–103); however, compared to the transcendence of the Creator in
Byron's vision, it remains an essentially immanentized 'something'. For defence of
the poem's residual transcendence, as evidence of a 'panentheistic' epiphany, see
William A. Ulmer, *The Christian Wordsworth, 1798–1805* (New York, NY: SUNY
Press, 2001), p. 42ff.

BYRON AND THE TRESPASSING OF ONTOLOGY

42 T.S. Eliot, 'East Coker', V, *Four Quartets*.

43 In foregrounding the poet's preference for an anonymous immanence, I am not concurring with those critics who see Wordsworth's visionary vagueness as muddled thinking or an opportunistic evasion, in an attempt to be 'uplifting yet non-denominational', as Empson notoriously describes it (*Seven Types of Ambiguity* (London: Chatto & Windus, 1930), p. 154). Rather, I would suggest that the evasion of precise predication is itself paradoxically a referential strategy, which seeks to signify that which is beyond all names by way of a synonymic denomination. In other words, the semantic unit is not the individual act of naming, but rather the flux of referentiality as a whole, such that the meaning is generated performatively, *across* the individual predicative gestures, whose very inadequacy is harnessed as a way of evoking what they cannot name.

44 Barbour, '"Between Two Worlds": The Structure of the Argument in "Tintern Abbey"', in *Nineteenth-Century Literature*, 48:2 (1993), p. 159.

45 The assertion that 'not a beam, nor air, nor leaf is lost / But hath a part of being' – which is careful to leave no part of the natural order outside the participatory embrace of the divine – suggests that the difference between life and death in created phenomena is subverted by a transcendent continuity in the life of the divine, which annuls without abolishing ontic distinctions. For a discussion of this matter in general, see Jean-Luc Marion, *God without Being*, pp. 83–102.

46 Ibid., p. 89. According to Marjarum, this is Byron's characteristic stance on the matter: 'He [Byron] clings with particular tenacity to the notion of that death and life are "misnamed", not properly to be understood as contradictory terms like *being* and *extinction*, but different forms of existence.' See *Byron as Skeptic and Believer*, p. 62.

47 Ulmer, *The Christian Wordsworth*, p. 42.

48 Milbank, 'Sublimity: The Modern Transcendent', in *Transcendence: Philosophy, Literature, and Theology Approach the Beyond*, ed. Regina Schwartz (New York, NY: Routledge, 2004).

49 Ibid., p. 211.

50 Ibid., pp. 223, 212–13.

51 See stanzas 88–90.

52 While this calls into question a current consensus, it reaffirms for example the views of Ruskin, who defended Byron against accusations of blasphemy and argued – in comparison to Wordsworth – that Byron was 'certainly the more reverent' and who writes of a passage on man's Fall from *The Island*: 'perfectly orthodox theology, you observe; no denial of the fall, – nor substitution of Bacterian birth for it. Nay, nearly Evangelical theology, in contempt for the human heart; but with deeper than Evangelical humility, acknowledging also what is sordid in its civilization.' (Ruskin, 'Fiction, Fair and Foul', in *WJR*, vol. 34, p. 333.)

53 For other examples of man-made objects that appear to mediate something beyond them, see the statue of 'the Virgin Mother of the God-born child', who 'made the earth below seem holy ground' in *Don Juan* (XIII, 61) or the warrior's statue in *Marino Faliero*, in which the Doge believes there is a spirit 'that acts and sees, unseen, though felt' (III, i, 84–96).

54 Discussions of transcendence in Byron's verse have tended to concentrate exclusively on the ecstatic moment – that is, discrete experiences in which the self has a sense of being 'carried away' – which has had the effect of misleadingly diminishing

the apparent significance of the subject in the poet's work. The threefold model suggested above represents an attempt to bring into view the larger pattern of which such experiences are but a part.

55 *The Theology of Henri de Lubac*, trans. Susan Clements (San Francisco, CA: Ignatius Press, 1983), p. 13. For a lucid summary of this highly complex and contested teaching, see Guy Mansini, 'The Abiding Theological Significance of Henri de Lubac's Surnaturel', in *The Thomist*, 73:4 (2009).

56 *CHP*, III, p. 14; *The Giaour*, p. 1139.

57 Henri de Lubac writes as follows of the ancients, though it also seems relevant to the Byronic hero: 'When they did not succeed in extinguishing [that organic spark of uncertainty, of longing and of discontent which lies at the depths of mankind's inmost being], it obsessed or even deranged them. It could only raise nature too high, or bring it down too low. A fragment of the divine, or the dust of the earth, or a chance and unsteady mixture of the two.' See *The Mystery of the Supernatural*, trans. Rosemary Sheed (Montreal: Palm Publishers, 1967), p. 170.

58 John Milbank, *The Suspended Middle: Henri de Lubac and the Debate concerning the Supernatural* (London: SCM, 2005), p. 27.

59 *The Mystery of the Supernatural*, pp. 147–48. I am conscious of the incongruity of invoking the Calvinist doctrine of 'total depravity' alongside a Catholic understanding of grace and nature as a way of illuminating Byron's theological anthropology. However, this corresponds to an incongruity in Byron's views, which, as Earnest Lovell observes, were shaped by his early 'Calvinistic-generated categories' and 'the Catholic sympathies of his later years', which meant that while he was unable fully 'to accept either one of these two great faiths', the poet was nevertheless influenced by both (*The Record of a Quest*, p. 192).

60 '"Eden's Door": The Porous Worlds of *Childe Harold's Pilgrimage* and *Don Juan*', in *The Byron Journal*, 37:2 (2009).

61 Buber, *I and Thou*, p. 77.

62 For a dogmatic anti-metaphysical reading, see Robert Gleckner, *Byron and the Ruins of Paradise* (Baltimore, MD: Johns Hopkins University Press, 1967), in which he writes as follows of the transcendental aspirations in *Childe Harold's Pilgrimage* and the ecstasy between man and God in *The Giaour*: 'That promise is illusory [...] just as the mind's aspirations are vain; for man is man, not God, and his love, therefore, however full and complete, is imperfect. Its momentary glimpse of Eden also precipitates its loss' (p. 262). It's hard to see on what grounds it is possible to assert so categorically that the poet's metaphysical claims are 'illusory' and 'vain'. That 'man is man, not God' is hardly conclusive, especially since from a theological point of view man – *as* man – is made in the image of God and thus has 'a profound ontological kinship with the divine origin' (Milbank, *The Suspended Middle*, p. 15).

63 'Burnt Norton', I, *Four Quartets*.

64 As Vincent Newey affirms: 'Byron never does renounce transcendental aspiration, though he knows its ends cannot be achieved except in flashes, at least while life continues' (Newey, 'Authoring the Self: *Childe Harold* III and IV', p. 177).

65 According to Anne Mellor, the poet's description of intoxication in *Don Juan* (II, 178ff) may also be seen as expressing 'a kind of self-transcendence – an expansion of human possibility, a widening of the senses and the spirit that is the closest they [human creatures] can come to divinity'. See *English Romantic Irony*, p. 46.

This makes even more sense when it is recalled that the phrase 'sober inebriation' is how the Church Fathers (following Philo) referred to the state of holy ecstasy.

66 Meister Eckhart, *Selected Writings*, trans. Oliver Davies (London: Penguin, 1994), p. 51.

67 See Jean-Louis Chrétien, *The Call and Response*, trans. Anne A. Davenport (New York, NY: Fordham University Press, 2004).

68 See, for example, Lovell, *Byron: The Record of a Quest*, in which he claims 'it is impossible to regard the pantheistic expressions produced in the summer of 1816 as anything other than purely "literary" effusions, the product of a limited literary influence' and that subsequent expressions of 'mystical' experience 'represent nothing more nor less than Byron recalling his own earlier productions' (pp. 127, 123).

69 Pafford, 'Byron and the Mind of Man: *Childe Harold III–IV* and *Manfred*', in *Studies of Romanticism*, 1:2 (1962), pp. 111, 122.

70 G.K. Chesterton, *Orthodoxy* (New York, NY: Doubleday, 1959), p. 19.

71 See, for example, Peter Cochran, 'Byron, Body and Soul'.

72 *CHP*, IV, p. 49 [emphasis added].

73 In emphasizing Byron's setting of limits and the religious significance of this, I am indebted to Vincent Newey's 'Authoring the Self: *Childe Harold* III and IV'.

74 See, for instance, Francis de Sales's *Treatise on the Love of God*, which distinguishes between three kinds of rapture, including the ecstasy of living. See also Karl Barth, who speaks of the spiritual life as an 'eccentric' [*ekzentrisch*] mode of existence. See Barth, *Die Kirchliche Dogmatik* (Zurich: TVZ, 1932–1970), IV/1, p. 830; IV/2, pp. 893–94; IV/3.2, pp. 629–31.

75 *DJ*, III, 101–103; *The Siege of Corinth*, 33, 947ff.

76 Beatty, 'Fiction's Limit and Eden's Door', in *Byron and the Limits of Fiction*, pp. 29–33.

77 Jean-Luc Marion, 'The "End of Metaphysics" as a Possibility', in *Religion after Metaphysics*, ed. Mark A. Wrathall and trans. Daryl Lee (Cambridge: Cambridge University Press, 2003), p. 176.

78 'If I am sincere with myself', Byron famously remarks of his journal writing, 'every page should confute, refute, and utterly abjure its predecessor' (*BLJ*, III, p. 233). Something of this seems to be apparent at a clausal level, too.

79 Bernhard Jackson, *The Development of Byron's Philosophy of Knowledge*, pp. 53, 49.

80 O'Connor, *Mystery and Manners* (New York, NY: Farrar, Straus & Giroux, 1970), p. 162.

81 C.S. Lewis, *English Literature in the Sixteenth Century, excluding Drama* (Oxford: Oxford University Press, 1954), p. 4.

82 For a related discussion of 'magic idealism' in Novalis and Coleridge, see Alison Milbank, 'Apologetics and the Imagination: Making Strange', in *Imaginative Apologetics: Theology, Philosophy and the Catholic Tradition*, ed. Andrew Davidson (London: SCM Press, 2011).

83 Preface to *The Vision of Judgment*.

84 See also stanzas XXVIII and LIV, in which the poet reflects on the problems of representing the transcendent by means of 'earthly likenesses' and 'comparisons from clay'.

85 Williams, *Grace and Necessity*, p. 21.

86 'The Harp the Monarch Minstrel Swept'; *The Prophecy of Dante*, II, 6–7; *CHP*, IV, 24; *CHP*, IV, 55; 'Sonnet on Chillon'.

87 In *Don Juan*, the poet claims: 'my tale is / "De rebus cunctis et quibûsdam aliis"' (XVI, 3).

CHAPTER THREE

Byron and the Noonday Demons

Mary Hurst

Thou shalt not be afraid for the terror by night;
Nor for the arrow that flieth by day;
Nor for the pestilence that walketh in darkness;
Nor for the destruction that wasteth at noonday.

(Psalm 91: 5–6)

In his journal of 1821, Byron sets out a problem that concerns the secular, aristocratic condition of *ennui*:

What is the reason that I have been all my lifetime, more or less *ennuyé*? [...] I presume that it is constitutional, as well as the waking in low spirits which I have invariably done for many years. Temperance and exercise, which I have practised at times, and for a long time vigorously and violently, made little or no difference. Violent passions did.[1]

Ennui, a state of melancholic boredom, is associated with aristocrats and aesthetes, those with time on their hands. Byron, himself an aristocrat and aesthete, had an experimental approach towards the resolution of his condition. He tries temperance and exercise with no success, but he finds that 'violent passions' help in combating the condition. Byron, perhaps sadly or most probably wryly, associates his problem with a particular time of the day, 'waking in low spirits'. His analysis that it is 'constitutional' is roughly similar to the Augustinian notion of Original Sin or the now fashionable reference to DNA and genetic inheritance, in that he feels that he was born into his condition and, despite continuous efforts, cannot easily change it. Byron's analysis is not wholly solipsistic but is it, in any way, spiritual? This essay sets out to present a sequence of ideas that locates the secular categories of *ennui* and melancholy more precisely as the silhouettes of the Greek and Scholastic theological term *acedia*, which has been loosely translated from the term that describes a spiritual condition of the Desert Fathers, understood as 'the noonday demon'.[2]

Such an argument is not without precedent. Jerome McGann, in his essay 'Byron's Lyric Poetry', observes: 'Romanticism is regularly and usefully characterised in terms lifted from a certain set of adjectives, such as: subjective, impassioned, personal, sincere, spontaneous, reflective, self-conscious.'[3] These terms, while they are secular characteristics of the psychological realms of the poetry of the period, also fit comfortably into the medieval concept of the spiritual condition of *acedia*.

The epigraph to this essay is taken from a well-known psalm, traditionally used at Compline, which in its origins concerns what were considered to be real demons causing personal, physical harm.[4] In the Douay version, based on the Septuagint and Vulgate, demons/devils are specifically cited: 'thou shalt not be afraid [...] of the business that flieth about in the dark; of invasion or of the noonday devil' (Psalm 91: 5–6).[5] These devils are more powerful at certain times of the day, especially at noon and night. Historical accuracy of the dating of these psalms is much disputed, though approximately a thousand years after their formulation, the Christian Desert Fathers retain the literally demonic understanding of the text but give a more psychological version of the condition. Evagrius, in his writings on the Seven Deadly Sins, describes it as:

> the noonday demon [...] he instils in the heart of the monk a hatred for the place, a hatred for his very life itself, [...] he induces the monk to forsake his cell and drop out of the fight.[6]

Evagrius pinpoints the hottest part of the day, when sleepiness, hunger and lethargy are most likely to occur. He suggests that the demons attack through various routes: 'they attack men of the world chiefly through their deeds [...] but they attack desert solitaries by means of thoughts'.[7] For the desert solitary, these demons of thought brought boredom with the religious life and the constraints of the monastic cell, which in turn agitated the monk so much that he was tempted to quit the cell and flee from his community. There is a move here from the idea that waste places are physically inhabited by demons to a more psychological sense that solitude brings out such demons of thought. In making space in one's mind, a demon will attempt to control that mental space. Evagrius' demarcations between 'men of the world' and 'desert solitaries' have resonances that reverberate throughout Byron's own continuing considerations of his demon. While not an obviously spiritual figure, Byron is clearly a 'man of the world', who is, at the same time, aware of the vexations of demons and, in an unconscious agreement with Evagrius, articulates the effect and origins of the demon as intellectual – 'The blight of life – the demon, Thought' (*CHP*, I, 'To Inez', 6), to which I will return.

After criticism by Francis Jeffrey that the poet 'delights too exclusively in the delineation of a certain morbid exaltation of character and feeling', Byron appears to be aware not only of the condition but of the effect that such an attribution may have on his public persona.[8] He complains to Moore that he 'will never be able to shake off [his] sables in public imagination'.[9] His commercial judgment is sensitive to the imputation of a figure of darkness and melancholy, a criticism levelled once again at Byron by William Hazlitt, who detected elements of a melancholic demon in Byron's writing – a demon he judged would be deleterious to the reading public:

> He hangs the cloud, the film of his existence over all outward things – sits in the centre of his thoughts, and enjoys dark night, bright day, the glitter and gloom 'in cell monastic' – we see the mournful pall, the crucifix, [...] the agonized brow of genius, the wasted form of beauty – but we are still imprisoned in a dungeon [...].[10]

Enforced or voluntary solitude in 'cell monastic' and 'imprisoned in a dungeon' is a vocabulary that involves an unwitting nod in the direction of the spiritual condition of *acedia*. Hazlitt's depiction – 'He hangs the cloud' – begins to describe the poet's struggle; though my emphasis is on 'begin', while Hazlitt's observations come to rest on Byron as the 'pampered egotist'.[11] Despite Hazlitt's criticism, Byron's concerns, quoted above, are more than an ego-centred desire to alleviate *ennui*. Yet Hazlitt gets closer and closer to the condition, arriving at the precise location in 'cell monastic' of the *acedeic* demon. The cloud of melancholy, for Hazlitt, seems deliberately hung by Byron like a pall over all aspects of life, but Hazlitt refers to the poet's melancholic aspect in its nineteenth-century poetic sense, which is one that is inseparable from aestheticism.[12]

Aesthetically, the melancholy of Hamlet and that described by Robert Burton in *The Anatomy of Melancholy* is a specifically secular condition. During the reign of Elizabeth I and 'for some centuries thereafter', a melancholic mood was 'a fashionable mark of intellectual or aesthetic refinement'.[13] In *The Anatomy of Melancholy*, a copy of which Byron owned, Burton amalgamates both the spiritual and psychological natures of *acedia* under the general heading of 'melancholy'.[14] While Burton does not use the word *acedia*, he does suggest that melancholia is associated with a personality that is 'meditative, sombre, thoughtful [and] prone to reflection'.[15] His main concern is the psychological aspect of the condition: '[the victims endure] the most intolerable torment and insufferable anguish of conscience'.[16] Yet for Burton and the desert monks, such torment has an adventitious dimension, in that it negatively points beyond the present, in generating an agitated inability to rest content with this-worldly satisfactions.[17]

Hazlitt's description of the melancholic state straddles 'dark night', 'bright day', the agony across 'the brow of genius' and the point where the form of beauty is 'wasted'. Indeed, 'all outward things' are paradoxically shrouded by way of a kind of negative ecstasy in 'the film of his existence'. While such a psychological understanding of the condition might, as Phillip Martin notes, 'reinforce the Romantic cult of introversion wherein isolation of the private poet is seen as a necessary condition of gifted perception',[18] introversion or solipsism are not, I suggest, the most precise or appropriate models for describing the relationship between Byron, his poetry and his demons. I propose, instead, that the spiritual origins of *acedia* provide us with a vocabulary that foreshadows aspects of Byron's persona and poetry, which secular terms such as melancholy and *ennui* do not. The condition of being visited by 'the noonday demon', as experienced by the Desert Fathers, involved an overwhelming feeling of sorrow and an urgent desire to leave their cells in order physically and psychologically to wander. Byron's condition, if viewed in this light, becomes more than the 'sensibility of a gifted perception' and moves closer to the *distrait* of the 'noonday demon'.

Hazlitt observes that Byron has habits of mind and recurring preoccupations that are concerned with the perplexities of the human personality and consciousness, as if he is actually besieged by demons as the poet sits in 'the centre of his thoughts'. This view of Byron, linked with the solitude and rigour of the 'cell monastic', encompasses not merely Romantic solipsism, but an *acedeic* self-focus on his ritual listlessness: 'His object seems to be to stimulate himself and his readers for the moment – to keep both alive, to drive away *ennui*, to substitute a feverish and irritable state of excitement for listless indolence or even calm enjoyment.'[19] This is exactly what Byron says when he observes that violent passions work as a counter to *ennui*. Several years earlier,

Byron intimated in his preface to *Hours of Idleness* (1807) that some of his poems were written during the 'disadvantages of [...] depression of spirits': 'Poetry, however, is not my primary vocation; to divert the dull moments of indisposition, or the monotony of a vacant hour, urged me "to this sin".'[20] In these early days of Byron's writing, his vocabulary of 'vocation' and 'sin' suggests that poetry is not merely the transmission of empirical evidence, and he certainly does not seem to suggest that it is 'the product of a gifted perception'. In the first instance, his comment is humorous, although Byron's jokes often reveal his characteristic opinions. His vocabulary here suggests a spiritual awareness that he implicitly associates with the employment of writing poetry. Yet his sole declared motivation is to escape 'dull moments of indisposition', so writing poetry becomes an indulgence, a 'sin', as if he is at the same time betraying poetry. The word 'sin' becomes shorthand for this activity; however, the activity of writing poetry paradoxically emerges from his restless boredom and depressed spirits. For the reader, this is no 'sin' because it is a condition of the poetry's existence, but for Byron it reveals a condition of sinfulness – a condition in which he genuinely believed. His 'flagrantly confessional' style, noted by McGann, evidences such a belief in the intimacy of the public/private nature of the confession of his 'sin' for him here in his preface.[21]

*

Byron was of course not a mystic, at least in any straightforward sense; though he may have experienced something analogous to the suspensions or semi-trances of some of his characters. Nevertheless, he is always intrigued by the indeterminacy between body, mind and spirit, and the condition of *acedia* is indeterminate in precisely this sense. As we have seen, noonday demons were originally considered to be spiritual or supernatural beings that caused observable harm, which came to be interpreted as primarily a spiritual attack, though it had physical symptoms of quasi-paralysis alternating with restlessness. Thus, the condition is exactly that puzzling mixture of spirit and matter which fascinated Byron:

> Childe Harold bask'd him in the noon-tide sun,
> Disporting there like any fly; [...]
> He felt the fullness of satiety:
> Then loath'd he in his native land to dwell

Which seem'd to him more lone than Eremite's sad cell.
(*CHP*, I, 4)

Byron blends two very different things here – satiety (of sex, food or varied experiences) and the solitude of the Eremite's cell. Yet his conjunction brings solitude and satiety together, as if they went hand-in-hand and were not opposed. Harold seeks to flee satiety in the same way that the monk or hermit may wish to escape the ascetic life: 'Then loath'd he in his native land to dwell / Which seem'd to him more lone than the Eremite's sad cell.' The double emphasis of 'the fullness of satiety' demands the most obvious antithesis – a period of asceticism. The colon after 'satiety' imputes a logical solution to the problem; however, Byron adds the next illogical sensation, which suggests knowledge of, and is extraordinarily close to, the desert monk abandoning his cell.

Knowledge of the Eremite would naturally encompass knowledge of their ascetic discipline. Byron himself had ascetic streaks in his temperament, and well-documented periods in his life were spent horse-riding, eating a Spartan diet to reduce his weight, reading, writing and thinking in solitude. Teresa Guiccioli noted:

> There is no doubt that Lord Byron loved solitude for no one knew better than he the art of living with oneself – the art – such a difficult one, of knowing how to be alone.[22]

If we are to believe Teresa, Byron achieved some success in combating the demon while acknowledging the 'difficult' aspects of 'the art'. Behind Byron's thought in the *Childe Harold* extract is a common moral thought, to which he returns frequently, that pleasure is the sternest moralist.[23] In the relentless pursuit of pleasure, the human tires of it and becomes bored. But Byron seems to suggest that such boredom may lead to an activation of conscience – as if pleasure has its own limits and constructs its own morality. Such thoughts, for Byron, are ingrained with characteristic demonic agitation – 'fulness', 'satiety', 'loath'd' and 'lone' – which the narrator attempts to regulate by what Jerome Christiansen interestingly refers to as 'inaugural askesis, a position of security unjeopardized by desire'.[24] Whatever the reasons were for Byron's condition, he writes from that most difficult of positions – that of knowing that he is enduring some form of debilitation without knowing why. Byron is of course both the accursed wanderer and happy wanderer 'So late into the night', whose spirits revive when he travels.[25] Yet during his periods of wandering, perhaps through his 'violent passions' – which seem to seek, by way of excess, a place 'unjeopardized by desire' – he engages in combat with the demon.

Here we should perhaps pause to make another distinction. We have seen how melancholy differs in understanding through literary history, but how were demons understood? The popular image in Byron's day is best illustrated by the demon summoned in Mathew Lewis's *The Monk*. In this novel, the demon appears at the behest of Matilda: 'The Spirit sank upon his knee, and with a submissive air presented to her the branch of Myrtle.'[26] The demon in this case is melodramatic and behaves like a pet. Similarly, at the end of the novel, the demon is merely a flying monster with talons, which picks up Ambrosio and drops him in the same way that Southey is dropped into a lake from the sky at the end of Byron's *The Vision of Judgment*, which is perhaps a comic allusion to Lewis's Ambrosio. Lewis's demon is thus a supernatural being that is subject to Matilda's command. In *Manfred*, however, while the protagonist is emphatically not subject to the spirits,[27] the spirits for their part are far less compliant and more antagonistic than those that appear in *The Monk*. In contrast to Lewis, then – whose spirits are more of a plot device – Byron represents the noonday demons of *acedia* as infernal entities that attack the human spirit, as they tempt him, make him restless and melancholic. In this respect, Byron seems closer to Evagrius, who does not use the term 'demon' in a metaphorical sense: 'He believed that there really were demons. "Thoughts" were simply the most common mechanism by which the solitaries encountered demons.'[28]

Thoughts could be demons for Byron, too. Despite stretching himself out on tombstones at Harrow, Byron was partly a man of worldly sensibility. Yet if we probe his descriptions of *ennui*, we cannot progress very far without reference to the spiritual vocabulary of demons. Indeed, his wordliness frequently spurs him into awareness of the agitations endured by monks and hermits:

> The laughing dames in whom he did delight,
> Whose large blue eyes, fair locks, and snowy hands
> Might shake the saintship of an anchorite [...]. (*CHP*, I, II)

Byron is attentive here to the idea of an inner life in his acknowledgement of the anchorite's saintship, as he is thinking of well-known pictures of Anthony the hermit being tempted by visions of women. In 'shake', he also acknowledges the discipline of the anchorite, who must sit tight, while enduring the onslaught of demons that tempt him with lustful thoughts. And in 1822, Byron references the plight of St Francis in *Don Juan* VI: 'The devil being overcome, retired immediately, and the holy man returned victorious to his cell.'[29] Like the hermit, Harold both seeks and suffers from solitude, in which he encounters and does battle with demons. In *Childe Harold* IV, we can see *acedia* at its deepest level fused across body, mind and spirit, in the speaker's restless wandering and in Byron's own wandering after escaping England:

> But my soul wanders; I demand it back
> To meditate amidst decay, and stand
> A ruin amongst ruins [...]. (*CHP*, IV, 25)

Meditating amidst decay is another familiar melancholic posture, typical of the 'Graveyard School', of which Byron is an obvious heir. There are, however, illuminating differences between them. Melancholia in Edward Young's *Night Thoughts* (1742–1745), for example, retains its religious overtones and has a profound Christian emphasis, as the poet evangelizes – through his melancholy – a message of Christian redemption.[30] Likewise, James Hervey's *Meditations and Contemplations* (1746–1747) offers thoughts of man's unpreparedness for death, his mortality and redemption, which are prompted by what the author sees on the monuments in graveyards – a characteristically Gothic haunt of demons.[31] Melancholy, in these examples, represents a capacity for infinite feeling, which results from a period of reflective development, culminating in a kind of visionary sensibility, which almost amounts to a blessed condition. It makes the sufferer aware of a sense of human mortality and instructs the heart to wean itself away from worldly preoccupations. In contrast to Byron's meditations, the concerns of these poets are not with demons but rather on the moral reflections of the landscape and a sense of terror in contemplating death.

The ancient ascetic notion that demons, through thought, try to prevent the individual's salvation can be seen in Byron's lyric 'To Inez'. In its form and position, Byron presents careful thought mirroring a silent combat with the demon's strategy. The idea of demons as self-perpetuating beings that sap the spiritual energy of the sufferer runs parallel to, but is not the same as, *ennui*:

3

> It is not love, it is not hate,   845
> Nor low Ambition's honours lost,
> That bids me loathe my present state,
> And fly from all that I priz'd the most:

4

It is that weariness which springs
From all I meet, or hear, or see: 850
To me no pleasure Beauty brings;
Thine eyes have scarce a charm for me.

                           5
It is that settled, ceaseless gloom
The fabled Hebrew wanderer bore;
That will not look beyond the tomb,   855
But cannot hope for rest before.

                           6
What Exile from himself can flee?
To Zones, though more and more remote,
Still, still pursues, where'er I be,   860
The blight of life – the demon, Thought. (*CHP*, I, 'To Inez')

Like Shelley's divine wanderer, Harold physically aims to stray from
the agitating thoughts but to no avail: 'What Exile from himself can
flee?' (857). He must confront the demon of his own 'weariness' (849).
Yet such demons occasion a relentless focus on his plight – 'Still, still
pursues, where'er I be' (859) – resulting in disquiet and restlessness,
so much so that the mind cooperates with them against itself, for
the repetition of 'still' not only halts the progress of the line but also
intensifies the relentlessness of the pursuing blight, in its antithetical
position within the dialectic of flight and pursuit. The poet-speaker,
however, does not wholly acquiesce and, instead, engages in a form of
striving against his weariness in psychologically confronting the demons
while simultaneously attempting to quell the desire to be perpetually
wandering. Despite attempts to quell such reflections, thoughts on
morality and silent meditation come upon the speaker unbidden and
beckon to him to surrender to them. There is a striking similarity here
between the conjunction of 'thought' and 'demon' in the Evagrian
sense, where demons directly influence what Latin tradition called the
cogitationes or thoughts of the ascetic, which try to get at the basis of
his consciousness and turn his spiritual life into a blight.

                                   *

It will be helpful at this point to remind ourselves of, and make clear,
some distinctions. *Ennui* is associated with aristocrats and is socially
contexted. Melancholy is a medical condition that concerns the emotions
and is associated with genius. *Acedia*, however, is a spiritual condition,

which attacks spiritual people. In *Childe Harold's Pilgrimage* Canto IV, the poet has dispensed with Harold, as if his thoughts, agitating though they are, have now led him to consider the value of his existence more directly. In doing so, Byron returns to a more intense strain of *ennui*, which reveals, with surprising explicitness, its relation to *acedia*:

> Clear as its current, glide the sauntering hours
> With a calm languor, which, though to the eye
> Idlesse it seem, hath its morality.
> If from society we learn to live,
> 'Tis solitude should teach us how to die;
> It hath no flatterers; vanity can give
> No hollow aid; alone – man with his God must strive:
>
> Or, it may be, with demons, who impair
> The strength of better thoughts, and seek their prey
> In melancholy bosoms, such as were
> Of moody texture from their earliest day,
> And loved to dwell in darkness and dismay,
> Deeming themselves predestin'd to a doom
> Which is not of the pangs that pass away;
> Making the sun like blood, the earth a tomb,
> The tomb a hell, and hell itself a murkier gloom. (IV, 33–34)

The impressionistic slowing down of time – 'sauntering', 'languor' and 'Idlesse' – seems poetic. However, 'Idlesse', from medieval Romance and probably mediated by Thomson's *The Castle of Indolence*, carries the line over into the territory of *acedia*, which involves 'solitude', 'melancholy', 'demons' and 'thoughts'.[32] These are furthermore, again in association with the monastic tradition of Evagrius, informed by a recognition of the deadliest sin, Pride, which Byron characteristically articulates as 'vanity'. In making this association and recognizing the need for God as an ally in the battle against the demon, Byron opens up an explicitly spiritual framework for the melancholy that his poetic contemporaries secularized. We can be even more precise. The passage oscillates between an ascetic orientation in the first stanza, a fatalism that perhaps emanates from Calvinistic predestination in the second, and the spirituality contained in the battle against the demonic agitation of one's thoughts throughout. Byron's comment 'though to the eye / Idlesse it seem' detaches the speaker from the fashionable melancholy of the period, which is synonymous with *dolce far niente*, and reveals it to be – for the poet of *Childe Harold's Pilgrimage* at least – an inescapably spiritual condition: 'man with his God must strive: / Or it

may be, with demons who impair / The strength of better thoughts.'
It may be a helpful or harmful striving, but either way the condition
'hath its morality'.

*

As we have seen, the general development of religious thought tended
to move from the ontological conception of demons to a psychological
understanding, without wholly discarding the sense that something
extra-psychological was at play. But did Byron really believe in demons?
I want to suggest that the poet's understanding of them is, in a sense,
a reversal of this thesis. To illustrate what I mean by this, and to show
that Byron's demons are real or on the edge of being real, rather than a
literary device to describe psychological processes, I will examine briefly
his dramatic poem *Manfred*.

We have noted that there is an elision between the vocabularies of
melancholy, solitude, wandering and striving with the demon of *acedia*.
Acedia causes the sufferer to realize a certain gratuitousness in his or her
existence which brings the subject into confrontation with nothingness.
In *Manfred*, nothingness and emptiness preclude any apparent activity
of the soul – a condition which stands in stark contrast to that of the
comparative fullness of the Hunter and Abbot's souls, even though these
seem lesser spirits than Manfred himself. An empty soul *per se* creates
its opposite notion – that of a soul open to the reception of spiritual
renewal from outside:

> MAN. [*alone*].   There is a calm upon me –
> Inexplicable stillness! which till now
> Did not belong to what I knew of life. [...]
> It hath enlarged my thoughts with a new sense,
> And I within my tablets would note down
> That there is such a feeling. (III, i, 6–8; 16–18)

The '[i]nexplicable stillness' that is 'seated in my soul' (III, i, 14) is a
new mode of existence, which simultaneously brings calm and exudes
its innate potentiality to 'enlarge [...] thoughts with a new sense'. The
expansive potential in this is noted by Manfred. Potentiality is what
Manfred wishes himself, as he no longer cares for spirituality and
becomes his 'own destroyer' (III, iv, 139), as an 'all-pitiless demon'
dashes him 'back / Into the gulf of [...] unfathom'd thought' (II, ii,
138; 143–44). Yet, as his soul ebbs from him, he continues to wrestle
with demons: 'I do not combat against death, but thee' (III, iv, 112).

The struggle is intensified for Manfred, as he resists both spirits and the ministrations of the Abbot: 'I'll die as I have lived – alone' (III, iv, 90). Manfred is apparently consumed by the psychological effects of guilt and memory. However, the play does dramatize a conflict with real spirits, and Manfred's sense of exaltation and risk seems to depend upon their existence. Spirits appear in many other poems but are not central to any of them until *Cain*. Manfred ends in a spiritual place and condition, which replaces 'the difficult air of the mountain's top' with a death that is 'not so difficult'. This transition is from spiritual combat to a condition beyond striving. The 'nothingness' of which Manfred is aware is neither melancholy nor *ennui* but an insight into the abyss of temptation, which only a spiritual searcher would encounter. Such unusual movements of what may be viewed as a Faustian or Satanic searching here mirror, in an inverted way, the eventual attainment of the anchorite. Byron is often associated with the former, but the blend of self/soul/spirit is an area of struggle with unknown forces that are both within and without him. Of course, *Manfred* is a play, and spirits and demons live within the sphere of an imagined dramatic space. We might say that is the only place that they live. Byron, however, uses the idea of demons that inhabit areas of wasteland again in *Heaven and Earth* (1823): 'Avaunt! ye exulting demons of the waste' (I, iii, 114). The thrust of Romantic criticism in recent years has been to the psychological basis of the Lake Poets' cult of imagination and the historical and material contexts in which Byron and others wrote. But Byron's poetry will not be wholly caught by such emphases. Manfred lives neither in his imagination nor in history. He lives, as does Japhet, in a world where spirits and demons have powers, and he feels both kinship with those powers and a sense of threat. Byron does not show a closed-in consciousness or one that depends simply on its own resources. He is acutely aware of unknown pressures that operate both without and within consciousness and which reinforce a moral order rather than simply confirming an imaginative one. In this way and in this sense, Byron belongs to Evagrian tradition more than he belongs to the more recent cults of melancholy introspection and aristocratic *ennui*.

Notes

1 Leslie A. Marchand, *Byron: A Portrait* (London: Cresset, 1987), p. 339.
2 Cassian [c.360–435] translates the Greek word into Latin and so into the tradition of the Western Catholic Church. He writes that *acedia* is 'a weariness of the heart' – *taedium cordis*. The etymology of *acedia* or *accidie* may be traced according to the

OED throughout the thirteenth to sixteenth centuries, but then the word seems to disappear from use. It appears again in 1891 within a collection of sermons by Francis Paget, entitled *The Spirit of Discipline*, which contains an introductory essay concerning '*Accidie*'. See the present author's unpublished thesis, *Byron and the Catholic Persuasion* (Liverpool, 2005).

3 Jerome McGann, 'Byron's Lyric Poetry', in *The Cambridge Companion to Byron*, ed. Drummond Bone (Cambridge: Cambridge University Press, 2005), p. 209.

4 Leopold Sabourin, *The Psalms* (New York, NY: Alba, 1974), p. 384.

5 'A sagitta volante in die a negotio perambulante in tenebris ab incursu et daemonio meridiano.' See *The Vulgate Psalter*, ed. A.B. Macaulay (London: Dent, 1913).

6 William Harmless, S.J., *Desert Christians* (Oxford: Oxford University Press, 2004), p. 325.

7 Ibid., p. 327.

8 D. Smith Nichol, ed. *Jeffrey's Literary Criticism* (London: Froude, 1910), pp. 149–50.

9 *BLJ*, V, p. 186.

10 William Hazlitt, *The Spirit of the Age: or, Contemporary Portraits*, in *CWWH*, vol. XI, p. 71.

11 Ibid., p. 125.

12 The connection between melancholy and aestheticism has been recently discussed by Giorgio Agamben, who notes that dandyism 'presents itself as a paradoxical re-evaluation of sloth, whose etymological meaning is, in fact, lack of care (from *a-chedomai*)'. In doing so, however, he also points out that it was a 'patristic description of the slothful man [that] furnished the model for modern literature'. See Giorgio Agamben, *Stanzas*, p. 8, n. 4.

13 *OED*, 'melancholy', 3a.

14 According to his reading list, Byron had read Burton's *Anatomy* and described it as an 'instructive medley, of quotation and Classical anecdotes'. He goes on to warn the 'superficial Reader' of the 'intricacies' of the text. See *CMP*, pp. 6–7.

15 'Acedia Bane of Solitaries', available at: www.hermitary.com/solitude/acedia.html (accessed 13.11.12).

16 Bergen Evans, *The Psychiatry of Robert Burton* (New York, NY: Columbia University Press, 1944), p. 57.

17 Agamben similarly notes that *acedia*, from a theological point of view, 'does not have only a negative value' and was seen by the Church Fathers as a *tristitia salutifera* (saving sorrow) or 'golden goad of the soul', since – on account of its 'dialectal leavening capable of reversing privation as possession' – it represents 'not only a flight from, but also a flight toward, which communicates with its object in the form of a negation and a lack'. See *Stanzas*, p. 7.

18 Philip W. Martin, 'Heroism and History: *Childe Harold* I and II and *The Tales*', in *The Cambridge Companion to Byron*, p. 77.

19 Hazlitt, *The Spirit of the Age*, p. 181.

20 *CPW*, I, p. 33.

21 Jerome McGann, 'Byron's Lyric Poetry': 'In one view Byron's poetry seems to lack intimacy despite its flagrantly confessional character' (p. 212).

22 Teresa Guccioli, *Lord Byron's Life in Italy*, ed. Peter Cochran, trans. Michael Rees (Newark, NJ: University of Delaware Press, 2005), p. 338. This aspect of Byron's temperament is also noted by Marchand, *Byron: A Portrait*, p. 422.

23 The notion that pleasure is the sternest moralist is linked in part, perhaps, to

the eighteenth-century graveyard meditations and poems such as Young's *Night Thoughts*, in which solitude, night, landscape, etc. are occasions for religious and moral reflection.

24 Jerome Christensen, *Lord Byron's Strength* (Baltimore, MD: Johns Hopkins University Press, 1993), p. 71.

25 'So, We'll Go No More A Roving'.

26 Mathew Lewis, *The Monk: A Romance*, ed. Howard Anderson (Oxford: Oxford University Press, 1973), p. 277.

27   ALL THE SPIRITS. Prostrate thyself, and thy condemned clay,
      Child of the earth! or dread the worst.
      MAN.   I know it;
      And yet ye see I kneel not. (II, iv, pp. 34–37)

28 Harmless, *Desert Christians*, p. 327.

29 Ernest Hartley Coleridge, *The Poetical Works of Lord Byron* (London: Murray, 1905). The citation of St Francis is a correction from the first edition, in which Byron mistakenly refers to St Anthony – the first desert hermit. What is significant here, I think, is that Byron recalls the details of the two saints and, in his characteristic desire for accuracy, corrects his error in the second edition.

30 Edward Young, *Night Thoughts*, ed. Stephen Cornford (Cambridge: Cambridge University Press, 1989).

31 James Hervey, *Meditations and Contemplations* (London: Cornish, 1855).

32 James Thomson, *The Castle of Indolence*, ed. James Sambrook (Oxford: Clarendon Press, 1986). In the opening stanzas of *The Castle of Indolence*, Thomson sets out 'in the manner of Spenser' ideas of 'fiend' (13), 'listless climate' (17) and *'Idless'* (40). Thomson, in the first canto, argues for indolence and *idless* and writes in a rich poetical style. The second canto, which deplores *idles*, is in a flatter, less poetic manner. In his reading list of 1807, Byron writes that amongst English 'minor poets', 'Gray, Goldsmith, and Collins or Thomson might have been added as worthy of mention' (*CMP*, p. 3).

CHAPTER FOUR

Conjuration and Exorcism:
Byron's Spectral Rhetoric

Dale Townshend

In 1880, over half a century after Byron's death, one Quevedo Redivivus published in London his *Spiritual Interview with Lord Byron [...] With Some Interesting Information About the Spirit World. With Notes Explanatory and Elucidatory*, a half-serious, half-tongue-in-cheek account of his encounter with the poet's ghost.[1] Signing himself 'Qeuvedo Redivivus' – the nom de plume that Byron himself used in *The Vision of Judgment* – the writer of this short anti-Spiritualist tract conjures up through his choice of authorial pseudonym the spectre of what was already, in Byron's poem of 1822, the ghost of a poetic identity in the figure of Franciso de Quevedo, the Baroque Spanish poet and politician, whom Byron's satirical jesting in the poem had purported to restore to life. As Susan J. Wolfson has pointed out, Byron's resuscitation of Quevedo in *The Vision of Judgment* is only one instance of the poet's concerted 'ghosting' of his own poetic authority, not only in this poem, but at seminal moments throughout his verse, to the extent that, behind the spectral Junius, who makes his appearance in stanza 73, we might descry none other than the figure of the anti-monarchical Byron himself – the ghostly poet who simultaneously masks and discloses himself through the name of one who signed his own anti-Hanoverian rants as 'stat nominis umbra'.[2] Once translated and decrypted as 'the shadow of a name [who] stands here', it is easy to see that the historical Junius's peculiarly spectral mode of authorial inscription is rendered strikingly literal in the context of Byron's poem: tall, thin and grey-haired, the Shadow of Junius, we are told, 'look'd as it had been a shade on earth' (75); 'The man', the poem continues, 'was a phantasmagoria in / Himself – he was so volatile and thin!' (77). Culturally consigned to pseudo-

97

nymity, marginality and invisibility while yet alive, the poets Quevedo and Junius, invoked by Byron in *The Vision of Judgment* as his noble spectral ancestors within the same oppositional line of political and aesthetic practice, have been relegated to the realm of the ghostly long before their actual deaths. As such, they are incapable of effecting their supernatural return as anything other than the mere ghosts of ghosts or, at an even greater remove, as the ghosts of ghosts of ghosts: pale and somewhat ineffectual spectres caught up in an infinite, ever-receding line of regression. Sycophants the likes of Pye and Southey, by contrast, remain spectres firmly of the first order, even as they, unlike Byron's ghostly avatars, flee and gibber off to their almost certainly hellish destinations towards the poem's end. Self-consciously mirroring the ways in which the poetic spirit of Byron takes possession of the names and identities of other dead poets in order to represent and articulate itself in *The Vision of Judgment*, the author of *Spiritual Interview with Lord Byron* stages the ghostly return of Byron via a medium that is spectral by at least two removes: this Quevedo Redivivus is the ghost of an already ghostly Byronic author.

As its playful echoing of *The Vision of Judgment* suggests, Quevedo Redivivus's *Spiritual Interview* betrays an intimate knowledge of the configuration of ghosts and spectres in Byron's own writings, not least of all in its structural reliance upon the oppositional but complementary gestures of conjuration and exorcism: the calling up of Byron's spirit in the medium's darkened drawing-room, followed by the rationalist dismantling of belief in the supernatural via the sceptical narrator's doubts concerning the medium's possible charlatanism. As I shall argue in this chapter, Byron's conceptualization of the ghostly is founded upon a similar logic, a comparable dynamic of spectral conjuration and exorcism. A little more detail may help to introduce this.

As it turns out, this Quevedo Redivivus is no late-Victorian caught up in the rage for congress with the world of spirits so much as a sceptical onlooker who witnesses before him a dubious act of conjuration by an unnamed 'Materializing Medium'. Redivivus, the narrator, enters the medium's drawing-room in order to witness before him by weak gas light the props and accoutrements of professional spectral conjuration, including a screen of curtains or shawls dividing the drawing-room into two, behind which is placed a single chair. Following some curious rapping and a series of confused verbal ejaculations, the curtains of this makeshift stage part, so as to reveal 'a figure seated in the chair';[3] dark though it is, the narrator is just about able to make out some rather iconic Byronic features: 'he seemed to be dressed in a long cloak, and had the large collars so well known in Lord Byron's pictures'.[4] Having appeared before him, the ghost of Byron engages his equally ghostly namesake in intense but humorous conversation, the topics of which range from his dislike of a certain statue that Disraeli erected in his memory; the vulgarity of Scottish cultural nationalism; the state of American literature; his approval of the writings of Swinburne; his dislike for George Eliot, Robert Browning and Alfred Tennyson in particular; and his despair at the condition of contemporary English letters in general. Of all his many sources of disaffection though it is the very spectral nature of his being that the spirit of Byron finds the most disconcerting: in addition to not being able to deny the charges of false attribution made in his name, 'to have to hear and read many things about oneself and not be able to say a word about anything' is 'by far the worst of being a Spirit'.[5] In keeping with the promise of the tract's title, the spirit of Byron, if only through an egregious act of self-promotion, furnishes Quevedo with a graphic sense of the poetic afterlife, rather as Byron himself had done in *The Vision of Judgment*:

> We are all very much at sixes and sevens as we were in the world, Cowper, Coleridge, who eats opium still, Southey and the cakers and the tea and bread and butter school, give tea parties in which Hannah Moore and Mrs. Hemans meet.[6]

Timeless though it may seem, this particular version of the hereafter, Byron assures the narrator, is governed by the same temporal laws as those characterizing mortal existence, so that while he might know that Homer exists, he has 'never had the honour of an introduction to him', and while, thanks to Horace, he has had the pleasure of an introduction to Virgil, he has not managed to form a firm acquaintance with the man due to their linguistic differences and the considerable time it takes to traverse geographical space and historical time. "'[W]e haven't'", he assures Quevedo, "'much the pull over you, with your railways and your steamers, though the literary men stick together and generally call on each other when they travel.'"[7]

Byron's ghost disappears in the *Spiritual Interview* almost as rapidly as it materialized. Anxious to end the proceedings so as to attend another appointment, the spirit of Byron bids Quevedo Redivivus good evening as the curtains of the makeshift stage are drawn. Emerging from behind the curtains as the room lightens, the medium enquires of his client's levels of satisfaction with his conjuration, but as he does so, the narrator registers 'a slight sound in his voice not unlike that of the lordly Spirit with whom [he] had so lately conversed'.[8] Faint though it may be, this is enough to engender in the narrator serious misgivings concerning the authenticity of the séance that he has just witnessed; belief, once deftly suspended, is quickly threatened with collapse, for what was initiated in earnest as a real conjuration becomes conceivably little more than an elaborate hoax, the product of the same spurious smoke-and-mirror deceptions brought to mind by the medium's connections with the firm of Maskelyne and Cooke – the two late nineteenth-century magicians renowned for their debunking of the fraudulent Spiritualism of the brothers Davenport. Seemingly reluctant to strain the boundaries of his belief any further, Quevedo bids both the medium and his readers a hasty farewell, paying the former his fee and leaving with an experience of otherworldly timelessness not unlike that which was described during the interview with the spirit of Byron himself: 'The interview had only lasted, I found, on looking at my watch, forty minutes though it had seemed an age.'[9]

A flippant and somewhat facetious gibe at late-Victorian Spiritualism though it undoubtedly is, Quevedo Redivivus's *Spiritual Interview with Lord Byron* helpfully highlights the strategy of ghostly invitation and expulsion that is elaborated across Byron's *oeuvre* and which serves to frame and punctuate both the beginning and end of his poetic career. In 'A Fragment', for instance – the early Ossianic poem that first appeared in *Fugitive Pieces* (1806) – the speaker, lyrically indistinguishable from the figure of Byron himself, imagines the moment of his own death in the lines 'When, to their airy hall, my fathers' voice, / Shall call my spirit' (1–2). The Freudian fantasy of the primal scene, in which the subject narcissistically imagines being able to gaze at its own origins at the moment of its sexual conception, is rewritten here as the speaker's fantasy of immortality after death. But the effects are equally narcissistic, for here the young and ambitious poet, jettisoning the conventional modes of remembrance accorded to individuals of lesser distinction, anticipates his own ghost's gazing upon his much sought-after fame as it accretes and gathers around his name:

> Oh! may my shade behold no sculptur'd urns,
> To mark the spot, where earth to earth returns:
> No lenthen'd scroll, no praise encumber'd stone;
> My epitaph shall be, my name alone. (5–8)

Byron's name, so the ending of the poem asserts, ought to constitute the sole support of the poet's posthumous reputation and renown, to the exclusion of all other modes of symbolic remembrance: 'Oh! may no other fame my deeds repay; / *That*, only *that*, shall single out the spot, / By that remember'd, or with that forgot' (10–12). Death here marks not the termination of poetic dialogue so much as its spectral commencement. Charged with the responsibility of ensuring the ongoing remembrance of the poet beyond the time of his physical death, Byron's name – though initially an inanimate epitaph – comes to speak for, and in place of, the absent poet. Byron here stages what Paul de Man, apropos Wordsworth's conceptualization of the functions of the poet's name in *Essays upon Epitaphs*, describes as prosopopeia, namely:

> the fiction of an apostrophe to an absent, deceased or voiceless entity [in the form of his own name], which posits the possibility of the latter's reply and confers upon it the power of speech. Voice assumes mouth, eye and finally face, a chain that is manifest in the etymology of the trope's name, *prosopon poien*, to confer a mask or a face (*prosopon*). Prosopopeia is the trope of autobiography, by which one's name [...] is made as intelligible and memorable as a face.[10]

Through this rhetorical trope, the face that is erased by the poet's death is restored and reconfigured in the name that comes to speak, spectre-like, in his place. Given the poet's notoriously complex relationship with his own corporeality – a profound body-dysmorphia, expressed through Byron's incessant dieting, the manipulation of his physical appearance and his comments about his own disability – the wish for a spectral disembodiment articulated in this poem seems hardly coincidental.

Already, the prosopopeia of 'A Fragment' serves to encode at least three instances of spectrality: the ghost of Byron returns from beyond the grave in order to gaze upon the fame that accretes posthumously around his name, with both fame and the name being imbued with certain haunting, spectral qualities, the effects of which are actively courted and invoked. The connections between spectrality and the functions of the name drawn upon here are conceptually not too far removed from aspects of Jacques Derrida's reflections on the functions of the authorial signature and proper name at several points throughout his writing. In the early essay 'Signature Event Context', for instance, Derrida maintains that, since iterability is the necessary condition of the signature – that is, its ability, *qua* signature, to be repeated meaningfully in countless contexts, situations and conditions, irrespective of the presence of the author, the signatory, the addresser or the addressee – the signature is necessarily a bearer of death: bound up in absence, its function is to take the place of the present signatory.[11] Like Byron's sense of the functions of his own name in this early poem, each authorial signature for Derrida is also necessarily the author's epitaph.

Simultaneously present and absent, but neither fully one nor the other, the author of the signature is relegated to the realm of the spectral. This ghostly relegation, however, is precisely that which the early Byron wishes to exploit; as it is so literally rendered in Quevedo Redivivus's *Spiritual Interview with Lord Byron*, fame is an evanescent, ghostly entity that is supported and underpinned by the functions of the poet's name – the name as it might be lodged in cultural memory, circulated in literary discourse and emblazoned in gold lettering on the covers of so many of the poet's publications.

At least where literary renown and celebrity were concerned, the wishes of the young Byron seem to have been granted. As Jane Stabler has argued, Elizabeth Barrett Browning's 'Stanzas on the Death of Lord Byron' and Felicia Hemans's 'The Lost Pleiad' both figured Byron's reputation as a form of haunting, spectrally rendering him in these two poems as 'a violent collision of presence and absence'.[12] In Tom Mole's account, Byron's name, alongside his frequently circulated visual image, became a veritable commodity or 'brand name' during the poet's lifetime, a sign that guaranteed a certain literary product and one that drove the production, marketing and reception of his publications.[13] At certain moments, Byron's verse shows an awareness of the currency of his own name and claims to extend its powers of ghostly immortalization to those about whom he chooses to write. In 'To Ianthe', a poem added to the seventh edition of the first canto of *Childe Harold's Pilgrimage* in 1814, for instance, Byron, in sentiments strongly suggestive of Shakespeare's sonnets, promises the poem's addressee, the young Lady Charlotte Harley, a form of immortality in and through the functions of the name as it is enshrined alongside those of 'Harold' and 'Byron' within the verse itself: 'Such is thy name with this my verse entwin'd; / And long as kinder eyes a look shall cast / On Harold's page, Ianthe's here enshrin'd / Shall thus be first beheld, forgotten last' (37–40). Though its narcissistic strains have been slightly attenuated, Byron exploits here a version of the proper name as the deathly support of its subject's ghostly immortality presented in 'A Fragment', even as 'To Ianthe' employs – for the sake of modesty and the generation of readerly intrigue (described by Mole as Byron's 'hermeneutic of intimacy') – a pseudonym in order to represent it. The name of the poem's eponymous figure itself of course had been subject to a process of ghosting, as Byron substituted the original 'Childe Burun' of the manuscript form for the more autobiographically remote Harold.

In his caustic response to the negative reception of his early poetry in *English Bards and Scotch Reviewers: A Satire* (1809), Byron expressed his early aristocratic contempt for literary professionalism by employing a distinction between those inferior hacks who write for money and those who, like Byron himself, seek out the ephemeral, ghost-like status of the appellation of bard or 'poet': 'when the sons of song descend to trade, / Their bays are sear, their former laurels fade. / Let such forgo the poet's sacred name, / Who rack their brains for lucre, not for fame' (175–78). Byron's disregard for what he later describes as the work of the 'prostituted Muse, and hireling Bard' (182) is directly related to his attack on the commercial imperatives driving the writing and publication of Gothic fiction in the poem.[14] This sets in place a crucial distinction in Byron's verse: if fame is a ghost, it is not to be confused with the gibbering spectres of the Gothic – that popular cultural mode in which ghosts, in the work of Matthew Gregory Lewis and his followers, most insistently stalk:

> Oh! wonder-working LEWIS! Monk, or Bard,
> Who fain would'st make Parnassus a church-yard!
> Lo! wreaths of yew, not laurel, bind thy brow,
> Thy Muse a Sprite, Apollo's sexton thou!
> Whether on ancient tombs thou tak'st thy stand,
> By gibb'ring spectres hailed, thy kindred band;
> Or tracest chaste descriptions on thy page,
> To please the females of our modest age,
> All hail, M.P.! from whose infernal brain
> Thin sheeted phantoms glide, a grisly train [...]
> (*English Bards and Scotch Reviewers*, 265–74)

In apostrophizing Matthew Lewis in the same terms used by the weird sisters to greet the regicide Macbeth in Shakespeare's play, Byron recalls the accusation of 'state-parricide' that T.J. Mathias had levied at *The Monk* in the fourth book of *The Pursuits of Literature* (1797),[15] while simultaneously setting in place a link between Gothic visions of spectrality and a certain moral and aesthetic culpability: Macbeth, like Lewis in Byron's estimation, sees the ghost of Banquo in an external projection of his aesthetic and psychological guilt. Byron's railing against the Gothic endeavours of Lewis and Scott in their collaborative *Tales of Terror* makes much the same point: 'If tales like thine may please, / St. Luke alone can vanquish the disease: / Even Satan's self with thee might dread to dwell, / And in thy skull discern a deeper hell' (279–82). At work here, then, is Romanticism's familiar offering of itself, via Shakespeare, as an antidote to Gothic excess, a movement in keeping with the sentiments expressed by Wordsworth in the 1802 preface to *Lyrical Ballads*:

> The invaluable works of our elder writers (I had almost said the works of Shakespeare and Milton) are driven into neglect by frantic novels, sickly and stupid German tragedies, and deluges of idle and extravagant stories in verse. When I think upon this degrading thirst after outrageous stimulation, I am almost ashamed to have spoken of the feeble effort with which I have endeavoured to counteract it.[16]

Though ghostly, Romanticism's poetic fame is by no means Gothic; *The Giaour* (1813), in fact, sets up a hierarchy of spectral beings, according to which the vampire – that master trope of Gothic writing in the Byron and Shelley circle – is figured as a 'spectre more accursed' than the less menacing 'Gouls' and 'Afrits' (786). Accordingly, it remains up to such plunderers and grave-robbers as Lord Elgin in *English Bards and Scotch Reviewers* to pursue the 'shade of fame' (1028) in its most illegitimate, ghastly and Gothic manifestations – a point upon which Byron will elaborate in *Childe Harold's Pilgrimage*.

*

In addition to being qualitatively distinct from the popular cultural excesses of the Gothic, Byron's sense of spectral fame is also not to be confused with the promises of immortality enshrined in the call to noble, honourable death at war in the national and international political discourse of early nineteenth-century Europe. In the first canto of *Childe Harold's Pilgrimage*, Byron encounters the opposite of posthumous regard in the vision of the many broken bodies that litter the battlefields of the Peninsula War – the remains of those who, at the behest of the political tyrants of Europe, have sacrificed their lives in the name of military glory. Such victims to 'Vain Sophistry' (I, 42), Byron claims, 'barter breath for fame: / Fame that will scarce reanimate their clay, / Though thousands fall to deck some single name' (I, 44). While fame offers immortality through its insistent haunting of posterity, military glory rewards its subjects with nothing more than death. During the account of the Siege of Ismail in *Don Juan*, Canto VII, Byron satirizes the promise of heroic immortality articulated in the political call to military service-through-sacrifice by foregrounding just how non-conducive such unpronounceable names as Strongenoff, Strokonoff and Tschitsshakoff are to the mnemonic functions of versification: 'but Fame (capricious strumpet) / It seems, has got an ear as well as trumpet' and cannot, the next stanza continues, 'tune those discords of narration, / Which may be names at Moscow, into rhyme' (VII, 15–16). While the singularity of the names of the Russian soldiers might be favourable alternatives to the lack of originality plaguing the surnames of the English – sixteen amongst them, Byron humorously observes, are called Thomson and nineteen Smith – the appearance of the names of the fallen in '*bulletins*' is small compensation for 'a *bullet in*' the body (VII, 21). And even if their appearance in newspapers and other printed media might avoid the embarrassment of misspelling, the names of those who fall in national wars inevitably impose upon their bearers, even once duly listed and recorded, a dreadful form of anonymity:

> But here are men who fought in gallant actions
>   As gallantly as ever heroes fought,
> But buried in the heap of such transactions
>   Their names are rarely found, nor often sought. [...]
> Of all our modern battles, I will bet
> You can't repeat nine names from each Gazette. (VII, 34)

As remote from 'honest fame' as conceivably possible, the 'gore' of military glory purportedly offered by the inscription of the names of the dead is, in effect, no different from the trivial and meretricious 'modern fame' witnessed in the figures of the Amundevilles, with their departure for their country seat in Canto VIII being recorded in the fashionable columns of the London newspapers (XIII, 51).

Meaningless though it is, the paradox that is consistently explored in *Childe Harold's Pilgrimage* is that the remembrance and monumentalization of those who die in the name of military glory is entirely necessary if their terrifying return, as spectres, is to be avoided. Jacques Lacan articulated the standard psychoanalytic line on the link between inadequate practices of mourning and the appearance of ghosts in his reading of Shakespeare's *Hamlet*:

> This explains the belief we find in folklore in the very close association of the lack, skipping, or refusal of something in the satisfaction of the dead, with the appearance of ghosts and spectres in the gap left by the omission of the significant rite.[17]

As the case of old Hamlet attests, that which remains inadequately mourned is likely to return as ghost, a sentiment entirely in accordance with the configuration of the supernatural in so many Gothic romances, dramas and chapbooks of the late eighteenth century.[18] The case of the bleeding nun in Lewis's *The Monk* is entirely representative in this regard: 'The bones of Beatrice continued to lie unburied, and her Ghost continued to haunt the Castle.'[19] At certain moments, Byron's verse gives expression to a similar set of assumptions, albeit largely as a means of employing a further distinction between the desirable haunting that is fame and the undesirable hauntings staged in the Gothic mode. Indeed, as the poem 'Darkness' from *The Prisoner of Chillon and Other Poems* (1816) so clearly demonstrates, the poet's diction is often the most Gothic when pathologies of mourning are at stake: in the dark, apocalyptic landscape of the poem – a Gothic wasteland plagued by bloodshed, famine, death and internecine strife – the remains of the unburied and unmemorialized dead are to be found, their bones as 'tombless as their flesh' (45). Surveying the Spanish battlefields of the Peninsula War, the Childe of Canto I bitterly recommends the bloody traces left by the corpses of 'the unburied slain' (I, 88) as the only means of monumentalization that is available to them: 'Let their bleach'd bones, and blood's unbleaching stain, / Long mark the battle-field with hideous awe' (I, 88). Sad and inadequate as such a means of commemoration undoubtedly is, it remains a salutary alternative to the graphic scene of haunting figured in Canto III. In making the passage from the Rhineland to the Alps, Childe Harold encounters the battlefield of Morat, where the Swiss defeated Charles the Bold, Duke of Burgundy, in 1476. Solely commemorated, like the fallen of the Peninsula War, by the mere fact of their unburied bones, the dead at Morat have been inadequately mourned: 'Here Burgundy bequeath'd his tombless host, / A bony heap, through ages to remain, / Themselves their monument' (III, 63). Despite serving for Byron as evidence of the inevitable victory of his Whiggish principle of Liberty, the site of battle, starkly lacking in the appropriate rituals of remembrance and grief, has been plagued ever since by the spectral return of the dead. Byron's register at this moment is appropriately Gothic: 'the Stygian coast / Unsepulchred they roam'd, and shriek'd each wandering ghost' (III, 63). Byron's note to Canto III only augments the links between curtailed funeral rites and the appearance of the ghost. Interred in a plain and simple sepulchre, Petrarch, Canto IV continues, has received no due commemoration beyond that provided by the texture of his own verse (III, 31), while the 'injur'd shade' of Tasso returns to restore the peace that was denied the poet in life (IV, 39). Canto IV, in fact, is replete with acts of mourning that have been variously denied, interrupted or curtailed: Scipio's tomb on the Appian Way has been disturbed and plundered (IV, 79); Dante lies far away from his native Florence at Ravenna (IV, 57); Petrarch's grave at Arqua has been 'rifled' (IV, 57); and the tomb of Boccaccio is '[u]ptorn' (IV, 58). Recalling the ghost of Old Hamlet's description of himself as 'Unhousel'd, Unanointed, Unanel'd', these poets share in the lamentable fate of those who are '[w]ithout a grave, unknell'd, uncoffin'd, and unknown' (IV, 179). Against these images of lack, the tomb of Caecilia Metella along the Appian Way (IV, 99–104) appears to be excessive in the extreme. Proffering the texture of its own verse as a mechanism of sound and appropriate monumentalization, *Childe Harold's Pilgrimage* links the public with the private, the social with the intimate, the famous with the obscure: Rousseau is mourned alongside Julia Alpinula; the loss of the unknown casualties of war are mourned alongside such figures of personal significance as Edleston, Wingfield and the poet's mother. 'But these are deeds which should not pass away', as Canto III urges: 'And names that must not wither, though the earth / Forgets her empires with a just decay, / The enslavers and the enslaved, their death and birth' (III, 67). Inadequate mourning marks the advent of the Gothic via the horrifying return of the dead; memorialization in Byron's verse, by contrast, bestows upon the dead the enviable spectrality that is fame.

*

Already, by the time of the publication of the third canto of *Childe Harold's Pilgrimage* in 1816, there is evidence of Byron's growing disillusionment with the pursuit of ghostly fame. In lines that strongly recall the links that Shelley drew between spectres and various forms of poetic and emotional immaturity in 'Hymn to Intellectual Beauty' (1816/1817) – 'While yet a boy I sought for ghosts, and sped / […] with fearful step pursuing / Hopes of strange converse with the storied dead' (49–52) – the older, somewhat jaded persona of Canto III records a marked change in the course and trajectory of his ghost-hunting, from the pursuit of the ever-elusive external object that is fame to the quiet contemplation of his own haunted subjective interiors: 'Fame is the thirst of youth, – but I am not / So young as to regard men's frown or smile, / As loss or guerdon of a glorious lot; / I stood and stand alone, – remembered or forgot' (III, 112). This acknowledgement serves to recast Byron's characterization of the eponymous figure of *Lara* (1814) in the poem of two years earlier as a figure of his own poetic identity. Described as 'a stranger in this breathing world, / An erring spirit from another hurled' (315–16), the Byronic Lara, already spectral, pursued the ghost of fame in the jejune fashion of the Byronic Childe: 'And troubled manhood followed baffled youth; / With thought of years in phantom chase misspent' (324–25). Fame, the persona of *Childe Harold's Pilgrimage* insists, like ambition, strife, love and sorrow, is no longer imbued with the power to '[c]ut to his heart again with the keen knife / Of silent, sharp endurance' (III, 5). The passage of time has brought with it the knowledge that forbearance no longer resides in the poet's difficult pursuit of literary renown so much as in the endurance of the ignominy that his name has come to signify: on the back of scandal and public intrigue, Byron has had his 'name blighted' by 'foaming calumny' (*CHP*, IV, 135–36). As Canto I puts it: 'But one sad losel soils a name for aye, / However mighty in the olden time' (I, 3); 'Nor all that heralds rake from coffin'd clay, / Nor florid prose, nor honied lies of rhyme', the poem continues, '[c]an blazon evil deeds, or consecrate a crime' (I, 3). If a name, as an epitaph, can serve as the ghostly support of its bearer's poetic fame in the afterlife, it can also, once sullied, function as its demon – the host to what *Don Juan* fittingly describes as 'the ghost of Scandal' (XII, 47). At moments such as these, Byron encounters a ghostly independence of the name similar to that theorized by Derrida in his later study *On the Name*.[20] Here, Derrida builds upon the sense of death and spectrality inscribed within the signature in order to figure the proper name as an entity that enjoys a spectral existence quite independently of the wishes and demands of the narcissistic subject. Although the subject, like Byron in 'A Fragment', might, according to a certain 'naïve rendering' or 'common illusion [*fantasme courant*]', presume that all the achievements and functions of the name will inevitably return 'in a direct or indirect way, in a straight or oblique line' as a veritable 'profit' for his/her narcissism, the name prohibits such gratification in order to sever itself off from the referent, assuming a spectral, ghostly quality all of its own. As Derrida maintains: 'that which bears, has borne, will bear your name seems sufficiently free, powerful, creative, and autonomous to live alone and radically to do without you and your name'.[21] Inevitably slipping free of its narcissistic moorings, the name, as spectre or demon, comes to articulate nothing so volubly as the violent death of the subject of narcissism: 'What returns to your name, to the secret of your name, is the ability to disappear *in your name*.'[22] Thus, when the Byron of Canto III of *Childe Harold's Pilgrimage* invokes the haunting powers of his name, it is no longer in a narcissistic affirmation of his poetic renown but, in a more modest, private and sentimental register, as a means of effecting contact with Ada – a form of ghostly father-daughter converse that might occur beyond the grave, even without the medium of the proper name:

Yet, though dull Hate as duty should be taught,
I know that thou wilt love me; though my name
Should be shut from thee, as a spell still fraught
With desolation, – and a broken claim:
Though the grave closed between us, – 'twere the same,
I know that thou wilt love me [...]. (III, 117)

Canto IV similarly registers the limitations of the name as a spectral agent of fame in the painful event of that name – though ideally the property of public renown – having been sullied by the effects of private scandal or intrigue. Even so, Byron persists in envisaging for himself a spectral afterlife via his return as '[s]omething unearthly, which they deem not of', his defiant conquering of corporeal mortality and his ghostly haunting, '[l]ike the remembered tone of a mute lyre', which '[s] hall on their softened spirits sink' (IV, 137). Similar fantasies of Byron's own spectral afterlife infused the elegiac mourning of his friends, John Wingfield and John Edleston, at end of Canto I and the beginning of Canto II of *Childe Harold*, respectively. The death of Wingfield occasions in the poet a flight of fancy that details a Platonic fusion of spirits or souls in the afterlife: 'And Fancy hover o'er thy bloodless bier, / Till my frail frame return to whence it rose, / And mourn'd and mourner lie united in repose' (I, 92). With Edleston having been kept alive within the poet through the haunting effects of memory – 'can I deem thee dead, / When busy Memory flashes on my brain?' (II, 9) – Byron can phantasmatically negotiate the possibility of spectral unification in the afterlife: 'Well – I will dream that we may meet again, / And woo the vision to my vacant breast' (II, 9). No longer dependent upon the fame that accretes narcissistically – and to the exclusion of all others – around the personal name, the Byron of Canto IV phantasmatically imagines his ghostly return from exile to England after death, so as to take up his place alongside the many other poets canonized within the nation's literary pantheon and language:

Perhaps I loved [England] well: and should I lay
My ashes in a soil which is not mine,
My spirit shall resume it – if we may
Unbodied choose a sanctuary. I twine
My hopes of being remembered in my line
With my land's language [...]. (IV, 9)

If his fame, as the final lines of the stanza continue, 'should be, as my fortunes are, / Of hasty growth and blight' and if anonymity or 'dull Oblivion' should, like the break between stanzas 8 and 9, serve as the

impediment to bar '[m]y name from out the temple where the dead /
Are honoured by the nations' (IV, 9–10), Byron records his apparent
indifference: 'let it be – / And light the laurels on a loftier head!' (I,
10). However, this can only be read as disingenuous in a poet who once
pursued the ghost of evanescent fame inscribed within the haunting
effects of a personal name with such insistence. Byron's identification
with Dante, Petrarch and Boccaccio later in the canto only reinforces
the hollow ring to his denouncements: though these 'Etruscan three'
(IV, 56) have been denied national commemoration through burial
alongside other renowned Italian poets in the Church of Santa Croce,
Byron is comforted by the fact that each receives proper and adequate
monumentalization, both in and through his own name. These are
poets, he continues, '[w]hose names are mausoleums of the Muse'; as
such, they are 'gently prest with far more reverent tread / Than ever
paced the slab which paves the princely head' (IV, 60). It is difficult
not to see in these identifications with the Italian poets evidence of
Byron's narcissistic fantasy of old: the return of his own ghost to earth
to witness the haunting effect of his own name/fame or, in the words
of Canto IV, 'to dream of fame, / And wipe the dust from off the idle
name / We never more shall hear' (IV, 166).

*

Fame, for the young Byron, was ghostly insofar as it ambivalently
evoked in him the sentiments of terror and delight, fear and fascination.
However, in the poet's later work, fame is spectral insofar as it is remote,
inaccessible and perhaps even an entirely phantasmatic construction.
This marked shift in Byron's conceptualization of fame, from a positive
ghostly entity that is actively pursued and invoked to a negative
phantasm that is to be wholeheartedly rejected or exorcized, is best
exemplified across the various cantos of *Don Juan*. Byron's famous
critique of the Lake Poets in the Dedication to the poem figures fame
and posthumous regard as an over-subscribed and hotly contested fray
into which he wisely refuses to enter. This over-subscription, the poem
implies throughout, pertains to matters both aesthetic and political,
and those who, like Cumberland, Prince Ferdinand, Wellesley and
Napoleon, pursue fame in the broad political arena are eventually
drained of their lifeblood so as to become spectres similar to those that
are made to appear before the regicide Macbeth in Shakespeare's play:
'Each in their turn like Banquo's monarchs stalk, / Followers of fame,
"nine farrow" of that sow' (I, 2). In a marked relocation of the ghostly,

the once-spectral fame has assumed a horrible porcine embodiment, with those who court it becoming, in effect, grey, disembodied spectres drained of all vitality. Elsewhere in *Don Juan*, though, fame maintains its ghostly credentials, albeit with ghostliness now serving as an image through which Byron can signify literary renown's evanescent qualities. Intoxicating, impermanent and intangible, the spectre of literary fame is smoke-like in the extreme: 'Yet there will still be bards; though fame is smoke, / Its fumes are frankincense to human thought' (IV, 106). Byron's familiar linking of the aesthetic and political in *Don Juan* occurs again Canto XI, when the persona describes Poets' Corner in Westminster Abbey as 'yon shrine where Fame is / A spectral resident – whose pallid beam / In shape of moonshine hovers o'er the pile – / Make this a sacred part of Albion's isle' (XI, 24). That '[y]e shades / Of Pope and Dryden' (III, 100) continue to haunt at all, however, is attributable more to contingency than to any innate aesthetic merit; as a mere 'lottery, / Drawn by the blue-coat misses of a coterie' (IV, 109), fame is spectral, because its presence is wholly without guarantee, arbitrarily dependent 'more upon the historian's style / Than on the name a person leaves behind' (III, 90).

As this suggests, the Byron of *Don Juan* has wholly lost faith in the power of the name to effect a haunting of posterity. Although 'Epistle to Augusta' (1816) records, with considerable confidence, the attainment of the goals that Byron had phantasmatically negotiated in 'A Fragment' – fame, like love, this poem reads, 'came unsought and with me grew, / And made me all which they can make – a Name' (13) – Canto I of *Don Juan* moves beyond the unconvincing disavowal of fame in the earlier poem in order to interrogate the spectral nature of the poet's name itself. Though fame might, indeed, furnish the poet with a name, that name is, as 'Epistle to Augusta' puts it, 'all' that fame can bestow. Forever confined to the level of the purely nominal, the name no longer bears the potential to serve as that through which the poet negotiates his spectral afterlife:

> What is the end of fame? 'tis but to fill
>   A certain portion of uncertain paper:
> Some liken it to climbing up a hill,
>   Whose summit, like all hills', is lost in vapour;
> For this men write, speak, preach, and heroes kill,
>   And bards burn what they call their 'midnight taper',
> To have, when the original is dust,
> A name, a wretched picture, and worse bust. (I, 218)

A name is conceivably all that might remain once the passage of life has moved from womb to tomb. If poetic fame here is anything but guaranteed, even less so is the possibility of the name effecting a haunting of the future; instead, it remains forever confined to, and circumscribed by, the deathly functions of the epitaph: 'The priest instructs, and so our life exhales, / A little breath, love, wine, ambition, fame, / Fighting, devotion, dust, – perhaps a name' (*DJ*, II, 4).

As Jerome McGann in *Byron and Romanticism* has argued, Byron's *The Prophecy of Dante* (1821) figures his own poetic identity as an avatar of the great Tuscan poet to the extent that, in lines such as the following, one may read Byron's sense of being forced to live a marginal, ghostly existence long before the advent of actual death.[23] Here, the living poet becomes spectral via an appropriation of the ghost's lines from *Hamlet*, Act I, scene v, 'I could a tale unfold':

> I am not of this people, or this age,
> And yet my harpings will unfold a tale
> Which shall preserve these times when not a page
> Of their perturbed annals could attract
> An eye to gaze upon their civil rage
> Did not my verse embalm full many an act
> Worthless as they who wrought it: 'tis the doom
> Of spirits of my order to be rack'd
> In life, to wear their hearts out, and consume
> Their days in endless strife, and die alone;
> Then future thousands crowd around their tomb,
> And pilgrims come from climes where they have known
> The name of him – who now is but a name [...].
> *(The Prophecy of Dante, I, 143–55)*

In a reversal of the supernaturalism of the early poems, ghostliness has become the condition of the poet long before death – a condition similar to that presented in Byron's identification with the ghosts of Quevedo and Junius in *The Vision of Judgment*, as well as his figuring of his own poetic identity in the character of Lara. In this state of affairs, death brings no supernatural afterlife so much as a deathly 'embalming' in a mere name. The most poignant expression of these sentiments occurs across stanzas 100 and 101 of Canto IV in *Don Juan*, in which Byron, having contemplated the extended spectral afterlife of poets who, in the fashion of Dryden and Pope, have 'come down to us through distance / Of time and tongues, the foster-babes of Fame' (IV, 100), is led somewhat radically to conclude that that which seems supernatural is, in effect, nothing other than the illusory effect of naming:

> Where twenty ages gather o'er a name,
> 'Tis as a snowball which derives assistance
> From every flake, and yet rolls on the same,
> Even till an iceberg it may chance to grow,
> But, after all, 'tis nothing but cold snow. (IV, 100)

Such a version of the 'explained supernatural' would not be out of place in the Gothic romances of Ann Radcliffe. As the next stanza continues: 'And so great names are nothing more than nominal, / And love of glory's but an airy lust' (IV, 101). Names are no longer the vehicle of the poet's ghostly afterlife, and death, even when it is recorded in an epitaph, is tantamount to erasure, illegibility and anonymity: 'Where are the epitaphs our fathers read? / Save a few glean'd from the sepulchral gloom / Which once-named myriads nameless lie beneath, / And lose their own in universal death' (IV, 102). As the speaker of 'Churchill's Grave: A Fact Literally Rendered' puts it, the epitaph of the dead poet is as illegible as the epitaphs on the tombstones of the undistinguished that surround it '[w]ith name no clearer than the names unknown' (6). Although the closing couplet of this poem emphasizes the doubleness of the poet's name and its ability to serve as both a means of 'Obscurity' and 'Fame', the overwhelming note to the Sexton's homily is one of obliteration: 'The Glory and the Nothing of a Name' (43). At the grave of the dead poet, Byron's persona in 'Churchill's Grave', like Hamlet in the graveyard scene, confronts the inevitability and finality of death. As Canto IX of *Don Juan* shows, Byron's verse has come full circle, from the wish for spectral disembodiment in the proper name as it is expressed in 'A Fragment' back to the ineluctable reality that is Hamlet's too, too sullied flesh:

> 'To be or not to be! that is the question',
> Says Shakespeare, who just now is much in fashion.
> I am neither Alexander nor Hephaestion,
> Nor ever had for *abstract* fame much passion;
> But would much rather have a sound digestion,
> Than Buonaparte's cancer: – could I dash on
> Through fifty victories to shame or fame,
> Without a stomach – what were a good name? (IX, 14)

Fame in *Don Juan* is ghostly only because, like a ghost, it does not really exist; names are not agents of haunting but only so many reminders of death. While early Byron had written in pursuit of ghosts, the later Byron writes in pursuit of money – either that, his narrator tells us, or '[t]o make some hour less dreary' (XIV, 11). The mortality of the corruptible body and recording of mortality in the legible (though also potentially illegible) epitaph is life's only certainty. When Byron uncannily returns to the task of imagining his own death in the late poem 'On This Day I Complete My Thirty-Sixth Year' (1824), his sense of the poetic afterlife has been thoroughly stripped of his narcissistic fantasy of spectral return: 'Seek out – less often sought than found – / A Soldier's Grave, for thee the best; / Then look around, and choose thy Ground, / And take thy Rest!' (37–40). No longer the watershed that opens up onto a posthumous haunting, death has become for Byron a point of termination, an end both in and of itself.

*

Byron's disillusionment with the project of literary renown in *Don Juan* is cognate with the poem's parodic but good-humoured engagement with the ghosts of Gothic romance in the famous Black Friar episode narrated across cantos XV–XVII. Insofar as the tale of the Black Friar marks the return of the frequently disavowed popular cultural mode that is Gothic to the 'high' reaches of the Romantic epic-turned-lyric poem, the last two cantos of *Don Juan* are crucial to the ongoing critical fascination with the relationship between these two contemporary but aesthetically opposed impulses.[24] As Coleridge's review of Matthew Lewis's *The Monk* in the *Critical Review* of February 1797 as well as his condemnation of the 'trash of the circulating libraries' in a lengthy footnote to *Biographia Literaria* (1817) had made clear, the ghosts that shrieked, rattled and howled in so many early Gothic fictions, chapbooks, dramas and phantasmagoric visual entertainments of the Romantic era were symptomatic of the depraved aesthetic 'appetites' of the age's popular readership. By contrast, Byron's narrator, at least initially, deliberately seeks to exploit what even Wordsworth described as 'this degrading thirst after outrageous stimulation' in order to present the Gothic vogue for ghosts in a somewhat more positive light: 'And now, that we may furnish with some matter all / Tastes, we are going to try the supernatural' (XV, 93). Momentarily refusing such blanket Romantic condemnations of the Gothic as the sign of depraved popular taste, Byron figures the rage for ghosts as one particular literary predilection among many, and one that is not necessarily less legitimate than others. Positioning his 'Grim reader' (XV, 95) at this moment more as the fevered, feminine reader of a Gothic romance than the restrained, masculine subject of literary epic, Byron's narrator begins to spin his yarn of supernatural imagining. Recalling the ways in which Gothic

fictions of the period frequently appropriated Shakespearean configu-
rations of the supernatural as literary precedent – 'I could a tale unfold',
the ghost's lines from *Hamlet*, are used by Ann Radcliffe as epigraphs
in both *A Sicilian Romance* and the second chapter of *The Mysteries
of Udolpho* – the narrative of the Black Friar, as McGann's editorial
notes point out, is couched in allusions to *Hamlet* and *Macbeth*.[25] More
overtly, the beginning section of Canto XV self-consciously conjures up
a Gothic scene of story-telling, with its midnight setting, shrieks of owls
and distinctly Walpolean portraits of dead ancestors which scowl down
upon the living and, as in *The Castle of Otranto*, appear to leave their
frames. In another allusion to the self-authenticating gestures of early
Gothic romance – in particular, the tendency of writers to present their
fictions as fragmented documentary remainders of empirical historical
truth – the narrator's tale, for all its supernaturalism, emphasises its truth
value throughout: 'But of all truths which she [his muse] has told, the
most / True is that which she is about to tell. / I said it was a story of a
ghost –' (XVI, 4). In yet another instance of cross-dressing in the poem,
Don Juan, abed in his 'Gothic chamber' (XVI, 15) replete with stained
glass, wainscoting and pointed arches, assumes the characteristic pose
of a Radcliffean heroine, as the ghost of the Black Friar makes its first
appearance. Evaporating and disappearing shortly thereafter, Adeline's
ballad the next morning describes the Black Friar as the remainder of
historical change, a recalcitrant spectral residue which, in its defiant
return, resisted Henry VIII's dissolution of the monasteries, and which
not even the process of architectural improvement and modernization at
the Abbey has been able to eradicate.[26] That night, the ghost makes its
second appearance '[w]ith awful footsteps regular as rhyme' (XVI, 113).
Though this spectre, with its sweet breath, dimpled chin and glowing
bust is all too voluptuous a thing of 'flesh and blood' (XVI, 123), Don
Juan's reactions betray the sub-Cartesian distinctions between spectral
disembodiment and gross corporeality that informed Byron's earlier
spectral fantasies in such poems as 'A Fragment': 'His own internal
ghost began to awaken / Within him', we are told, 'and to quell his
corporal quaking – / Hinting that soul and body on the whole / Were
odds against a disembodied soul' (XVI, 118). With the disclosure of
the Duchess of Fitz-Fulke's spectral transvestitism in the last line of
Canto XVI – a scene of clerical cross-dressing that recalls the figure of
Rosario/Matilda in *The Monk* – Byron, at least at the superficial level
of narrative entertainment, exorcizes the Gothic ghost in a gesture
that once again recalls the Radcliffean technique of the explained
supernatural: no waif-like spectre this, but only the staged amatory

deceptions of the passionate Duchess. Canto III of *Don Juan* employed a similar strategy: though long-presumed dead, Lambro returns home not as an uncanny spectre but merely as a man who now experiences his once homely abode as decidedly unhomely. In both instances, Byron has recourse to a decidedly Gothic strategy in order to lay the ghosts of the Gothic to rest.

However, as Bernard Beatty's close reading of the final cantos of the poem has pointed out, the process of Gothic denouement effected in this bathetic disclosure does little to explain away other, more complex and less crudely rendered versions of the supernatural – namely, the numerous manifestations of ghostliness that persist and remain in place, wholly unexorcized, at the poem's end. As Beatty puts it, the spectral encounter at Norman Abbey 'remains as a force to disturb daylight experience' when Don Juan and Fitz-Fulke breakfast together the following morning.[27] Both of them seem, by the light of day, to have become spectral themselves, with Juan described as '[b]eing wan and worn, with eyes that hardly brooked / The light' and Her Grace as pale and shivering, 'as if she had kept / A vigil, or dreamt rather more than slept' (XVII, 14). Moreover, given the differences in circumstance and poetic execution between them, it is by no means certain that Juan's first ghostly visitant was, indeed, the amorous Duchess; rather, in retrospect, it seems fair to surmise that, upon learning of the legend of the Black Friar as it was narrated to Juan in her presence, Fitz-Fulke cannily exploited the tale's potential for erotic conquest. In Julian Wolfreys's terms, the haunting effects of the poem's ending have become irreducible to the apparition, the pervading field of spectrality far exceeding the singular example of the Black Friar's ghost.[28] 'I leave the thing a problem, like all things', the narrator teasingly asserts (XVII, 13), and in a characteristic moment of Byronic uncertainty, ghostliness spills over the contrived 'Gothic' ending of the Fitz-Fulke episode.

In Peter Cochran's estimation, Byron appears at this moment to be 'having it both ways', gratifying both the sceptical and credulous sides of his personality simultaneously.[29] But perhaps the matter is more decisive than this. For this dispersal of ghosts across two textual axes – the one parodic and temporary and the other permanent and enduring – marks out the difference between the Gothic and Romantic modes, respectively: behind Byron's dispensing with the ghosts of the Gothic at the end of *Don Juan* lies a decidedly Romantic concern with the ghostliness of everyday life, in spectres that refuse to answer to the convenient narrative strategies of invocation and expulsion, but persist in manifesting themselves in spite of the conscious wishes of those whom they haunt. Beneath the comic resolution of the poem, that is, lies a concern with tragic interiority.[30] In a manifestation of what Terry Castle has identified as the 'invention' of the uncanny in European culture of the late eighteenth and early nineteenth centuries, external ghosts are explained away only to be introjected as psychic phantoms on the outer limits of consciousness.[31] The existence of this inner, psychic field of Romantic spectrality and its difference from the superficial claptrap of the Gothic had already been alluded to in the poem's account of the 'internal ghost' of Don Juan, which had been awakened within him during his encounter with the Black Friar (XVI, 118): 'I hate all mystery, and that air / Of clap-trap, which your recent poets prize', the anti-Gothic narrator of *Don Juan* had claimed earlier (II, 124). But this is not enough to deter Byron from figuring the interior of the Childe's psyche as a haunted, spectral space.

It is across the various cantos of *Childe Harold's Pilgrimage* that this particular configuration of the spectral is given its most sustained treatment. Abandoning the pursuit of fame and turning inwards towards 'the soul's haunted cell', Byron's persona in Canto III presumes to consort there with a host of spectres: 'With airy images, and shapes which dwell / Still unimpair'd' (III, 5). Time and again, the subjective poetic interior to which Byron increasingly gives lyrical expression across the four cantos is presented, via certain Lockean underpinnings, as a flat internal surface or private interior space that has been variously 'written upon' or 'populated by' the legible effects of the subject's empirical experiences across time. Almost invariably, these experiences are negatively rendered, with the breast of the lyrical poet described as being '[w]rung with the wounds which kill not, but ne'er heal' (*CHP*, III, 8) or ineradicably marked by the painful inscriptions of trauma: 'What deep wounds ever closed without a scar? / The heart's bleed longest, and but heal to wear / That which disfigures it' (III, 84). As Byron phrases it in *The Giaour*, 'sterner hearts alone may feel / The wound that time can never heal' (920–21). Though as invisible as a ghost and as bitter as a scorpion's sting, the countless 'griefs subdued' that compose the 'mask' of subjective authenticity that Byron fashions for himself at such moments can be awakened and reactivated through memory by so slight a sensory impression as music, wind or the sight of the ocean. Compounding the Lockean dimensions, Byron invokes the Associationist paradigm of David Hartley in his presentation of sensory impressions as being capable of '[s]triking the electric chain wherewith we are darkly bound' (*CHP*, IV, 23), one impression invoking another in a limitless chain of ghostly substitutions. The scientific metaphors of lightning, electricity and galvanism employed here soon give way to the more familiar Byronic field of the spectral, as awakened memory 'calls up to view / The spectres whom no exorcism can bind, / The cold – the changed – perchance the dead – anew, / The mourn'd, the loved, the lost – too many! – yet how few!' (*CHP*, IV, 24). Byron's lyrical persona is deeply, enduringly haunted.

Ghosts appear as symptoms of trauma on a broader scale, too, as Princess Charlotte, mournful and pale, appears with her baby in the gulf that is 'thick with phantoms' (*CHP*, IV, 167) as a powerful expression of the nation's unhealable wounds: 'Such as arises when a nation bleeds / With some deep and immedicable wound' (IV, 167). On both an individual and collective level, experience across time populates the Romantic subject with ghosts and apparitions, which, refusing the strategies of exorcism and banishment, return to haunt through the most unintentional invocations of memory. Byron elaborates upon this inner field of the haunted psyche amidst his reflections upon, and identifications with, the poets Petrarch, Tasso and Dante in stanza 34 of Canto IV: these are poetic souls plagued by 'demons, who impair / The strength of better thoughts, and seek their prey / In melancholy bosoms', making 'the sun like blood, the earth a tomb, / The tomb a hell, and hell itself a murkier gloom.' Gothic images of demons, melancholy and interminable hellfire inhabit the poetic psyche; infernally locked into a form of living death, the life of the Byronic poet is, once again, rendered spectral long before the advent of mortality. Jettisoning the surface conventions of the Gothic in order to employ the ghost as a suitable metaphor for the poet's troubled psyche, Byron in *Childe Harold's Pilgrimage*, rather like Coleridge in 'Frost at Midnight', grounds the spectre in what, by implication, is the more legitimate realm of Romantic interiority and depth psychology.[32]

*

Its concerns with an intractable field of psychic spectrality aside, *Childe Harold's Pilgrimage*, like *Don Juan*, relies in other respects heavily upon the rhetorical, thematic and structural practices of invocation and exorcism, spectral invitation and ghostly banishment. The ghosts of Canto I of *Childe Harold's Pilgrimage* announce their presence through the forces of structural interruption and spatio-temporal dislocation: amidst Byron's account of contemporary Spain of the Peninsula War, the poem turns to Mount Parnassus, the legendary home of the Muses in Ancient Greece. Upon first impression, the Greece of *Childe*

Harold's Pilgrimage seems to be a landscape populated with spectres: the determined absence of spectral activity on the sacred mountain implied in the lines 'Though here no more Apollo haunts his grot, / And thou, the Muses' seat, art now their grave' (I, 62) swiftly gives way to a more abiding sense of ghostly presence at Parnassus, and one that curiously renders the use of the verb 'haunts' in line 634 as a synonym for embodied, non-spectral activity: 'Some gentle Spirit still pervades the spot, / Sighs in the gale, keeps silence in the cave, / And glides with glassy foot o'er yon melodious Wave' (I, 62). If only momentarily, ancient Greece seems to be presided over by what, in classical Roman religion, was a genius loci – a protective spectral being that has survived Christianity's systematic eradication of pagan belief structures and persisted into the speaker's present. Though 'Glory fly her glades,' the poem continues, the nation seems to be protected by 'such peaceful shades / As Greece can still bestow' (I, 64). Despite the sense of comfort and security conjured up in these lines, the use of the auxiliary 'can' already seems to point to a certain lack at the heart of the supernatural: those few ghosts that still haunt and populate the national landscape seem to be doomed to failure and inadequacy, a point that will be further developed in Canto II.

When Byron returns to the topic of Greece in the second canto, he presents Childe Harold as a 'gloomy wanderer' (II, 16) melancholically traversing the 'graveyard' that is contemporary Athens. Its ancient monuments in ruins, the city has become the 'nation's sepulchre' (II, 3), but one that still appears at this point to be haunted by the 'shade of power' (II, 2), the remnant or memory of the political and cultural grandeur that once was. As this suggests, much of what drives the second canto of *Childe Harold's Pilgrimage* is the desire for congress with the dead – that is, with the wistful *anticipation* of the ghostly return rather than with the spectral return itself. In stanza 8, for instance, Byron records the clash between classical and Judeo-Christian belief systems in order to express a wish that the souls of the sages Zoroaster and Pythagoras would 'shame' the Sadducean discrediting of belief in the afterlife by returning from the grave:

> Yet if, as holiest men have deem'd, there be
> A land of souls beyond that sable shore,
> To shame the doctrine of the Sadducee
> And sophists, madly vain of dubious lore;
> How sweet it were in concert to adore
> With those who made our mortal labours light!
> To hear each voice we fear'd to hear no more!

> Behold each mighty shade reveal'd to sight,
> The Bactrian, Samian sage, and all who taught the right! (II, 8)

While the prosopopoeic addressal of the absent entity rests securely on the corollary of that entity's subsequent response, the speaker of Canto II, somewhat more tentatively, can merely anticipate, in the realm of fantasy, an audible and comprehensible spectral reply. The lack of any firm belief in the existence and power of ghosts implied here is taken further in Byron's figuring of Thomas Bruce, the seventh Earl of Elgin, as a veritable 'grave-robber' who has plundered Athens of its antique treasures. With '[h]er sons too weak the sacred shrine to guard' (II, 12), Anthena's spectral children have failed to protect the city against Elgin's depredations; regrettably, Sadducean scepticism regarding the spirit world seems to have triumphed over pagan spirituality. Earlier evocations of the existence of genius loci appear unsustainable, as the Childe's prosopopoeic address to the dead seems to echo and resound into an afterlife that has been drained and emptied of all supernatural beings:

> Where was thine Aegis, Pallas! that appall'd
> Stern Alaric and Havoc on their way?
> Where Peleus' son? whom Hell in vain enthrall'd,
> His shade from Hades upon that dread day,
> Bursting to light in terrible array! (II, 14)

The only part of Greece that remains untouched by cultural depredation is the natural world, for what Elgin has effected in the realm of aesthetic objects, the programme of Turkish nationalism has effected in the political arena. In this regard, too, however, Greece has been let down by its spectres. In its invocation of the 'lost Liberty' (II, 75, 714) of the vanquished nation, the verse reads as a rousing yet desperate call for the resurrection and valorous return of the nation's ghosts from the otherwise silent and empty tomb:

> Fair Greece! sad relic of departed worth!
> Immortal, though no more! though fallen, great!
> Who now shall lead thy scatter'd children forth,
> And long accustom'd bondage uncreate?
> Not such thy sons who whilome did await,
> The hopeless warriors of a willing doom,
> In bleak Thermopylae's sepulchral strait –
> Oh! who that gallant spirit shall resume,
> Leap from Eurotas' banks, and call thee from the tomb? (II, 73)

In the context of Byron's insistence that the cultural and political spirits of Greece have failed to present themselves, the line '[w]here'er we tread 'tis haunted, holy ground' (II, 88) reads more as wish-fulfilment on the Childe's behalf than anything else: indeed, the preceding stanzas of the canto have pointed to nothing if not to the sad absence of all supernatural activity in modern-day Athens. This spectral lack is mirrored in the absence of the ghost of Edelston towards the end of Canto II, even as Byron's prosopopoeic address in stanza 95 – 'Thou too art gone, thou lov'd and lovely one!' (II, 95) – conjures up the spirit of his dead friend as the implied addressee of the speaker's elegiac mode. When, in *The Giaour* (1813), Byron metaphorically figures ancient Greece as the corpse of a woman, her loveliness parting 'not quite with parting breath', the only ghost that subsequently appears is the beauty of the corpse, which 'haunts' the body to the tomb (92–100). Assuming the responsibilities of protection and resistance that should ideally have been wielded by spectres, Byron's persona renders itself ghostly in metaphorically deploying the city of Athens as a consecrated churchyard in which the act of grave-robbing becomes a prohibited and sacrosanct activity: 'Let such approach this consecrated land, / And pass in peace along the magic waste: / But spare its relics – let no busy hand / Deface the scenes, already how defac'd!' (*CHP*, II, 93). A similarly spectral fate awaits the 'self-exiled Harold' in Canto III; for, realizing '[t]hat all was over on this side the tomb' (III, 16), the Childe's existence becomes that of the living dead. But when, in Canto IV, the mask of the Childe is discarded in the process of Byron donning the apparently more 'authentic' persona of lyrical self-expression, his disappearance into the abyss of death – the place of ultimate oblivion, '[t]hrough which all things grow phantoms' (IV, 165) – reads as the dissolution and erasure of his once-spectral being:

> He is no more – these breathings are his last;
> His wanderings done, his visions ebbing fast,
> And he himself as nothing: – if he was
> Aught but a phantasy, and could be class'd
> With forms which live and suffer – let that pass –
> His shadow fades away into Destruction's mass [...]. (IV, 164)

Like the chance that drives fame, haunting – Canto II implies – would be a fine thing, if only because populating the empty void of modern existence with spectres would ward against the devastating isolation expressed in the Childe's sense of himself as 'alone on earth, as I am now' (II, 98).

In what we might call a moment of 'negative Gothic', then, the real terror that underlies much of Byron's political commentary on the state of contemporary Greece and Rome in *Childe Harold's Pilgrimage* is the realization that spectres may not, indeed, exist; that phantoms are nothing more than phantoms; and that the dead are not indubitably bound to make a ghostly return from the grave. If they do, they have certainly failed to present themselves here: failing to come to the rescue of the two nations that require their protection and assistance the most, the ghosts of Europe have let the continent down. In his *Communist Manifesto* of 1848, Karl Marx had, with some confidence, announced that 'A spectre is haunting Europe'; for Byron, writing in the period from 1816 to 1818, the very opposite appears to be the case. As a result, Byron repeatedly finds himself in the position of a spectral conjurer, calling up spirits, as Shelley put it in 'Mont Blanc', '[n]ear the still cave of the witch Poesy, / Seeking among the shadows that pass by, / Ghosts of all things that are', inviting through poetic utterance '[s]ome spectre, some faint image'. The numerous spectral adjurations of the eponymous Manfred in Byron's dramatic poem of the same name illustrate this pose well:

> Mysterious Agency!
> Ye spirits of the unbounded Universe!
> Whom I have sought in darkness and in light –
> Ye, who do compass earth about, and dwell
> In subtler essence – ye, to whom the tops
> Of mountains inaccessible are haunts,
> And earth's and ocean's caves familiar things –
> I call upon ye by the written charm
> Which gives me power upon you – Rise! appear! (I, i, 28–36)

The act of spectral conjuration reaches its crescendo in Canto IV of *Childe Harold's Pilgrimage*, as Byron's poetic persona, having set the seal of magical incantation, welcomes the ghosts of ancient Rome as a prelude to restoring the city's lost noble heritage: 'Now welcome, thou dread power / Nameless, yet thus omnipotent, which here / Walk'st in the shadow of the midnight hour / With a deep awe, yet all distinct from fear' (IV, 138). Though Rome was sacked in ancient times by the Goths, its destruction was nothing like the political and cultural sacking of Greece in the present day by both the Turkish and British empires, respectively. Even so, the ruins of the Coliseum lend themselves to Byron as a makeshift spectral circle in which the act of conjuration might be performed: 'Then in this magic circle raise the dead: / Heroes have trod this spot – 'tis on their dust ye tread' (IV, 144). While this might recall the sense of Athens as 'haunted, holy ground' from Canto II, the very act of summoning up the spirits, both here and earlier, is necessitated by the acknowledgement that the ghosts of the noble, antique past are no longer present and by no means guaranteed to materialize. The primary strategy that the poet has at his disposal for the summoning of ghosts, the poem suggests, is the creative power invested in the faculty of the poetic imagination itself. In the context of Byron's spectral preoccupations in the poem, the often-quoted lines from Canto III – ''Tis to create, and in creating live / A being more intense, that we endow / With form our fancy' (III, 6) – might be read as a statement on the ability of the mind to create spectres out of nothing, projecting them into the emptiness as we proceed. Intensity, here, becomes a byword for Romantic sublimity, with creative idealism 'lending splendour' to what, for Shelley, was the everlasting universe of empirical things. As Canto IV continues, the ghostly and phantasmatic 'beings' of the poetic mind 'are not of clay' and, as such, are '[e]ssentially immortal' (IV, 5); opening us up to the experience of sublime intensity, they 'multiply in us a brighter ray / And more beloved existence' (IV, 5). Accordingly, when the poet encounters the ghosts of an old man and young woman in the Pantheon in Rome, they are explained as 'phantoms of the brain' (IV, 148), as the ideal projections of the creative consciousness, albeit without the infernal Macbethian connotations of the Gothic imagination set up in *English Bards and Scotch Reviewers*. Like romantic love, the ghosts of ideal poetic creation are capable of 'replenishing the void' (*CHP*, IV, 5), thus providing a salutary 'refuge' from the 'Vacancy' that is old age (*CHP*, IV, 6).

*

At first glance, it might seem that Byron's poetry, in its insistent issuing of a call to spectres to rise up and assume a range of predetermined roles and pre-ordained functions, forecloses upon the possibility of an ethical encounter with the ghost such as that provisionally outlined by Derrida in his influential *Specters of Marx*.[33] Challenging the psychoanalytically inflected practices of spectral exorcism that have informed many aspects of Western cultural tradition, Derrida advocates here an ethics of ghostliness – a praxis that involves the extension of an attitude of 'absolute hospitality' to the ghosts that might arrive, in however unprecedented, unrecognizable and hitherto inconceivable a form, from an ethical future, announcing, as they do so, a programme of 'the good' that remains, as yet, unthought.[34] As *arrivant*, Derrida's ethical spectre instantiates a new order of justice and ethics and ought, as such, to be welcomed rather than exorcized and invoked rather than eradicated. This ethics of welcome and hospitality, however, is one that, for Derrida, ought to remain free of the obligations of reciprocation, as Derrida prepares the way for 'the absolute surprise of the *arrivant* from whom or from which one will not ask anything in return and who or which will not be asked to commit to the domestic contracts of any welcoming power'.[35] As this suggests, the Derridean spectre might only serve as a vehicle for ethics insofar as it remains fundamentally unknown and unknowable, as an 'experience of the impossible' and an 'alterity that cannot be anticipated'.[36] Articulating 'the messianic without messianism',[37] the spectre issues out of some future configuration of ultimate justice that cannot yet be anticipated. As Colin Davis in this regard has pointed out, the Derridean ethical spectre occupies the place of Levinas's absolute Other, shattering the security of all existent knowledge systems and eradicating the grounds of current morality and epistemology in the process.[38] The ghosts invoked by Byron, in contrast, seem, at least in some senses, to be phantoms that the persona presumes to know, understand and even manipulate to his own advantage: a ghostly supplement to the Whiggish myth of Liberty, which he sees corrupted before his eyes in contemporary Spain and Greece, the spectral remnant of antique glory that he sees in ruins in modern-day Rome. Characteristically putting words of his own devising into the mouths of the dead, Byron's verse, from a certain perspective, seems to preclude the possibility of ethical spectrality through the rhetorical trope of prosopopeia. Conjured into existence, rendered animate and purportedly given a voice of their own, all that the ghosts of Byron's verse ever really seem to achieve is the ventriloquizing of the poet's own political position, as complex, provisional and undoubtedly oriented towards his own conceptualization of 'the good' as it might be.[39] As Michael Riffaterre has argued, prosopopoeia as de Man theorizes it is narcissistic in the extreme: 'the address calls for a reply of the addressee, the gaze that perceives animation invites gazing back from the animated object to the subject daydreaming a Narcissistic reflection of itself in things'.[40] The primacy of the narcissistic ego marks the failure of Derrida's spectral ethics.

However, as the irreducible haunting that exceeds the figure of the ghost in the Black Friar episode in *Don Juan* indicates, there remains in place another, more radical field of spectrality tacitly written into Byron's *oeuvre* – one which, in defying all imaginary demands for knowledge, opens up the possibility of an ethical spectral relation that is conceptually cognate with that of Derrida. Manifesting themselves through interruption in temporal schemas that remain, in *Hamlet*, as in *Don Juan*, forever 'out of joint' (IX, 41), these are the voices of the dead that return to frustrate the narcissistic trappings of prosopopeia, chiasmically imposing, as they do in 'The isles of Greece' inset in Canto III of *Don Juan*, a stony silence upon those who have dared to invoke them:

> What, silent still? and silent all?
>   Ah! no; – the voices of the dead
> Sound like a distant torrent's fall,
>   And answer, 'Let one living head,
> But one arise, – we come, we come!'
> 'Tis but the living who are dumb. (III, 731–36)

Frustrating the speaker's demand for mirror-like identification, the ghost of Leila in *The Giaour* appears only as a cipher of non-reflective blankness, as a radical ghostly absence that refuses the comforts of love and imaginary recognition:

> And rushing from my couch, I dart,
> And clasp her to my desperate heart;
> I clasp – what is it that I clasp?
> No breathing form within my grasp,
> No heart that beats reply to mine,
> Yet, Leila! yet the form is thine!
> And art thou, dearest, chang'd so much,
> As meet my eye, yet mock my touch? (1285–92)

Even as she is clasped in the speaker's arms, the empty spectre that is Leila, who is hailed indecisively in terms that recall Brutus's responses to the ghost of Caesar as 'shape or shade! – whate'er thou art' (1315), remains fundamentally unknown and unknowable, a radical otherness that engenders in the speaker so many unresolved problems and unanswered questions. In *Manfred*, too, the ghost of Astarte serves only as a reminder of radical otherness that exceeds the structures of human knowledge and rationality, a sense implicit even in the optimistic yet doubt-infused, incantation that Nemesis uses to call her up:

> Shadow! or Spirit!
> Whatever thou art,
> Which still doth inherit
> The whole or a part

> Of the form of thy birth,
> Of the mould of thy clay,
> Which returned to the earth,
> Re-appear to the day! (II, iv, 84–91)

Even as Manfred invokes her, he knows neither the question he will ask
of her nor the answers that he would like to receive: 'I know not what I
ask, nor what I seek' (II, iv, 132). Though repeatedly adjured by Nemesis
and Manfred himself to speak, the ghost of Astarte remains defiant in
her muteness: 'and in that silence', Manfred acknowledges, 'I am more
than answered' (II, iv, 111). As with the ghost of Leila, there is something
in this that approaches Derrida's sense of the spectre as a 'messianism
without content';[41] insofar as the ghosts of Astarte and Leila exceed
the field of human understanding, Byron conserves what, in Derridean
terms, is respect for 'the heterogeneity of the other'.[42] While this is
undoubtedly to the chagrin of morally complex Byronic heroes, like
Manfred and the Giaour, it does, in and through the very frustration
it provokes, open up an ethical alternative in relation to spectres, one
that resides in the alterity of the ghost and its defiance of the anthropomorphic, somewhat violent gestures of invocation and exorcism. Figured
as an utterly intransigent nymph, for instance, Astarte's ghostly version
of Echo refuses vocally to reflect the verbal ejaculations of Manfred's
Narcissus, even as so many other spirits answer his call:

> For I have call'd on thee in the still night,
> Startled the slumbering birds from the hush'd boughs,
> And woke the mountain wolves, and made the caves
> Acquainted with thy vainly echoed name,
> Which answered me – many things answered me –
> Spirits and men – but thou wert silent all. (II, iv, 136–41)

Beyond the ken of humans and other spirits alike, Astarte is a spectral
manifestation of that which is radically other – indeed, of the very
other of Otherness itself; as even the ghostly Nemesis is led to observe:
'She is not of our order, but belongs / To the other powers. Mortal! thy
quest is vain, / And we are baffled also' (II, iv, 116–18). It is in this field
of absolute alterity, though, that the key to Manfred's existence lies.
Going to the grave with the very secrets that would make the lives of
the living bearable and meaningful, the dead in *Manfred* hold within
their gift a salutary ethical alternative, but one which, at least to the
living, remains always inaccessible and forever beyond the realms of
fathomable knowledge. As such, the dead remain as 'sceptred sovereigns,
who still rule / Our spirits from their urns' (III, iv, 40–41). Byron's

fragment 'Could I remount the river of my years', explores a similar dilemma. 'Absent are the dead', the speaker observes, though they persist in haunting us, as if through a dreary shroud, from their afterlife of tranquillity ('A Fragment', 11–13). Like the ghosts of Leila and Astarte, these too are spectres that refuse the narcissistic structures of recognition and knowing; 'for they are cold', the persona continues, 'And ne'er can be what once we did behold' (15). In this state of absence and longing, in which the dead remain permanently separated from the living as if by a barrier as large as the earth and as deep as the sea, the only possibility of reconciliation between the two worlds lies in the fact of death itself: 'In the dark union of insensate dust' (22). Until that moment, the ghosts of the absent dead will continue to haunt the living, either remaining, as Astarte does, utterly mute and incommunicative – 'in their silent cities dwell / Each in his incommunicative cell' (27–28) – or speaking, if and when they do, in languages that remain utterly unintelligible for the living: 'Or have they their own language – and a sense / Of breathless being – darkened and intense – / As midnight in her solitude' (29–31). The crux of the matter, though, lies in the precise nature of the secrets that the dead have taken with them to their graves. As in *Manfred*, spectres in the foregoing fragment are figured as holding for Byron the promise of an ethical tomorrow:

> and the key
> Of thy profundity is in the grave,
> The portal of thy universal cave –
> Where I would walk in Spirit – and behold
> Our elements resolved to things untold,
> And fathom hidden wonders – and explore
> The essence of great bosoms now no more. (34–40)

The impossible position in which the living poet characteristically finds himself, then, is that while the dead continue to speak to the living in tongues that are unknown, the 'essences' in their breasts and the 'hidden wonders' of their ways – in short, their functions as harbingers of the ethical future – will remain secretive, inaccessible and undisclosed. Even though their messages are incapable of being transmitted by even the most indefatigable of conjurors, Byron's ethical shades still mark out their difference from the falsehood-dealing phantoms of Abraham and Torok's psychoanalytic schema.[43] While psychoanalysis arrogates to itself the power to penetrate the secrets of the dead and exorcize the ghostly symptoms that their silences have called up in the living, the Byronic poet acknowledges only his permanent exile, *qua* living being, from the spectre's unknown and unknowable ethical promise. His only hope lies in the gesture of ghostly invocation itself, as ineffectual as the act of conjuration in a poem such as *Childe Harold's Pilgrimage* might be. Either that, Byron's verse teaches us, or else in the poet's much-anticipated access to the spectral realm via the assumption of the gift of death – a fantasy that had fuelled the poet's utterances from the outset.

Notes

1 Quevedo Redivivus, *Spiritual Interview with Lord Byron. In Which His Lordship Gave His Opinions and Feelings About His New Monument and Gossip About the Literature of His Own and the Present Day, With Some Interesting Information about the Spirit World. With Notes Explanatory and Elucidatory* (London: Samuel Palmer and Sons, n.d.). In the absence of any indication on the title page, there is some doubt concerning the precise year in which Quevedo Redivivus's tract was published. The British Library tentatively ascribes the date of 1880 to the copy held there, while the National Library of Scotland catalogue suggests a publication date of 1876. However, other sources suggest a date as early as 1840. For a scholarly discussion of the possible date of publication, including the convincing argument that the text is of American provenance, see Barbara Melchiori, 'Lord Byron Among the Ghosts', in *Arte e letteratura: Scritti in ricordo di Gabriele Baldini* (Rome: Edizioni di Storia e Letteratura, 1972), pp. 241–57.

2 See Susan J. Wolfson's arguments in both '*The Vision of Judgment* and the Visions of "Author"', in *The Cambridge Companion to Byron*, pp. 171–85 and 'Byron's Ghosting Authority', pp. 763–92.

3 Quevedo Redivivus, *Spiritual Interview with Lord Byron*, p. 5.

4 Ibid.

5 Ibid., pp. 5–6.

6 Ibid., p. 9.

7 Ibid., p. 10.

8 Ibid., p. 13.

9 Ibid.

10 Paul de Man, 'Autobiography as De-facement', *MLN*, 94:5 (December 1979), p. 926.

11 Jacques Derrida, 'Signature Event Context', in *Limited Inc*, trans. S. Weber and J. Mehlman (Evanston, IL: Northwestern University Press, 1988), pp. 1–23.

12 Jane Stabler, *Byron, Poetics and History* (Cambridge: Cambridge University Press, 2002), p. 2.

13 Tom Mole, *Byron's Romantic Celebrity: Industrial Culture and the Hermeneutic of Intimacy* (Basingstoke: Palgrave Macmillan, 2007), p. 16.

14 For a recent account of Byron's relationship with the Gothic, see the various essays in *The Gothic Byron*, ed. Peter Cochran (Newcastle upon Tyne: Cambridge Scholars Press, 2009) and, particularly, Cochran's essay in this collection, 'Byron Reads and Rewrites Gothic', pp. 1–78.

15 T.J. Mathias, *The Pursuits of Literature: A Satirical Poem. Part the Fourth and Last* (London: Printed for T. Becket, 1797), p. iv.

16 William Wordsworth, 'Preface to *Lyrical Ballads* (1802)' in *Romanticism: An Anthology with CD-ROM*, 2nd Edition, ed. Duncan Wu (Oxford: Blackwell, 2000), p. 359

17 Jacques Lacan, 'Desire and the Interpretation of Desire in *Hamlet*', trans. J. Hulbert and ed. J.A. Miller, in *Yale French Studies*, 55: 56 (1977), p. 39.

18 See my argument 'Gothic and the Ghost of *Hamlet*', in *Gothic Shakespeares*, eds. J. Drakakis and D. Townshend (Abingdon: Routledge, 2008), pp. 60–97.

19 Matthew Lewis, *The Monk: A Romance*, ed. Howard Anderson (Oxford: Oxford University Press, 1973), p. 175.

20 Jacques Derrida, *On the Name*, trans. David Wood, John P. Leavey, Jnr., and Ian McLeod (Stanford, CA: Stanford University Press, 1995).

21 Ibid., p. 13.

22 Ibid. Emphasis in the original.

23 Jerome J. McGann, *Byron and Romanticism*, p. 107.

24 For the most influential account of the relationship between these two modes, see Michael Gamer, *Romanticism and the Gothic: Genre, Reception, and Canon Formation* (Cambridge: Cambridge University Press, 2000).

25 See, for instance, the allusion to *Hamlet*, Act IV, scene v, lines 43–44, in *Don Juan*, XV, 99; *Hamlet*, Act II, scene ii, line 103, in *Don Juan*, XVI, 1; and *Macbeth*'s 'sisters weïrd' in *Don Juan*, XVI, 21.

26 See, in this respect, the political reading of the ghost of the Black Friar advanced in Malcolm Kelsall, 'The Gothic Ghost: The Return of the (Politically) Repressed', in *The Gothic Byron*, pp. 119–25.

27 Bernard Beatty, *Byron's 'Don Juan'*, p. 31.

28 Wolfreys, *Victorian Hauntings: Spectrality, Gothic, the Uncanny and Literature*, p. 6.

29 Peter Cochran, 'Byron Reads and Rewrites Gothic', p. 73.

30 For an account of the dynamic interchange between the comic and the tragic in Byron's *oeuvre*, see Alan Rawes's argument in *Byron's Poetic Experimentation: Childe Harold, The Tales, and the Quest for Comedy*.

31 See Terry Castle's argument in the last three chapters of *The Female Thermometer: Eighteenth-Century Culture and the Invention of the Uncanny* (New York, NY: Oxford University Press, 1995).

32 See, in this regard, Jerrold E. Hogle's argument in 'The Gothic Ghost as Counterfeit and Its Haunting of Romanticism: The Case of "Frost at Midnight"', *European Romantic Review*, 9:2 (Spring 1998), pp. 283–92.

33 Jacques Derrida, *Specters of Marx*.

34 Ibid., p. 168.

35 Ibid., p. 65.

36 Ibid.

37 Ibid., p. 63.

38 Colin Davis, *Haunted Subjects: Deconstruction, Psychoanalysis and the Return of the Dead* (Basingstoke: Palgrave Macmillan, 2007), p. 83.

39 For a searching account of Byron's complex political stance, see Malcolm Kelsall's 'Byron's Politics', in *The Cambridge Companion to Byron*, pp. 44–55, as well as Kelsall's full-length study, *Byron's Politics* (Brighton: The Harvester Press, 1987).

40 Michael Riffaterre, 'Prosopopeia', in *Yale French Studies*, 69 (1985), p. 112.

41 Derrida, *Specters of Marx*, p. 63.

42 Ibid., p. 29.

43 In outlining the differences between psychoanalytic and deconstructive approaches to the spectre, Davis argues the following: 'Abraham and Torok's crucial theoretical and therapeutic innovation is their designation of the phantom as a liar, a purveyor of falsehood in the psychic life of the subject rather than an apparition which restores the truth. For Derrida, the spectre neither lies nor tells the truth in any conventional sense because it does not belong to the order of knowledge; yet Derrida's spectres command respect in a manner that Abraham and Torok's lying phantom never could, so that their versions of haunting are very different from those of popular culture and from each other' (Davis, *Haunted Subjects*, p. 73).

CHAPTER FIVE

Byron avec Sade:
Material and Spectral Violence
in *Childe Harold's Pilgrimage* Canto IV

Piya Pal-Lapinski

In a provocative essay entitled 'Kant Avec Sade', Lacan aligns these two (apparently) polarized Enlightenment thinkers in terms of their pursuit of a pure abstraction of form: Kant's insistence on the purity of the 'categorical imperative' as the basis of the moral law is mirrored and reconstituted through Sade's search for a pure form of violence, which remains tied to the moral law – to the idea of prohibition – even as it tries to break with it.[1] Commenting on this 'ideal couple', Žižek asks whether the 'sublime disinterested ethical attitude is somehow identical to, or overlaps with, the unrestrained indulgence in pleasurable violence?'[2] Both are emptied of pathological feelings or motivations and both aim to achieve a strict purity of structure divorced from pathos. Additionally, Alenka Zupančič has shown how Kant's grounding of the moral law in the 'endless progress of the immortality of the soul' is replicated in the Sadean fantasy of an immortal body that is tortured endlessly but does not display or succumb to the marks of violence.[3] In other words, material violence becomes translated into a spectral, figural version of itself.

In this chapter, I am proposing an alignment of another couple, Byron and Sade, which both enacts and moves beyond the kind of mirroring that we see in Lacan's reading. This link between Byron and Sade has been articulated before, most famously by Sainte-Beuve in his 1843 article in *La Revue des Deux Mondes*:

... j'oserai affirmer, sans crainte d'être démenti, que Byron et de Sade (je demande pardon du rapprochement) ont peut-être été les deux plus grands inspirateurs de nos modernes, l'un affiché et visible, l'autre clandestine – pas trop clandestin.[4]

Repeating the split between the material and spectral, the visible and invisible, Sainte-Beuve posits Sade almost as Byron's spectral other and connects them both to modernity. This connection was taken up also by Gustave Flaubert, as noted by Mario Praz, whose chapter on Sade in *The Romantic Agony* culminates with Byron.[5] Recent essays on both Sade and Byron by Geoffrey Wall and Joshua Gonsalves have developed this further, but the focus remains on eroticism – 'volupté' – rather than the way that both writers anatomize violence.[6] In biographical terms, Sade appears to have entered Byron's life at a chaotic moment, when his marriage to Annabella Milbanke was falling apart. Byron had read Sade's *Justine* (1791) in 1815. Annabella discovered his hidden copy of the novel prior to their separation; during these weeks, Byron also ordered Sade's works from the library and apparently threatened to enact the ideas found within. Drawing on Augusta Leigh's correspondence, Benita Eisler describes this incident, claiming that Sade's writings 'offered Byron a manual for moral suicide'.[7] However, given that Annabella used the discovery of *Justine* to demonize Byron and accuse him of insanity (a pathologization that Eisler curiously repeats in her account), it is more likely that Byron's interest in Sade at this time coincided with the violence of the entrapment he felt in his marriage – one that found dual expression in physical acts of material violence (such as breaking objects and firing pistols while his wife was giving birth) and an exploration of symbolic violence as the limit point of sexual relationships.[8] One of the more intriguing readings of the relationship of this situation to the composition of Canto IV comes from Paul Elledge, who suggests that the Bridge of Sighs 'configuration' at the opening of Canto IV 'suspends Byron in an ambiguous space between the (alleged) extremes of uneasy relationship and fatal estrangement, a bifurcated sector where his marital, paternal and artistic identities are interrogated'.[9]

This chapter approaches the connection between the two writers from a very specific perspective. It looks at the way Sade's 'demonic libertinism' and obsession with a pure corporeal violence (literally stripped down to its core) is transformed in *Childe Harold's Pilgrimage* IV (written 1817–1818) into a specifically Byronic discourse of violence. If this demonic libertinism is, as Pierre Saint-Amand has claimed, a radical form of transcendence that withdraws from bodies in favour of signs and usurps the place of divinity,[10] and if, as Baudrillard has suggested in *Seduction*, the demonic is an 'aesthetic possessiveness over signs',[11] then it may be argued that Byron is in this sense more 'demonic' than Sade. The legitimacy of that argument will be examined in this chapter.

Although demonic and other kinds of violence exist elsewhere in Byron – for example, in *The Giaour* and the war cantos of *Don Juan* – *Childe Harold's Pilgrimage* IV is the only poetic text that brings together the material violence of history and the spectral violence of the aesthetic sign, which it does through the 'body' of the ruin: 'Till I had bodied forth the heated mind / Forms from the floating wreck ruin leaves behind' (IV, 104). As Byron observed: 'if ever I did anything original it was in C—d H—d'.[12]

While the entire poem is concerned with the violence of historical process, it is in Canto IV, with its focus on Roman ruins and the Doge's Palace (Palazzo Ducale) in Venice, that the conversion of the material violence of history into a transcendent violence of aesthetic signs is at its most complete. In particular, the organization of architectural spaces within the Palazzo Ducale in Venice and the way these spaces conflate (and separate) the violence of war, politics, torture and eroticism sets the tone for the exploration of violence in Canto IV. It is also at the Doge's Palace that, in November 1816, Byron came across the portrait of the decapitated Doge Marino Faliero, concealed by a black painted veil.[13] In a moment that strangely echoes the Gothic terror 'behind the black veil' in Ann Radcliffe's *The Mysteries of Udolpho*, the violence of Marino Faliero's execution is transformed into an aesthetic artefact, which becomes the site of the signification of a double beheading: the historical one and the one endlessly repeating itself on the walls of the palace.

The Palazzo Ducale is, in some ways, not only the starting point, but also the symbolic centre of the intersection of material and spectral violence in *Childe Harold*. Canto IV is a poem of ruins, and the Ducal Palace, having been destroyed by fire and rebuilt several times over successive years, is the symbol of Venice's vanished sovereignty. As it rises from the waves, the prison haunts the palace as its ghostly double, both insubstantial, emerging from 'the stroke of the enchanter's wand':

> I stood in Venice, on the Bridge of Sighs;
> A palace and a prison on each hand:
> I saw from out the wave her structures rise
> As from the stroke of the enchanter's wand:
> A thousand years their cloudy wings expand
> Around me, and a dying Glory smiles
> O'er the far times, when many a subject land

Look'd to the winged Lion's marble piles
Where Venice sate in state, thron'd on her hundred isles! (IV, 1)

Such images of posthumous existence proliferate in the first few stanzas
of the Canto: Venice is a ruin, the gondoliers are 'silent' and 'songless'
and her buildings are 'crumbling to the shore' (IV, 3). She is haunted
by 'mighty shadows, whose dim forms despond / Above the dogeless
city's vanish'd sway' (IV, 4). The violence of Venice's sovereignty has
been translated into the spectrality of its aesthetic signs. This violence
is beautiful and erotic, 'but Beauty still is here' precisely because it has
withdrawn from the body (of Venice) in favour of the sign.

Violence in Derrida, Sade and Benjamin

Forms of violence that erupt within the text of *Childe Harold's Pilgrimage*
IV evoke the 'spectres' of several theorists: Walter Benjamin's strange
and compelling essay 'Critique of Violence' is relevant in this context,[14]
as is Derrida's 'Violence and Metaphysics'.[15] These two works, I suggest,
may help us answer the following questions: how does a 'spectral'
Byronic violence, in Canto IV, both encompass and move beyond the
Sadean elements in the text? How does it distinguish itself – if, indeed,
it does – from the ferocious distillation of the 'pure' materiality of
violence in Sade?

Since violence tends to be a theoretical space that is difficult to
separate from the idea of force, it may be fruitful to approach the
conceptual category of 'violence' in a somewhat unusual way – more
along the lines of Jacques Derrida's exploration of violence as inextricably
linked to the articulation of Being as an ontological category. In
Derrida's reading, violence remains connected with force, but can also
include a certain movement that is in 'excess' of physical force and
cannot be 'fixed' in terms of the materiality of force alone.[16] This is a
different idea from that of material violence exceeding representation – a
claim that is often made.[17] Instead, my point is that the representation
of violence is itself an act of (necessary?) violence, and that violence
both escapes and compulsively desires a return to an embodiment
that covers over its point of origin. Is there a 'transcendental violence',
Derrida asks in 'Violence and Metaphysics', at the root of signification?
Is there, he inquires,

> an original, transcendental violence, previous to every ethical choice, even
> supposed by ethical non-violence? Is it meaningful to speak of pre-ethical
> violence? If the transcendental 'violence' to which we allude is tied to

phenomenality itself, and to the possibility of language, it then would be embedded in the root of meaning and logos.[18]

If this is the case, one could say that there is a 'spectral violence' in various senses that hovers over attempts to materialize violence. My use of the term 'spectral' is also borrowed from Derrida: in *Specters of Marx*, he defines a spectre or ghost as 'a paradoxical incorporation'. It is, he writes,

> the becoming body, a certain phenomenal and carnal form of the spirit. It becomes rather, some 'thing' that remains difficult to name: neither soul nor body, and both one and the other. For it is flesh and phenomenality that give to the spirit its spectral apparition, but which *disappear* right away in the apparition [...].[19]

The spectre remains haunted by the trace of the body, even as this embodiment vanishes. For Derrida, the spectral remains intimately connected to history, and particularly in its return, in its *revenant* form as the repetition of the end of history, the end of discourse. It will be helpful at this point to bring in the work of Walter Benjamin.

In 'Critique of Violence', Benjamin describes three types of violence. The first two are law-making and law-preserving violence, which are linked to the legal order and, by extension, the state. Benjamin sees all law as founded in an originary, anterior violence. Derrida clarifies this distinction: law-making violence is that which 'institutes and positions law', whereas law-preserving violence is that which 'conserves, maintains and insures the enforceability of the law'. Derrida extends this concept by reminding us that 'there is no such thing as law that doesn't imply in itself, *in the analytic structure of its concept*, the possibility of being "enforced" or applied by force'.[20] For Benjamin, both types of violence converge in, and are appropriated by, the spectral form of police violence, which 'haunts' the modern state when it can no longer guarantee its ends through strictly legal means.[21]

The last section of Benjamin's essay takes, as Derrida points out, a 'most enigmatic, profound, and fascinating'[22] turn, and it is here that Benjamin posits his puzzling idea of 'divine violence'. This is a violence that somehow separates itself from any connection with the law or the state and bypasses the inevitable dilemma of means and ends. Citing classical myth (with Niobe and Prometheus as examples), Benjamin speaks of 'mythic violence' – the punishment delivered by the gods to mortals. This mythic violence remains tied to a legal dimension as it serves to establish a new law; however, there remains in these acts of violence some element that escapes or eludes legality. Benjamin is not clear about what this element is precisely; he speaks of it mainly as a form of violence that interrupts the usual connection between means and ends or is related to 'justified' or 'unjustified' means and/or ends in 'some different way'.[23] For Benjamin, there is always a gap, an element of irrationality, in the relationship between 'justified means' and ends with regards to violence, and the law does not succeed in closing this gap; in fact, it disavows it. He does state, though, that divine violence, in opposition to mythic violence, is 'law-destroying', 'lethal without spilling blood' and expiatory. Divine violence does not 'annihilate the soul' of the living, although it may strike at property.[24] While Benjamin's alignment of 'mythic violence' with the classical and 'divine' violence of the Judaic tradition is problematic and somewhat polarized, the significance of the concept lies in the idea of 'another violence', distinct from force and law. Here, Benjamin seems to be moving towards the concept of a spectral violence that is liberated from the state or perhaps history itself.

Sade's libertinism draws its energy from the gap between the law (as sign) and the founding act of violence that the law disavows (as Benjamin maintains). For Sade, this extends to the gap between culture and its violence, since the logic of culture depends on the invisibility of this violence. In *Justine*, the heroine falls into the hands of one 'vicious' libertine after another, including a surgeon who wants to dissect his own daughter.[25] And, of course, as critics have noted, the ultimate libertine, who violates her over and over again, especially with a bolt of lightning at the end, is God. Could this be seen as an example of 'divine violence', given that it does not result in the re-establishment of either social or sexual laws, since through this act of divine violence Justine escapes both? Throughout the novel, Justine is repeatedly told that 'law' and 'society' disavow or deny their relationship to and reliance on violence.[26] As Marcel Hénaff has put it: the libertine text '"thinks" [...] the unrepresentable relation of society to a violence that as yet has no name. It must not be known at the moment it is being done.'[27] Not only do the signs of culture, morality, politics and law contain multiple points of interaction with an invisible violence, but the distance itself – the gap in meaning, the ability of the sign to reverse itself and to absorb or disclose its relationship to violence – is itself a violent act that embodiment disguises and covers over.

In this way, Sade's libertines attempt to flatten the sign, to force it open, to penetrate to the pure core of violence itself, stripped of its signs (and its history). The ferocity of the erotic violence that the Sadean libertine visits on the bodies of the victims is invested with a particular form of panic: specifically, that *the symbolization of violence will always outstrip its corporeality*, its literalization. In many cases, therefore, the body of the Sadean victim remains somehow uninscribed by violence, and this lack of inscription points to the peculiar paradox at the heart of Sade's dynamics of violence. For example, at one point, Justine encounters a vampiric Count, who is aroused by the spectacle of his wife being bled on a regular basis. He has to see her bleeding in order to experience sexual arousal. However, her beauty remains untouched by the 'signs' of the bleeding; as Justine notices:

> what astonished me was that despite the slenderness of the Countess's figure, despite her sufferings, nothing had impaired the firm quality of her flesh [...] as if she had always dwelled in the depths of happiness [...] nothing spoiled, nothing damaged [...] the very image of a beautiful lily on which the honeybee has inflicted some scratches. (637)

The body thus masquerades as the sign that conceals its full relationship to violence and can be repeatedly torn open. The body repeatedly threatens to turn the actual corporeal act of violence into a signifier that disavows its physicality, its corporeality. The more the Sadean libertine attempts to isolate or 'uncover' the pure corporeality of violence, the more it eludes him, as the victim's body absorbs the signs of violence. The body as body and the body as sign conspire together to trick Sade. It is the radical transcendence of the sign – violence as a transcendent force – which Sade cannot bear. If violence escapes the body, it is this escape which is barred by the Sadean libertine.

Material versus Spectral Violence in *Childe Harold's Pilgrimage* Canto IV

In *Childe Harold's Pilgrimage* Canto IV, Harold, like Justine, wanders – in this case, through the ruins of Venice and Rome. For Byron, the ruin is the displaced Sadean body – a signifier of both material and spectral violence. Such ruins evoke Giorgio Agamben's notion of 'bare life' – a form of existence that is no longer viable in terms of a legal or political dimension, but which nevertheless remains connected to sovereign violence, representing its 'unconditional power over life and death' – a sort of spectral threshold, which allows sovereign power to verify itself through the simultaneous inclusion and exclusion of bare life. Caught between its previous historical/political life and the decay brought on through both time and nature, the ruin is the indistinct

zone between political *bios* and natural *zoe* that Agamben posits as the
space in which bare life articulates itself.[28]

History is transformed into an aesthetic play of signs that resist being
absorbed into a narrative where the relationship between the means
and the ends of violence are clear. The foundation of the state remains
anchored to a violence that the Enlightenment disavows through its
opposition of violence and rationality. By the fourth canto, 'Harold'
has achieved a sort of 'libertine apathy' – a form of detachment that
overcomes the impasse between apathy and passion. Passion is brought
back in once a mastery over instinct has been achieved and is refracted
through this control. It propels the libertine into a solitude in which,
once total control over desire has been achieved, there is nothing left
to desire except death itself.[29] The alternation of apathy and passion is
quite pronounced in the poem; at times, Byron/Harold stands apart
'in a satanic solitude', observing the intertwining of erotic and political
violence in the spectacle of history, and at times he attempts to project
himself violently into the spectacle. As Paul Elledge has remarked, in
Canto III, Harold's attempts to 'hurl himself into animate or inanimate
objects of identification' are violent.[30] Let us examine some of these
instances of violence in more detail.

Signs of torture take on ghostly forms that haunt the poem from
the very beginning. Byron's 'torn and bleeding' body (IV, 10) becomes a
form of 'bare life', occupying the space of erotic and aesthetic spectacle
interchangeably with the ruin: 'a ruin amidst ruins' (IV, 25). Italy is a
beautiful woman, a Gothic heroine whose body invites violence:

> Italia! oh Italia! thou who hast
> The fatal gift of beauty, which became
> A funeral dower of present woes and past [...]
> Oh God! that thou wert in thy nakedness
> Less lovely or more powerful, and could'st claim
> Thy right, and awe the robbers back, who press
> To shed thy blood, and drink the tears of thy distress [...]. (IV, 42)

Here, Byron is specifically aestheticizing the material core of sovereign
violence. The Falls of Terni evoke 'endless torture'. One of the strangest
passages in Byron follows, where he conflates the radiance of an iris (a
sort of rainbow-like effect of the sun) with a peculiar kind of specta-
torship of torture:

> Horribly beautiful! but on the verge,
> From side to side, beneath the glittering morn,
> An Iris sits, amidst the infernal surge,

> Like Hope upon a death-bed [...]
> Resembling, 'mid the torture of the scene,
> Love watching Madness with unalterable mien. (IV, 72)

While love and apathy cannot coexist in Sade's universe, in Byron the two converge. Love occupies the place of the libertine torturer. Like Benjamin and Sade, Byron is all too aware of the intimate but disavowed relationship between law, culture and violence. But in his eroticization of the signs of violence, Byron is simultaneously more demonic and more erotic than even Sade. For Byron, the aesthetic symbolization of history and sovereignty, the reversibility of their signs, contains a violence of its own that separates itself from relations of physical force yet maintains a disturbing connection to it.

Sade is afraid that the radical transcendence of the sign will swallow corporeal violence; Byron is afraid that the corporeal violence of history might outstrip the phantasmatic, symbolic violence of the aesthetic – the 'floating wreck of Ruin'. Byron recreates the beautiful historical artefact in order to subject it to a simulacrum of violence, which always remains in excess of actual physical violence; yet it is the link with bodies that gives it its specific aesthetic/erotic charge. Canto IV's focus, therefore, is not on the violence enacted on the actual physical body, but on displacing this violence onto specific political symbols, such as the landscape, the ruin and the imperial city. However, ruins also evoke the physical body: they 'body forth the heated mind'.

But what is specifically Byronic about these violent acts of signification? The answer emerges in three moves during the course of *Childe Harold's Pilgrimage* IV. In the first move, Venice is a beautiful woman who both arouses desire and defers its satisfaction, on account of the violence of history that consumes her from within. But Venice herself is also associated with sovereign violence – the state figured as feminine. Whereas for Sade, violence is repeatedly inflicted on the beautiful female body from outside, in an effort to flatten the signs of violence that escape the body, for Byron it is a violence self-engendered within beauty that allows it to signify itself and generate spectral signs that escape material violence. Byron pauses in his meditation on the destruction of Imperial Rome to gaze at the goddess who 'loves in stone' – the Venus de Medici at the Uffizi in Florence. The aesthetic violence of the Medici Venus's beauty almost turns the viewer to stone and 'plucks out' the eye: 'We gaze and turn away, and know not where, / Dazzled and drunk with beauty' (IV, 50). It is 'unnatural': 'We stand, and in that form and face behold / What Mind can make, when Nature's self would fail' (IV, 49).

Beauty here does not redeem the material violence of history; instead, it results in a moment of terror, a moment of petrification in which the historian loses his own gaze in the vortex of the aesthetic signs generated by the stone Venus. Excavated statues of Venus were linked with a history of archaeological violence and fragmentation; the recovery of both the Venus de Medici (found in fragments in Hadrian's Villa at Tivoli in 1580) and the Venus of Melos as part-objects was what made their beauty disturbing.[31]

What signifies Venice for Byron, what draws him, it seems, is not decay, it is *violence*: the statues are 'shiver'd' (IV, 15), the horses of St Mark's are 'bridled' and the sinking of Venice is envisioned as a single moment of destruction set against her '1300 years of freedom' (IV, 13). History can only be 'blasted open'[32] through this spectralization of violence. However, this is a form of transcendence that continually remains at war with a physical violence that threatens to swallow it. For Byron, unlike Sade, it is crucial that this gap remains unclosed, so that specific acts of material violence cannot lay claim to the truth of history by themselves. In the famous opening lines of Canto IV, the 'palace' and 'prison' have a dual existence: within the poem itself as locations of material violence, and as phantasms rising from the waves. Through its architecture and history, the Palazzo Ducale symbolized this double violence. Successive fires – one in 1574 and another soon after in 1577 – had repeatedly damaged the Doge's Palace and its self-representation as the iconic space of Venetian sovereignty. Its structural stability was compromised by the fire of 1577, and although Andrea Palladio was consulted on the restoration, this was not without controversy. Palladio felt that 'ruin' was inherent in the structural defects of the building itself: 'for all these causes one may with good reason sooner fear the ruin of this palace than hope that it can be reconstructed by any architect whatsoever'.[33] In his note to the prisons of the Ducal Palace in Canto IV, Byron commented on the signs of violence that replaced the violence of the prisons themselves: 'the inmates of the dungeons beneath had left traces of their repentance, or of their despair, which are still visible' and 'signatures [...] scratched upon the walls'.[34]

Meanwhile, the Baroque ceilings of the palace council chambers, where the business of the Venetian state was carried out, transformed state power into an elaborate labyrinth of aesthetic signs. The Sala dell'Anticollegio (anteroom for the reception of foreign ambassadors and delegations), Sala del Collegio (reception room) and Sala del Consiglio dei Dieci (for meetings of the Council of Ten) were all covered with heavily ornate frescos, painted mainly by Paolo Veronese. Here, the

violence of sovereignty was voluptuously 'embodied' and translated into
femininity, in eroticized panels such as *The Rape of Europa* (1576–1580)
or *Venice Enthroned with Peace and Justice* (1575–1578). The Sala della
Bussola (chamber of judicial decisions), similarly decorated by Veronese,
was linked vertically with the prisons – the 'pozzi' and 'piombi' noted by
Byron. Through these ceilings, with their curiously floating perspective,
the Doge's Palace transcends the material violence of the prisons. This
is most evident in the Sala del Maggior Consiglio, where Veronese's
'Triumph of Venice' (1582) depicts triumphant Venice as a blonde beauty,
'floating' above chaos and military violence. These representations are
juxtaposed with other works that – as Jane Stabler has pointed out in
an essay examining the impact of Italian art on Byron – 'provide a
visual index to the wholesale slaughter described in the siege cantos of
Don Juan'.[35]

Ruins in Canto IV are materially the product of three kinds of
violence: natural, historical and legal. In his *Historical Illustrations* to
Canto IV of *Childe Harold*, Byron's friend Hobhouse makes a point
of noting the effect of successive acts of legal or papal violence on the
monuments of Rome, in addition to the natural process of decay and
foreign invasions. Of the 'legal violence', Hobhouse notes:

> the injuries done by the Christian clergy to the architectural beauty of
> Rome may be divided into two kinds: those which were commanded or
> connived at by Popes for useful repairs or constructions, and those which
> were encouraged or permitted from motives of fanaticism.[36]

Yet these acts of material/historical violence are not specifically 'present'
in the canto. Instead, in the case of both Cecilia Metella's tomb and
the Coliseum – the two main 'ruins' depicted in the poem – we again
have phantasms of violence: in the former, the violence of domesticity
('Perchance she died in youth: it may be, bowed / With woes far heavier
than the ponderous tomb' (IV, 102)); in the latter, colonization. At
Metella's tomb, Byron meditates:

> I know not why – but standing thus by thee
> It seems as if I had thine inmate known,
> Thou tomb! and other days come back on me
> With recollected music [...]
> Yet could I seat me by this ivied stone
> Till I had bodied forth the heated mind
> Forms from the floating wreck which Ruin leaves behind [...]
> (IV, 104)

The spectral violence of the Coliseum's vanished crowds has overtaken the physical traces – 'the red gash' (IV, 140) of the Gladiator's mutilated body:

> But here, where Murder breathed her bloody stream;
> And here, where buzzing nations choked the ways [...]
> Here, where the Roman million's blame or praise
> Was death or life, the playthings of a crowd,
> My voice sounds much – and fall the stars' faint rays
> On the arena void – seats crush'd – walls bow'd –
> And galleries, where my steps seem echoes strangely loud.
>   (IV, 142)

While they float above the materiality of the ruin these phantasms – these 'echoes' – at the same time try to re-inhabit it: 'When the colossal fabric's form is neared: / It will not bear the brightness of the day' (IV, 143). In both of these cases, physical decay – or 'bare life' – lies in wait to consume the ruin. But for Byron there is always another level of violence which *must* escape the body.

In the second move, Byron conveys the importance of vengeance as a viable and ambiguous form of political existence – of violence outside the law – through the famous 'forgiveness' curse. For Byron, even forgiveness is a violent act. This famous curse is a phantom which escapes the 'ashes' of Byron's own corporeality:

> Though I be ashes; a far hour shall wreak
> The deep prophetic fullness of this verse,
> And pile on human heads the mountain of my curse!
>
> That curse shall be Forgiveness. (IV, 134–35)

Here again a connection with Derrida can be made. For Derrida, forgiveness has to be separated from the conditionality of Christian redemption. To be truly itself, forgiveness has to be unconditional. Conditionality is violent, yet to forgive what is unforgiveable opens up an abyss that also contains a paradoxical violence within it.[37] In Canto IV, this Byronic impossibility of forgiveness is both spectral (a forgiveness that leaves the body behind and never quite materializes) and violent in its enunciation.

And in the third move, finally, Byron's 'Ocean' at the end of the poem moves towards a form of violence that is neither purely 'natural' in the Sadean sense nor 'divine' in Benjamin's sense. Although Byron does not absolve the divine of the material consequences of violence in the way that Benjamin seems to, 'Ocean' does appear to come closer to the latter's conception of a violence that is attempting to divest itself completely of its connection with the state. In this way, Byron tries to separate the violence of history from appropriation by a legal order. 'Ocean' is not 'divine' or 'sovereign' as such; the Almighty's form is merely a broken reflection found within its tempests: 'in breeze, or gale, or storm, / Icing the pole, or in the torrid clime / Dark-heaving', producing 'monsters of the deep' (IV, 183). It is not a violence that 'governs and executes', to use Agamben's words, but one that 'acts and manifests' beyond means and ends.[38] At the same time, the violence of 'Ocean' signifies itself by returning to physical eroticism – to the sovereign libertine consciousness that is Sade's 'Nature' – while simultaneously transcending it. This also disconnects it somewhat from the Judaic dimension we find in Benjamin.

The question remains, however: can this spectral, 'transcendent violence' fully escape the founding violence at the origin of the state and law? For Byron, the pursuit of the pure materiality of violence itself is not without its seductiveness. Violence compulsively returns to materiality to signify itself, but its signs are never fully embodied. Aesthetics and history take shape within the violence of this gap – indeed, all attempts at closure generate a more shattering violence. This is the anguish of *Childe Harold* Canto IV. Harold finds his home in the void between the body of violence and its phantasmatic signs:

> – if he was
> Aught but a phantasy, and could be class'd
> With forms which live and suffer – let that pass –
> His shadow fades away into Destruction's mass [...]
>
> Through which all things grow phantoms [...]. (IV, 164–65)

Notes

1 Jacques Lacan, 'Kant Avec Sade', trans. James B. Swenson, in *October*, 51 (Winter 1989), pp. 55–75.

2 See Slavoj Žižek, 'Kant and Sade: The Ideal Couple', available at:http://www.egs.edu/faculty/slavoj-zizek/articles/kant-and-sade-the-ideal-couple (accessed 7.15.2013).

3 Alenka Zupančič, 'Kant with Don Juan and Sade,' in *Radical Evil*, ed. Joan Copjec (London: Verso, 1996), pp. 118–19.

4 '... I dare declare, without fear of contradiction, that Byron and de Sade (I apologise for the conjunction) have perhaps been the two greatest inspirations of our modern writers, the former blatant and visible, the latter clandestine, not too

clandestine'. Quoted in Geoffrey Wall, 'Thinking With Demons: Flaubert and de Sade', in *The Cambridge Quarterly*, 36:2 (2007), pp. 101–28, 111.

5 Mario Praz, *The Romantic Agony* (New York, NY: Oxford University Press, 1970), pp. 164–65.

6 See Wall, 'Thinking with Demons', and Joshua Gonsalves, 'Byron – In-Between Sade, Lautreamont and Foucault: Situating the Canon of "Evil" in the Nineteenth Century', in *Romanticism on the Net*, 43 (August 2006), available at: http://id.erudit.org/revue/ron/2006/v/n43/013591ar.html?vue=resume (accessed 7.15.2013).

7 See Benita Eisler, *Byron: Child of Passion, Fool of Fame* (New York, NY: Vintage, 2000), p. 479.

8 Ibid pp. 477–81. For a somewhat different reading of Byron's behaviour during his wife's labour, see Fiona MacCarthy, *Byron: Life and Legend* (New York, NY: Farrar, Strauss and Giroux, 2002), pp. 259–62. MacCarthy speculates that Annabella may have exaggerated the accounts of Byron's violence. In his commentary on *Childe Harold's Pilgrimage*, Canto IV, Jerome McGann notes that 'CHP IV is preoccupied with the aftermath of Byron's marriage separation.' See *CPW*, II, p. 317.

9 Paul Elledge, 'Byron's Separations and the Endings of Pilgrimage', in *Texas Studies in Literature and Language*, 37:1 (Spring 1995), pp. 16–53, 21.

10 Pierre Saint-Amand, 'The Immortals', in *Yale French Studies*, 94 (1998), pp. 116–29.

11 Jean Baudrillard, *Seduction* (New York, NY: St Martin's Press, 1979), p. 116. In his analysis of Kierkegaard's *Diary of a Seducer*, Baudrillard describes the process of seduction as an obsession with signs.

12 Byron to Murray, 26 April 1814. Quoted in MacCarthy, *Byron: Life and Legend*, p. 160. For critical readings of Canto IV that focus on the relationship of the ruin as sign to history, see Stephen Cheeke, *Byron and Place: History, Translation, Nostalgia*; Robert Gleckner, *Byron and the Ruins of Paradise*; and Martin Procházka, 'History and Ruins in Canto IV of *Childe Harold's Pilgrimage*', in *Litteraria Pragensia*, 7:14 (1997), pp. 54–68. For previous studies of Byron's approach to violence, see Ian Haywood, *Bloody Romanticism: Spectacular Violence and the Politics of Representation, 1776–1832* (New York, NY: Palgrave Macmillan, 2006), pp. 198–205; and Daniel Watkins, 'Violence, Class Consciousness and Ideology in Byron's History Plays', in *ELH*, 48:4 (Winter 1981), pp. 799–816.

13 Byron, 'Preface to *Marino Faliero*', *CPW*, IV, p. 303.

14 Walter Benjamin, 'Critique of Violence', in *Selected Writings, Volume 1 1913–1926*, eds. Marcus Bullock and Michael W. Jennings (Cambridge, MA: Harvard University Press, 1996).

15 Jacques Derrida, 'Violence and Metaphysics: An Essay on the Thought of Emmanuel Levinas', in *Writing and Difference*, trans. Alan Bass (Chicago, IL: University of Chicago Press, 1978), pp. 79–153.

16 See 'Violence and Metaphysics', pp. 116–17.

17 For example, writing on the Palestine-Israel conflict, Saree Makdisi makes the following point: 'In far too much media coverage, especially in the United States, the conflict between Palestinians and Israelis ends up being reduced simply to [...] those forms of violence that lend themselves in one way or another to televisual spectacle. This has the effect not only of decontextualizing the violence of both sides, but also overshadowing [...] the much less visible but equally deadly effects of the [...] apparatus of bureaucracy and control.' See Saree Makdisi, *Palestine Inside Out: An Everyday Occupation* (New York, NY: W.W. Norton, 2008), p. 268.

18 'Violence and Metaphysics', p. 125.

19 Derrida, *Specters of Marx*, p. 5 [emphasis added].

20 Derrida 'Force of Law: The Mystical Foundation of Authority', in *Deconstruction and the Possibility of Justice*, eds. Drucilla Cornell, Michel Rosenfeld and David Gray Carlson (New York and London: Routledge, 1992), p. 6. Emphasis in the original.

21 'In a far more unnatural combination than in the death penalty, in a kind of spectral mixture, these two forms of violence are present in another institution of the modern state: the police.' See Benjamin, 'Critique of Violence', p. 242.

22 Derrida, 'Force of Law', p. 51.

23 Benjamin, 'Critique of Violence', pp. 247–48.

24 Ibid., p. 250.

25 Marquis de Sade, *Justine, Philosophy in the Bedroom and Other Writings*, trans. Richard Seaver and Austryn Wainhouse (New York, NY: Grove Press, 1965).

26 The bandit Coeur-de-fer speaks to Justine of the thin veneer of law: 'All men are born isolated, envious, cruel and despotic, wishing to have everything and surrender nothing, incessantly struggling to maintain either their rights or achieve their ambition. The legislator comes up and says to them: "Cease thus to fight; if each were to retreat a little, calm would be restored"' (*Justine*, p. 494). In an earlier version of the novel, *The Misfortunes of Virtue* (1787), the surgeon Rodin rationalizes: 'Is the murder which is sanctioned by law of a different nature to the kind which we are about to commit […]? Is not the whole point of the wise laws which permit capital punishment that one life should be sacrificed to save a thousand others?' See *The Misfortunes of Virtue and Other Early Tales*, trans. David Coward (Oxford: Oxford University Press, 1992), p. 59.

27 See Marcel Hénaff, 'Naked Terror: Political Violence, Libertine Violence', in Special Issue of *SubStance* 86: 'Reading Violence', eds. David F. Bell and Lawrence R. Schehr, 27:2 (1998), pp. 5–32.

28 Giorgio Agamben, *Homo Sacer: Sovereign Power and Bare Life*, trans. Daniel Heller-Roazen (Stanford, CA: Stanford University Press, 1995). Agamben draws on the Greek distinction between *zoe* – the 'simple fact of living' – and *bios* – collective existence (pp. 1–5). The intersection of this 'bare' life and political existence is what is central to Agamben's discussion of sovereignty; that is to say, the ways in which bare life becomes either excluded or included within the state. Of Sade, Agamben says: 'At the very moment in which the revolution makes birth – which is to say, bare life – into the foundation of sovereignty and rights, Sade stages […] the *theatrum politicum* as a theater of bare life in which the very physiological life of bodies appears, through sexuality, as the pure political element' (p. 134). He goes on to mention the way that the Sadean text 'consciously invokes the analogy with sovereign power'.

29 Marcel Hénaff discusses this tension between apathy and passion in Sade's libertines in *Sade: The Invention of the Libertine Body* (Minneapolis, MN: The University of Minnesota Press, 1999), pp. 84–103. The libertine overcomes the 'logical impasse of apathy versus passion' and moves closer to a confrontation with his own death.

30 Paul Elledge, *Byron and the Dynamics of Metaphor* (Nashville, TN: Vanderbilt University Press, 1968), p. 75. Elledge comments on the 'violence of his [Harold's] attempts to identify himself with Nature' (p. 55).

31 See Caroline Arscott and Katie Scott, 'Introducing Venus', in *Manifestations of Venus: Art and Sexuality*, eds. Caroline Arscott and Katie Scott (Manchester: Manchester University Press, 2000), p. 16. Alan Rawes has analyzed Byron's Venus in Canto IV as a 'thought, a flash innate to Mind', although he sees it mainly as an instance of Byron's celebration of 'imaginative creativity'. See Alan Rawes, *Byron's Poetic Experimentation*, p. 124.

32 See Walter Benjamin, 'On the Concept of History', in *Selected Writings, Volume 4*, eds. Howard Eiland and Michael Jennings (Cambridge, MA: Harvard University Press, 2003), p. 395.

33 Quoted in Tracy Cooper, *Palladio's Venice: Architecture and Society in a Renaissance Republic* (New Haven, CT: Yale University Press, 2005), p. 209.

34 *CPW*, II, p. 218.

35 Jane Stabler, '"Awake to Terror": The Impact of Italy on Byron's Depiction of Freedom's Battles', in *Byron and the Politics of Freedom and Terror*, eds. Matthew J.A. Green and Piya Pal-Lapinski (Basingstoke: Palgrave Macmillan, 2011), p. 73. For a room-by-room layout of the interiors of the Palazzo Ducale, see *The Doge's Palace in Venice* (Milan: Musei Civici Veneziani, 2008).

36 John Cam Hobhouse, *Historical Illustrations of the Fourth Canto of Childe Harold: Containing Dissertations on the Ruins of Rome, and an Essay on Italian Literature* (London: John Murray, 1818), p. 71.

37 Derrida, *On Cosmopolitanism and Forgiveness*, trans. Mark Dooley and Michael Hughes (New York, NY: Routledge, 2001).

38 *Homo Sacer*, p. 65. For a reading of Ocean as the 'violent erasure of the "problem of history"', see Procházka, 'History and Ruins in Canto IV of *Childe Harold's Pilgrimage*', p. 62; and as a re-enactment of the Doge's wedding to the Adriatic, see Elledge, 'Byron's Separation', p. 46.

CHAPTER SIX

"'Twixt Life and Death':
Childe Harold's Pilgrimage, Don Juan
and the Sublime

Philip Shaw

From its inception, the discourse of the sublime has placed emphasis
on the failure of the mind to comprehend the grand, the vast and
the terrifying. At its most radical, in the neo-Lacanian revision of the
Kantian sublime proposed by Slavoj Žižek, the connection between
sublimity and Reason is brought to an absolute, nihilistic conclusion.[1]
For Žižek, since representations are always lacking – formed, that is,
on the basis of their exclusion of some contradictory, impossible object,
otherwise known as the Real – the truth is no longer a noumenal, freely
indeterminate beyond, but rather 'the ultimate emptiness of all our
gestures'.[2] In this essay, I seek to explore the relation between emptiness,
negation and the sublime as presented by Byron in the closing cantos
of *Don Juan*. I want to suggest that while Byron appears to share
Žižek's suspicion of the transcendental aspirations of the sublime, his
particular critique is not directed against transcendentalism *per se* but
rather against the ambitions of the sublime to take the place of religion.
In essence, this essay will claim that for Byron the encounter with the
sublime leads not to the triumph of Reason, nor to its nihilistic voiding,
but results, rather, in the opening out of consciousness to the haunting
of the divine.

As David L. Sedley has argued, the emphasis in discourses of
the sublime on cognitive failure originates in the sceptical tradition.
Sedley's argument, which focuses on the development of the sublime
in Montaigne and Milton, relates the destructive tendencies of the
concept to its origins in early modern doubt. In Montaigne's *Journal*

de Voyage (1580–1581), for instance, a sceptical attitude to historical accuracy leads to the creation of a grand or sublime style, which stems 'not from coherence but from fragmentation [...] not from the success of cognition but from cognition's collapse'.[3] The object of Montaigne's attention is the ruins of Imperial Rome. Whereas previous scholars invoked the Aristotelian category of *admiratio* to convey a passage from bewilderment to coherence, so that ancient ruins can become, after all, objects of knowledge, for Montaigne the idea that Rome cannot be known as a thing-in-itself precipitates a sense of cognitive failure, which fosters, in turn, a feeling for that which lies beyond the realms of representation. As with Kant, therefore, the truth of Rome hovers above the limitations of mere human understanding, but its status as a sublime object of desire has, as Sedley suggests, the unfortunate side effect of encouraging the violent return of the radical doubt from which it emerged.

At first glance, Byron's poetry would appear to lend support to this sceptical conclusion. In his treatment of the sublime in *Childe Harold's Pilgrimage*, for instance, the classical coupling of sublimity and *admiratio* is constantly undermined by an acknowledgement of the material effects of waste and ruin. This is seen, most obviously, in his withering description of contemporary Greece, his trenchant observations on the Battle of Waterloo and his ambivalent portrayal of Rome. For Byron, the controlled bewilderment of *admiratio* – controlled because bewilderment is orientated towards cognition – falters in the face of a prodigious accumulation of blood, bones and clay, which function like a Žižekian 'indivisible remainder' to void all claims to knowledge and understanding.[4] Like Montaigne, what Byron witnesses in Rome is a vast and empty sepulchre, a '[c]haos of ruins'; for

> who shall trace the void,
> O'er the dim fragments cast a lunar light,
> And say, 'here was, or is', where all is doubly night? (*CHP*, IV, 80)

And of what does the gladiatorial arena tell us, other than that 'man' is 'slaughtered by his fellow man' to glut the 'imperial pleasure' and that 'battle-plains or listed spot [...] are but theatres where the chief actors rot' (*CHP*, IV, 139)?

Yet still this wreck is 'impregnate with divinity', allowing '[s]pirits [to] soar from ruin' (*CHP*, IV, 55). And elsewhere, most notably in the stanzas devoted to the Pantheon, amidst the proliferation of ruinous speculation, grandeur is allowed its place: 'Simple, erect, severe, austere, sublime – / Shrine of all saints and temple of all gods':

Relic of nobler days, and noblest arts!
Despoiled yet perfect, with thy circle spreads
A holiness appealing to all hearts –
To art a model; and to him who treads
Rome for the sake of ages, Glory sheds
Her light through thy sole aperture; to those
Who worship, here are altars for their beads;
And they who feel for genius may repose
Their eyes on honoured forms, whose busts around them close.
    (*CHP*, IV, 147)

Montaigne, in his meditations on Rome, has little to say about the city's capacity for 'holiness', but for Byron the sacred emerges as a category in its own right, outshining and inspiring the endeavours of artists, worshippers and historians alike.

But what, specifically, does Byron have to say about the holiness of the Coliseum? In stanza 144, the 'rising moon' brings the dead to life within the ruin's 'magic circle'. But something more than magic is suggested by the recent history of the arena: in medieval times, the amphitheatre housed a Christian church and, more recently, had been endorsed by Pope Benedict XIV as a holy relic, sacred to the memory of Christian martyrs. When Byron visited in the spring of 1817, he would have been able to walk the Via Delarosa, created by Pope Benedict some fifty years earlier. Reframed by holy significance, and thus by a mode of grandeur exceeding the limitations of human artifice, the blood impregnating the arena, shed for the purposes of pagan entertainment, could now be read, retroactively, as the sacrificial blood of Christ. Life, not death, had triumphed in the arena.

Whether Byron felt moved as a historian, artist or Christian on his visit to the Coliseum is unclear, but I want to suggest that his invocation of divinity was more than merely procedural. Still further, I should like to argue that Byron's scepticism, which results in the creation of a grand or sublime style founded in fragmentation, lent itself to an earnest inquiry into the nature and significance of the divine.[5] What began as a critique of the aesthetic category of *admiratio* – so beloved of Renaissance historians and contemporary travel writers – thus became, almost despite itself, a critique of the limitations of human artifice. This critique took place on two fronts: the cognitive and the ethical. In terms of the former, Byron, like Montaigne, was eager to steer the discourse of the sublime away from a restricted economy of confusion and coherence. By allowing confusion to proliferate, the poetry worked – as a discourse of scepticism – to undercut the claims of cognition while, as a discourse of the sublime, it sought to awaken, perhaps, a sense of the divine. This latter claim is, I am aware, highly contentious, but by way of support it is worth attending to an early instance of Byron's critique of the ethics of the sublime.[6]

On his last day in Rome, Byron witnessed the execution of three criminals. As he wrote to Murray:

> I saw three robbers guillotined – the ceremony – including the *masqued* priests – the half-naked executioners – the bandaged criminals – the black Christ & his banner – the scaffold – the soldiery – the slow procession – & the quick rattle and fall of the axe – the splash of the blood – & the ghastliness of the exposed heads – is altogether more impressive than the vulgar and ungentlemanly 'new drop' & dog-like agony of infliction upon the sufferers of the English sentence. Two of these men – behaved calmly enough – but the first of the three – died with great terror and reluctance – which was very horrible [...].[7]

Surveying the scene through an opera glass ('I was close – but was determined to see – as one should see everything once – with attention'), Byron notes that the 'effect to the spectator [...] is very striking & chilling'. The first execution turns him 'quite hot and thirsty'; his hand shakes so badly that he can hardly hold the opera glass. But by the second and third death, he was, he confessed, quite unmoved, 'which shows how dreadfully soon things grow indifferent [...] though I would have saved them if I could'.

The emotional arc of this scene recalls the relations between sublimity and negation outlined earlier, only this time Byron registers a certain moral queasiness otherwise lacking in the elaborately choreographed sequences of the Kantian sublime. As Edmund Burke acknowledges: 'there is no spectacle we so eagerly pursue, as that of some uncommon and grievous calamity; so that whether the misfortune is before our eyes, or whether they are turned back to it in history, it always touches with delight'.[8] Disturbingly, the execution of a criminal or the destruction of a city both yield their own forms of perverse delight – call it the illusory delight of surveying and thus overcoming one's own extinction – but such delight is possible only on condition that the event does not involve any actual threat. For the sublime to take effect, death must be kept at a distance. Hence the importance of the opera glass, which acts as a framing device, creating the effects of proximity while shielding the viewer from the unsettling effects of reality. By the second or third death, however, the effects of this painful pleasure have started to wane. No longer functional as a theatrical 'horror', the scene, with its grotesque parody of Christ's journey to Golgotha, rebounds on the spectator, forcing him to take account of his moral obligations: 'I would have saved them if I could.' Here, with an echo of Augustine's critique of his own youthful fascination with the staging of pain,[9] Byron moves from wrapt fascination to indifference and finally to something approaching shame. The conventional pagan idea that theatricalized displays of violence are in some way cathartic – yielding insight into the horrific underpinnings of self and society – is challenged by this passage. When the aesthetic framework collapses, when the viewer is no longer held at a distance from the object of sublime terror, so that the object is revealed as a vulnerable subject, at *that* point the viewer becomes a witness implicated in the suffering of a fellow human being.[10]

Byron often seems to take account of the victims of spectacular violence. The impulse emerges, typically, during the course of a set-piece presentation of the sublime. In the stanzas that follow on from the description of the Coliseum, for example, the focus closes on a shadowy couple, a destitute young woman and her aged father. Somewhat disturbingly, the old man is discovered suckling from his daughter's breast. As an instance of human degradation, the scene, which Byron derives from the legend of the Caritas Romana, appears merely grotesque to modern eyes. Yet, out of such unpromising material, Byron raises an idea of greatness, which, on account of its intimacy, yields far more in terms of its cosmic significance than the studied theatricality of most conventional accounts of sublimity. Not for the first time, the poem's significance is derived from allusions to Catholic iconography; in this case the daughter – '[b]lest into mother' (*CHP*, IV, 149) – emerges as a Marian figure, offering 'to old age the food, / The milk of his own gift' (IV, 150). In the preceding lines, where attention is devoted to the beauty of the human form, to the blood as 'nectar' and the breast as fructifying 'fountain', a link between the spirit and the flesh is forged.[11] Contrary to the standard Enlightenment view of the sublime as the negative apprehension of the supersensible, Byron seems to insist on the continuity of the sensual and divine. To adapt the words of the contemporary theologian John Milbank, the scene, in its pathetic and, admittedly, unsettling beauty, seems 'to recover the sense that the unknown is not simply that which cannot be represented, but is also that which arrives, which ceaselessly but imperfectly makes itself known again in every new event'.[12] Like the 'Glory' shining through the amphitheatre's 'sole aperture', the return of the father's love gift, manifested in imperfect and all-too-human form, becomes a principle of restoration, working like prayer to reverse the vitiating effects of time:

The starry fable of the milky way
Has not thy story's purity; it is
A constellation of a sweeter ray,
And sacred Nature triumphs more in this
Reverse of her decree, than in the abyss
Where sparkle distant worlds: – Oh, holiest nurse!
No drop of that clear stream its way shall miss
To thy sire's heart, replenishing its source
With life, as our freed souls rejoin the universe. (*CHP*, IV, 151)

The link between the universal and the particular, which underpins this conception of the Byronic sublime, is granted theoretical perspective in the ensuing description of St Peter's Basilica, that 'vast and wondrous dome'. Here again, rather than blockage or disjunction – those stock features of the Wordsworthian and Kantian sublimes – it is the sense of a correspondence between the human and the divine that is stressed.[13] In this, the poem accords with Joseph Addison's belief that noble buildings, such as temples or cathedrals, 'imprint' the mind 'and fit it to converse with the divinity'.[14] 'Enter', writes Byron, 'its grandeur overwhelms thee not';

And why? it is not lessened; but thy mind,
Expanded by the genius of the spot,
Has grown colossal, and can only find
A fit abode wherein appear enshrined
Thy hopes of immortality; and thou
Shalt one day, if found worthy, so defined,
See thy God face to face, as thou dost now
His Holy of Holies, nor be blasted by his brow. (*CHP*, IV, 155)

The allusion in the penultimate line to Paul's first letter to the Corinthians is a reminder both of the limitations of mortal knowledge and a promise of the perfect understanding to come – an understanding based on recognition or love. What the dome allows the mind to glean is an intimation of the resulting correspondence of human and divine conceptions:

Our outward sense
Is but of gradual grasp – and as it is
That what we have of feeling most intense
Outstrips our faint expression; even so this
Outshining and o'erwhelming edifice
Fools our fond gaze, and greatest of the great
Defies at first our Nature's littleness,

> Till, growing with its growth, we thus dilate
> Our spirits to the size of that they contemplate. (*CHP*, IV, 158)

The stress on the dilation of human 'spirit' does not serve as a figure for the primacy of mind or reason, but points rather to the analogical 'fit' between the mortal and the divine. Instead of insisting on the disjunction between sublime feeling and sensible expression – a disjunction that yields a negative intimation of the infinite – with Byron, though '[o]utshining' otherness 'outstrips' 'expression', the 'spirit' is able, as a result of its correspondence with the divine, to relay its participation in otherness to the 'gradual grasp' of 'sense'. Contra Kant, the faculty of Imagination does, after all, conceive the transcendental in sensible terms.

This, at least, is one potential pathway for the development of a critique of the Romantic sublime. At other times, pursuing his sceptical inclinations to the limit, as it were, Byron seems irresistibly attracted to the notion of a fatal divide between the human and the divine – a divide that maps neatly onto the division outlined earlier between cognition and wonder. At its bleakest, the emphasis on the impossibility of knowing suggests a form of nihilism.[15] In the late verse drama *Cain*, for instance, Lucifer pronounces what readers take to be the definitive expression of Byronic despair:

> Didst thou not require
> Knowledge? And have I not, in what I showed,
> Taught thee to know thyself?
> *Cain.*   Alas! I seem
> Nothing.
> *Lucifer.*   And this should be the human sum
> Of knowledge, to know mortal nature's nothingness [...].
>   (II, ii, 419–22)

The seeds of faith, hinted at within Canto IV of *Childe Harold's Pilgrimage*, would seem, on the evidence of Byron's later pronouncements, to have fallen on stony ground.

The knowledge of mortal nature's nothingness is taken up again in Canto XIV of *Don Juan*. Stanza 2 opens with an assertion of radical doubt: 'can you make fast, / After due search, your faith to any question?' (XIV, 2). The poem then goes on to endorse the sceptical view that philosophy, *qua* philosophy, is a matter of mere appetite: since 'system' eats 'system' (XIV, 1), it makes no sense to talk of Truth; better to rest content with the knowledge that there is no Truth, only the blind, empty pursuit of power. Within this proto-Darwinian realm, philosophical systems are judged on the basis of their indigestibility; that system is 'good' (XIV, 1) or 'best' (XIV, 2) that survives the longest in the gut.

Yet, here, at the very moment when the sceptic teeters on the edge of despair, something strange begins to happen. First, Descartes is invoked: 'Nothing more true than *not* to trust your senses' (XIV, 2). In his *Second Meditation*, after concluding 'that body, figure, extension, movement and place are only fictions of my mind', Descartes pauses to consider the nihilistic corollary 'that there is nothing certain in the world'.[16] As is well known, the philosopher entertains this position only briefly; structurally, this 'nothing' is retroactively informed by the irrefutable certainty of 'I am, I exist.' So there is something after all. But *Don Juan* serves to complicate this claim: 'And yet', the speaker goads, 'what are your other evidences?' (XIV, 2). Can we be certain that we exist on the basis that we think? Does the question mark at the end of this sentence grant 'fast' my faith that there is something in the world? And is the evidence of the mind any less delusory than the evidence of the body? 'For me', the speaker admits, aping Socrates and his own Lucifer, 'I know nothing.' But then, critically, 'nothing I deny, / Admit, reject, contemn' (XIV, 3), the reverse of which also holds true: 'He who doubts all things, nothing can deny' (XV, 88). Or, as the poet writes in Canto IX: 'So little do we know what we're about in / This world, I doubt if doubt itself be doubting' (17). The uncompromising sceptic turns out, after all, to be open to possibility:

> and what know *you*,
> Except perhaps that you were born to die?
> And both may after all turn out to untrue.
> An age may come, Font of Eternity,
> When nothing shall be either old or new. (XIV, 3)

This, it seems to me, is radical doubt of an altogether different flavour.[17]

But where is Byron's doubt taking us? Stanza 3 ends with an allusion – one of many in the poem – to *Hamlet* (III, ii, 65–68); specifically, a speech that draws in turn on Socrates's claim, in his *Apology*, that death would be good if it gave man sleep untroubled by dreams. Byron, in the following stanza, notes the impossibility of testing this hypothesis: 'and yet / How clay shrinks back from more quiescent clay!' (XIV, 4). It is, in other words, the dread of death that prevents most men from committing suicide; and yet, in a further dialectical twist, the poet avers that death, too, may have its attractions. The lines that pursue this thought draw, significantly, on the discourse of the sublime:

> when the mountains rear
>   Their peaks beneath your human foot, and there
>   You look down o'er the precipice, and drear
>   The gulf of rock yawns, – you can't gaze a minute
>   Without an awful wish to plunge within it. (*DJ*, XIV, 5)

The happy man holds back from this wish; but still, Byron insists, 'look into your past impression! / And you will find':

> The lurking bias, be it truth or error,
>   To the *unknown*; a secret prepossession,
> To plunge with all your fears – but where? You know not,
> And that's the reason why you do – or do not. (*DJ*, XIV, 6)

Socrates may know nothing, but the nihilist goes further and wishes to become nothing. That the lines in which this thought is expressed are not themselves nihilistic is a consequence of the stanza's framing commitment to uncertainty: we plunge or do not plunge because we 'know not' where we end. It is the saving gesture of faith – a faith founded paradoxically on doubt – which prevents the poem from succumbing to the appeal of its own abyss.

In the lines quoted above, the 'lurking bias' towards negation, which elsewhere, as we have seen, Byron identifies with the self-destructive tendencies of the sublime, is weighed alongside the prevailing instinct for survival: we choose, on the whole, 'not' to plunge to our deaths because we believe, reasonably enough, that to do so would mean the end of our lives.[18] In a sense, it is ignorance that keeps us going. Byron, throughout *Don Juan*, confronts the reader with a number of related moments of suspended thought. Most notably, in Canto I, the poet proclaims: 'Man's a phenomenon, one knows not what, / And wondrous beyond all wondrous measure.' The lines are a parody of Longinian *ekstasis* – an instance of the work-a-day poetics of wonder churned out by the dozen in 'this sublime world'. Fittingly, this expression of quasi-rapture, which functions as a mockery of the Wordsworthian 'something ever more about to be', ends with a chiastic joke: ''Tis pity [...] Pleasure's a sin, and sometimes sin's a pleasure' (I, 133). It takes a healthy dose of the finite to deflate man's visionary flight from the 'measure' of his own mortality. And yet, here again, the verse turns suddenly grave:

> Few mortals know what end they would be at,
>   But whether glory, power or love or treasure,
> The path is through perplexing ways, and when
> The goal is gain'd, we die you know – and then –

> What then? – I do not know, no more do you –
> And so good night. – Return we to our story […]. (*DJ*, I, 133–34)

That we will die is certain, is it not? Perhaps. But for Byron the 'hopes of immortality' (*CHP*, IV, 155) persist. In what follows, the desire for continuity beyond cognitive and expressive limits is signified by the diacritical dash, question mark and stanza break. Since knowledge is unable to inform these silences, the significance of which declines from wonder into incoherence as the dashes proliferate, the poet and, by implication, the reader must commit, once again, to their respective stories.

And yet, the blank space between the certainty of death and the return to narrative continuity resonates profoundly. In Lacanian thought, the significance of the space between the acknowledgement and acceptance of death is conveyed by the metaphor of 'being between two deaths', with the first death referring to physical death and the second to symbolic death.[19] For Lacan, the space between physical and symbolic death is literally 'un-dead' and since it cannot find a place in either realm, it keeps insisting or returning. Another term for this ghastly realm is, of course, the Real. As Felix Ensslin summarizes:

> the real, lacking representation, never appears in reality as such. It neither is given nor finds itself an order; it has no symbolic existence, that is, no name that remains, no space that persists, no place in the calculable and countable.[20]

In one sense, the Byronic Real is the impossible object that must be excluded so that life, or story, can continue. Yet, in another sense, it marks the existence of that deadly void or contradiction around which Byron's verse is orientated and towards which it is fatally attracted. In Canto XIV, stanza 8, for instance, 'poesy' is described as a 'paper kite, which flies 'twixt life and death'. Elsewhere, Don Juan himself is said to hover like a ghost between 'the real or ideal, – / For both are much the same' (X, 20), and when regarded from the point of view of the Lacanian Real, both are, indeed, more or less the same. In light of this, the desire expressed in other parts of the poem for contact with the divine might be regarded as an attempt to inform this fatal contradiction with symbolic significance. But it might also, from another perspective, be regarded as a reconfiguration of the Real, not as that which in the standard Lacanian sense marks the futility of signification, but rather as that which marks the return to signification of transcendental plenitude or, to adopt a Christian register, the return to language of divine rapture.[21]

Though I am uncertain of the extent to which *Don Juan* commits to either faith or doubt, it remains, of all the great Romantic poems, the poem that is most invested in ideas of God. More often than not, of course, divine significance is invoked by Byron only to succumb to the foil of scepticism: one thinks, for example, of the satirical treatment of the Noah story in the shipwreck episode (II, 91–95) or the debunking of the Fall in Canto IX, stanza 19, and Canto XIV, stanza 9. There are times, however, when the satire on religion seems merely conventional, as if, having reached the limits of signification, the poet felt compelled to recommit to the everyday business of narrative continuity. In a Lacanian sense, the return to 'story' thus becomes a way of fending off the terrifying sublimity of the Real.

To examine this point more thoroughly, I should like to return to Canto IX. In stanza 16 of this canto, *Hamlet* is quoted again: '"To be or not to be?" – Ere I decide, / I should be glad to know that which *is being*.' Having opened up this suicidal void – the space of 'between two deaths' outlined above – the poet draws on Montaigne's statement of radical self-doubt – 'Que sçais-je?' – to proclaim the end point of sceptical reason: 'I doubt if doubt itself be doubting' (IX, 17). Since, as the Sceptics proclaimed, nothing can be known in and of itself and that against every statement the contrary might be advanced with equal reason, then doubt, too, must be subjected to doubt. The doctrine of intellectual suspense turns out, after all, to be freighted by questions of faith.[22] Such questions, as the poem goes on to aver, may well be perilous: for while it is 'pleasant [...] to float, / Like Pyrrho, on a sea of speculation', what if the boat capsize? 'Swimming long', the poem reminds us, 'in the abyss of thought / Is apt to tire':

> a calm and shallow station
> Well nigh the shore, where one stoops down and gathers
> Some pretty shell, is best for moderate bathers. (*DJ*, IX, 18)

Like the suicidal gulf explored in Canto XIV, the abyss of thought leads the sceptic to the very limits of human understanding: is there something or nothing? Is it better to be or not to be? Faced with such unanswerable questions, it is better, perhaps, to stay close to shore so that we may commit, once again, to story.[23]

That Byron himself is not wholly convinced by this proposition is evident when one considers the verse's indebtedness to *Paradise Regained*. In Book 4, Christ rebukes Satan for his advocacy of Greek philosophy, arguing – by way of Augustine – for the primacy of wisdom (*sapientia*), which is divine, over knowledge (*scientia*), which is mortal. In the course of his speech, Christ singles out for special attention the Sceptics, who 'doubted all things'.[24] Finally, echoing *Ecclesiastes*, he criticizes those 'wise men' who, unable to bring wisdom to bear on their studies, become '[u]ncertain and unsettled',

> Crude or intoxicate, collecting toys,
> And trifles for choice matters, worth a sponge;
> As children gathering pebbles on the shore.
> (*Paradise Regained*, IV, 328–30)

In Byron's version of this speech, although the bather is portrayed as 'moderate' rather than 'intoxicate', he nevertheless remains a child, fixated with the fleeting beauty of 'some pretty shell' rather than the infinite glory of the divine.

Yet, though a sense of divine sublimity was granted earlier through the cognitive derailment of 'I doubt if doubt itself be doubting', the question of how to account for the inexpressible within ordinary language remains. For Byron, somewhat archly, it is the classical scholar – a man of *scientia*, rather than *sapentia* – who comes closest, as a consequence of literal drunkenness, to articulating the divine. This man is Shakespeare's Cassio:[25] 'well, God's above all and there be souls that must be saved [...] Let's ha' no more of this, let's to our affairs. God forgive us our sins!' (*Othello*, II, iii, 103–13); or as Byron has it: '"But Heaven [...] is above all, – / No more of this then, – let us pray!"' (*DJ*, IX, 19). As the stanza draws to its close, quotation from Shakespeare becomes the means by which Byron grants form to the overwhelming effects of divine unreason. It is fitting that, having begun with Hamlet's glimpse into the suicidal abyss, the verse should end with Hamlet's affirmation of the 'divinity that shapes our ends' (*Hamlet*, V, ii, 10): 'The Sparrow's fall / Is special providence' recalls the poet, more or less correctly (*DJ*, IX, 19). God is admitted, then, somewhat wearily and with a presiding sense of bathos – a remnant, perhaps, of the deflated balloon of scepticism – but God is admitted, nevertheless.

But what sort of God? Famously, towards the end of Canto XV, Byron turns to matters spiritual or, to be precise, to the ghostly. Teasing the boundary between the sublime and the ridiculous, the speaker insists that his 'belief is serious' (XV, 95). The paradox of serious laughter is a persistent theme in *Don Juan*, but in Canto XV, stanza 96, it is linked with the dissolving relation between fiction and reality. Referring to Hobbes's confession that what he read concerning apparitions almost convinced him of their existence, the poem turns at this point to reflect on the ability of fiction to create reality. Here, caught between two deaths, or as stanza 99 has it, ''Twixt night and morn', the poem once again reaches the limit point of understanding: 'How little do we know that which we are!' In a bid to overcome this abyss, the poem finds refuge in the taught paradox of Canto XVI, stanza 2: 'In some things, mine's beyond all contradiction / The most sincere that ever dealt in fiction.' Insisting that the ensuing ghost story is 'of all truths which she [the poem] has told, the most / True' (XVI, 4), the verse then goes on, in stanza 5, to cite Tertullian's proto-Kierkegaardian claim: 'sepultus resurrexit; certum est quia impossibile' ('[Christ] was buried and resurrected; this is certain because it is impossible').[26] In other words, believe in this miracle *because* of its absurdity.

The poem goes on, as many commentators observe, to complicate this claim.[27] Yet even as the ghost is shown to be merely absurd or ridiculous – the spectral presence that is haunting Juan turns out, after all, to be the Duchess of Fitz-Fulke disguised in a friar's habit – in another sense, the poem's materialist or comic solution to the problem of spirit is haunted by the persistently enigmatic status of Aurora Raby. There is a part of the poem, in other words, that remains in thrall to the '*quia impossibile*', to the idea of a higher truth shining through the fiction – the Symbolic Order? – that we mistake for reality.

Introduced in Canto XV, Aurora is linked, then, from the outset, with the religious sublime:

> In eyes which sadly shone, as seraphs' shine.
>   All youth – but with an aspect beyond time;
> Radiant and grave – as pitying man's decline;
>   Mournful – but mournful of another's crime,
> She look'd as if she sat by Eden's door,
> And grieved for those who could return no more. (*DJ*, XV, 45)

Combining the attributes of cherubim and seraphim, of infinite wisdom (*sapentia*) as well as infinite love, Aurora, as her name implies, is both luminous and unreachable. Residing 'beyond time' and '[a]part from the surrounding world', she naturally inspires 'awe in the homage which she drew' (XV, 47). Significantly, she is linked with stillness, quietness and calm, even, as Bernard Beatty has argued, with the benign indifference of the Buddha.[28] But whether Catholic or Buddhist, Aurora's 'depth of feeling', combined with her capacity 'to embrace / Thoughts, boundless, deep, but silent too as Space' (XVI, 48), is presented in the poem as a divine solution to the brute materialism of the Fitz-Fulke episode. Tellingly, by the end of the poem, Juan, too, is 'silent': 'the ghost', writes Byron, 'had done this much good, / In making him as silent as a ghost' (XVI, 107).[29]

So the flesh has become spirit, the real has become ideal, and we might, on the basis of this miraculous substitution, be ready to advance a Christian conclusion to Byron's epic poem. But *Don Juan* leaves us with a choice: either we interpret Juan's and Aurora's silences, by way of Lacan, as the stupefying sublimity of the empty 'thing' – the pure nothing or void around which signification coils – or else we respond with joy to the alternative posed in stanzas 107–108:

> And certainly Aurora had renewed
>   In him some feelings he had lately lost
> Or hardened, feelings which, perhaps ideal,
>   Are so divine, that I must deem them real: –
>
> The love of higher things and better days;
>   The unbounded hope, and heavenly ignorance
> Of what is called the world, and the world's ways [...].
>   (XVI, 107–08)

For Žižek, writing in the *Fragile Absolute*, the distinction between unbounded divine love and worldly progress corresponds to the fundamental tension between the Real and the Symbolic; as Žižek considers: 'what comes first, the signifier or some deadlock in the Real?' On the one hand, the conception of the Symbolic Order as that which cuts into or shapes the natural organism, forcing it to pursue an unreachable object of desire is 'clearly idealist; it is ultimately a new version of Divine intervention in the natural order'. On the other hand, the idea of the Symbolic as that which emerges as 'the answer to some monstrous excess in the Real' is clearly 'materialist', since it acknowledges, by way of Marx, the inherently contradictory nature of the world – the fact that it is driven from within to 'some kind of natural excess or imbalance, a malfunctioning, monstrous derailment'.[30]

Taking the materialist alternative first, the Byronic commitment to 'story' may thus be read as a secondary intervention, designed to 'gentrify' the ghastly, life-threatening excess of the poem's silences; thus, the interminable, suspended status of the ghost in Canto XVI is filled in, given life, and yet in a sense finally also killed off by the symbolic revelation that the ghost is, after all, merely a human being. But what of the idealist reading? Aurora, unlike the pantomime ghost, remains in this state of suspension; her silences seem to resonate beyond words and thus beyond the Symbolic. Can these silences, speaking volumes, be dismissed as a 'fantasy-construction', designed to conceal or render invisible the debilitating antagonism at the core of Byron's verse?

Writing to Thomas Moore on 8 March 1822, Byron proposed another version of this conundrum:

> As I said before, I am really a great admirer of tangible religion [...] What with incense, pictures, statues, confession, absolution, – there is something sensible to grasp at. Besides it leaves no possibility of doubt; for those who swallow their Deity, really and truly, in transubstantiation, can hardly find any thing else otherwise than easy of digestion.
>
> I am afraid that this sounds flippant, but I don't mean it to be so; only my turn of mind is so given to taking things in the absurd point of view, that it breaks out in spite of me every now and then. Still I do assure that I am a very good Christian. Whether you will believe me in this, I do not know [...].[31]

First, there is Byron's materialism: the miracle of transubstantiation, like the doctrines described at the beginning of *Don Juan*, Canto XVI, is hard to swallow. But for those who believe, this miracle, once digested, is the *'quia impossible' par exemplar*. And there is, no doubt, something absurd about such belief. As Žižek might argue, by way of Hegel, the sense in which the host *is* the body of Christ is a reminder of the essential materiality of the sublime. Where, for instance, in Kant, the mountain points to the existence of a supersensible realm beyond appearance, for Hegel there is an Idea – of the State or of God – only insofar as there is some thing – the finite body of the King or the vulnerable, mortal body of Christ – which prevents the Idea from attaining its full ontological identity. Indeed, as Žižek maintains, there is a sublime Idea only insofar as there is some material thing – in this case, a host – in which the Idea *cannot* be fully presented.[32]

Yet the point about the host is that it *is* the body of Christ. Unlike the Hegelian or Lacanian thing, the host is not an object that is orientated around a determinate lack, but rather it serves as the determinate expression of a divine plenitude. This is the real absurdity. But it is an absurdity rendered digestible by an act of faith. In Byron's letter to Moore, faith is manifested in the difference between the (apparent) flippancy of the opening statement and the (apparent) gravity of the closing statement. Byron does not know whether we believe him or not, but this state of suspension is, it seems to me, evidence enough of a yearning for the divine, both on his part and on ours.

Notes

1 Žižek, *The Sublime Object of Ideology* (New York & London: Verso, 1989).
2 John Milbank, 'Sublimity: The Modern Transcendent', p. 228. For a related discussion of the links between sublimity and nihilism, see Will Slocombe, *Nihilism and the Sublime Postmodern: The (Hi)Story of a Difficult Relationship from Romanticism to Postmodernism* (New York & London: Routledge, 2006).
3 Sedley, *Sublimity and Skepticism in Montaigne and Milton* (Ann Arbor, MI: University of Michigan Press, 2005), p. 40.
4 Žižek, *The Indivisible Remainder: Essays on Schelling and Related Matters* (New York & London: Verso, 1996).
5 As will become apparent, the argument presented here is influenced by Gavin Hopps's critique of sceptical reason in his introduction to *Romanticism and Religion from William Cowper to Wallace Stevens*, ed. Gavin Hopps and Jane Stabler (Aldershot: Ashgate, 2006). See, in particular, pp. 9–13. I have also benefitted from the arguments that John Milbank advances against the Kantian sublime in *Being Reconciled: Ontology and Pardon* (London and New York, NY: Routledge, 2003) and in 'Sublimity: The Modern Transcendent', pp. 211–34.
6 This claim to contentiousness ought, of course, to be set within context. The idea that Byron was, after all, a Christian poet, has been advanced by a number of commentators, including E.D. Hirsch, 'Byron and the Terrestrial Paradise', in *From Sensibility to Romanticism*, eds. Frederick Hilles and Harold Bloom (Oxford and New York, NY: Oxford University Press, 1965), pp. 56–95; G. Wilson Knight, *Poets of Action*, p. 263; Michael G. Cooke, *The Blind Man Traces the Circle: On the Patterns and Philosophy of Byron's Poetry* (Princeton, NJ: Princeton University Press, 1969), p. 212; M.K. Joseph, *Byron the Poet* (London: Gollancz, 1964), pp. 305–08; Bernard Beatty, *Byron's 'Don Juan'*, *passim*; and, most recently, by the contributors to two notable essay collections, *Byron, the Bible, and Religion*, ed. Wolf Z. Hirst (London and Toronto: Associated University Presses, 1991); and the above mentioned *Romanticism and Religion from William Cowper to Wallace Stevens*, eds. Hopps and Stabler.
7 *BLJ*, V, pp. 229–30. Emphasis in the original.
8 Burke, *A Philosophical Enquiry into the Origin of Our Ideas of the Sublime and the Beautiful*, ed. Adam Phillips (Oxford: Oxford University Press, 1990), p. 43.
9 Augustine, *Confessions*, ed. James J. O'Donnell (Oxford: Oxford University Press, 1992), 3.2.2.
10 Bernard Beatty writes in a similar vein that the sublime, for Byron, 'is not there simply to give us Keats's dizzy pain at aesthetically realised scale but gives us moral insight. The focus of that moral insight is exactly the same as the Romantic Sublime – the relationship between human finitude and a graspable infinity – but the point is quite different.' See Beatty, '"An Awful Wish to Plunge Within it": Byron's Critique of the Sublime', in *Revue de l'Université de Moncton*, 'Byron and the Romantic Sublime', ed. Paul M. Curtis (Moncton: Université de Moncton, 2005), pp. 265–76, 273–74.
11 See Bernard Beatty's comments on these stanzas in 'Milk and Blood, Heredity and Choice: Byron's Readings of Genesis', in *Eve's Children: The Biblical Stories Retold and Interpreted in Jewish and Christian Traditions*, ed. Gerard P. Luttikhuizen (Leiden: Brill, 2003), pp. 143–55. The piety of Pero towards her father, Cimon, is

the subject of numerous paintings. Notable examples include studies by Rubens, Greuze, Mellin and Zoffany.

12 Milbank, 'Sublimity: The Modern Transcendent', p. 217.

13 Stuart Curran reads the St Peter's sequence as an allegory of Byron's quest for artistic and personal unity. For Curran, therefore, the claim to transcendence is regarded as a purely aesthetic phenomenon. This reading is challenged by Alan Rawes, 'Byron's Confessional Pilgrimage', in *Romanticism and Religion from William Cowper to Wallace Stevens*, pp. 130–31.

14 Peter de Bolla, *The Discourse of the Sublime: Readings in History, Aesthetics and the Subject* (London: Blackwell, 1989), p. 45.

15 As Gavin Hopps points out, it is this aspect of Byron that Jerome McGann pursues in support of his 'project in radical unbelief' (*Romanticism and Religion from William Cowper to Wallace Stevens*, p. 11). What McGann's emphasis on the sceptical Byron tends to ignore, however, is the extent to which the poet regards doubt as coeval with faith.

16 Descartes, *Meditations on First Philosophy*, trans. F.E. Sutcliffe (London: Penguin, 1968), p. 102.

17 For readings sympathetic to the secularizing tendencies of Byronic doubt, see Wolf Z. Hirst, 'Byron's Revisionary Struggle with the Bible', in *Byron, the Bible, and Religion*, pp. 77–100; and Terence Allan Hoagwood, *Byron's Dialectic: Skepticism and the Critique of Culture*.

18 Bernard Beatty, in a particularly fine discussion of this passage, suggests that the phrase '"the lurking bias" – is [...] an assault on the new cult of the untethered Sublime'. Beatty goes on to add that the 'comic tone' of the final couplet 'is a long way from the exalted Wordsworth on Snowdon's precipice'. In this, of course, Byron does not seek to disavow a relationship with the infinite; rather, his aim is to show that 'it is not only the vast spatial sweep that is sublime but a combined sense of finite and infinite which is not merely aesthetically grasped [...] but is the grandeur and limitation known to the moral understanding'. See '"An Awful Wish to Plunge Within It": Byron's Critique of the Sublime', pp. 269, 274.

19 Lacan, *The Ethics of Psychoanalysis 1959–1960*, trans. Dennis Porter (New York & London: W.W. Norton, 1992), p. 320.

20 Ensslin, 'Between Two Deaths: From Mirror to Repetition', in *Between Two Deaths*, eds. Felix Ensslin and Ellen Blumenstein (Berlin: Hatje Cantz, 2007), p. 2.

21 John Milbank mounts a spirited critique of Žižek's Lacanianism in his contribution to Slavoj Žižek and John Milbank, *The Monstrosity of Christ: Paradox or Dialectic?*, ed. Creston Davis (Cambridge and London: MIT Press, 2009), pp. 110–233.

22 As Gavin Hopps explains: 'one of the most surprising discoveries of postmodernity is that, if scepticism is pushed to its limits, it reflexively undermines [...] its own enterprise, and thus paradoxically opens up a route to that which it also calls into question – namely, faith' (*Romanticism and Religion from William Cowper to Wallace Stevens*, p. 11).

23 In *Don Juan*, VII, 5, Byron observes of Newton that 'he himself felt only "like a youth / Picking up shells by the great ocean – Truth"'. Peter Cochran (see http://petercochran.wordpress.com/?s=don+juan) notes that Joseph Spence provides the source for this anecdote: 'Sir Isaac Newton, a little before he died, said, "I don't know what I may seem to the world; but as to myself, I seem to have been only like a boy playing on the sea-shore, and diverting myself in now and then finding

a smoother pebble or a prettier shell than ordinary, whilst the great ocean of truth lay all undiscovered before me."' See Joseph Spence, *Observations, Anecdotes, and Characters of Books and Men*, ed. Edmund Malone (London: John Murray 1820), pp. 158–59. I am grateful to Tony Howe for alerting me to the source of this allusion.

24 *Paradise Regained*, IV, 296, in *The Poems of John Milton*, eds. John Carey and Alastair Fowler (London: Longman, 1968).

25 The following quotations from Shakespeare are taken from William Shakespeare, *The Complete Works*, eds. Stanley Wells and Gary Taylor (Oxford: Clarendon Press, 1988).

26 *Tertullian's Treatise on the Incarnation*, vol. 4, trans. Ernest Ewans (London: SPCK, 1956), pp. 18–19.

27 Most notably, Bernard Beatty, in the closing pages of *Byron's 'Don Juan'*, pp. 202–11. Having noted the complex interplay of '[l]aughter, unease, poise, absurdity and reverence' in stanzas 6–7, Beatty concludes that the encompassing tone of the poem is, ultimately, religious.

28 Beatty, 'Fiction's Limit and Eden's Door' in *Byron and the Limits of Fiction*, p. 35.

29 For a related discussion of Aurora's spiritual significance, see Gavin Hopps, '"Eden's Door": The Porous Worlds of *Don Juan* and *Childe Harold's Pilgrimage*', in *The Byron Journal*, 37:2 (2009), pp. 109–20, 117–18.

30 Žižek, *The Fragile Absolute – Or, Why is the Christian Legacy Worth Fighting For?* (New York & London: Verso, 2000), pp. 91–92.

31 *BLJ*, IX, p. 122.

32 Žižek, *The Sublime Object of Ideology* (New York & London: Verso, 1989), pp. 203–06.

CHAPTER SEVEN

Byron, Ann Radcliffe and the Religious Implications of the Explained Supernatural in *Don Juan*

Alison Milbank

At first sight, it may seem somewhat comical to associate the sceptical and famously transgressive Lord Byron with the productions of a middle-class novelist of non-conformist origins, who classed protagonists of his aristocratic arrogance and incestuous predilections alongside her darkest villains. And yet in proposing a Radcliffean Gothic structure to the ghost scenes of Canto XVI of Byron's unfinished epic, *Don Juan*, I hope to find a way both to explicate the complex nature of the poet's attitude to the transcendent and to clarify the overall philosophical trajectory of his poem. In suggesting that the explained supernatural is used by Byron to trace a middle path between idealism and a dead materialism, I also hope to mediate between the Christian idealism of Bernard Beatty's interpretation of these English Cantos and those, like Jerome McGann, who uphold Byron's ultimate scepticism and proleptic postmodernity.[1]

Byron is most often cited in relation to the Gothic novel as someone whose literary self-projections onto a series of poetic damned and brooding heroes contributed to the character of the Gothic anti-hero. Caroline Lamb made him the protagonist of her Gothic *roman-à-clef*, *Glenarvon*, while Polidori's *The Vampyre*, based on Byron's contribution to Gothic storytelling in the competition at the Villa Diodati in Geneva, which inspired Mary Shelley to write *Frankenstein*, in calling its villain Ruthven in imitation of Lamb's Satanic character, associated Byron with the aristocratic vampire figure.[2] As soon as Byron inherited his title and the ancient house that went with it, he immediately set about constructing a complex articulation of his ancestry as one of aristocratic power and also usurpation, reminiscent of Horace Walpole's Gothic novel, *The Castle of Otranto* (1764), in which Otranto's tyrant, Manfred, is haunted by the armour and furnishings of the castle his grandfather obtained by murder and a forged will. In a poem written in 1803, 'On Leaving Newstead Abbey', the young Byron uses a ballad form to hymn the exploits of his medieval ancestors and mourn the ruinous state of their house, while in the later 'Elegy on Newstead Abbey', a more correctly historical reading of Newstead's history charts the downfall of the monks (actually Augustinian canons) that inhabited the Abbey until the Reformation and their subsequent expulsion by Henry VIII. The usurper here is not the Byron family so much as Cromwell, the 'fierce Usurper', who 'seeks his native hell' (103) after the Civil War, in which the Byrons fought for the King and their house and lands were sequestered. By the end of the poem, Newstead has become the picturesque ruin of Radcliffe's abbey in *The Romance of the Forest*, amid whose cloisters and defenestrated arches La Motte and his family find an ambiguous refuge. Indeed, Fiona MacCarthy suggests that Radcliffe, who visited relations in nearby Mansfield and Chesterfield, actually based her ruined abbey on Newstead, which shares its sylvan setting, being situated in the middle of Sherwood Forest. Byron's elegy is certainly in the mode of Radcliffean Gothic and eighteenth-century 'graveyard' poetic style:

> Newstead! what saddening change of scene is thine!
> Thy yawning arch betokens slow decay;
> The last and youngest of a noble line,
> Now holds thy mouldering turrets in his sway.
>
> Deserted now, he scans thy gray worn towers;
> Thy vaults, where dead of feudal ages sleep;
> Thy cloisters, pervious to the wintry showers;
> These, these he views, and views them but to weep.
>   ('Elegy on Newstead Abbey', 137–44)[3]

In rhyming 'sway' with 'decay' and ending by weeping over his domain, the young Byron casts himself in a role quite different from that of the Gothicized heroes of his later poetry. His Manfred, like Walpole's, is a Satanic overreacher, whose theurgic art seeks to control the world of the spirits and who has committed unnamed crimes against his sister and apparently somehow caused her death, just as Walpole's Manfred seeks a quasi-incestuous marriage with his dead son's bride, and accidentally kills his own daughter. The latter's castle is central to his exercise of authority and control. Its proud battlements echo his own arrogance, and it becomes the engine of his will to power, as he imprisons one character after another in its voluminous recesses. In a manner akin to Greek tragedy, every act of power on Manfred's part – divorcing his wife to marry his dead son's bride, imprisoning Theodore as responsible for his son's death – leads only to his undoing.

Yet here in this early poem, Byron takes the stance and particular discourse of what might be called the 'female' Gothic of Radcliffe, rather than the male of Walpole and Matthew Lewis, in which the central (usually female) protagonist is the virtuous object of the villain's tyranny and who escapes incarceration in his castle to be revealed, eventually, as its true heir. Like Radcliffe's Adeline in *The Romance of the Forest* or Emily St Aubert in *The Mysteries of Udolpho*, Byron is the true heir of a great house that is already ruined and under the sway of time's ravages. The emphasis on the usurpation of Newstead by the Puritans allies the young Byron with the original medieval inhabitants as equally wronged and disinherited. The narrator's stance and tone imitates the pensive melancholy of the Gothic heroine, who stops to drop a tear over the rook-haunted ruined arch or empty cloister. Melancholy is the shared moral discourse of the society of the virtuous in Radcliffe's fiction and is carefully differentiated from the dominatory attitude of the villain, who can never admire or mourn over a landscape but must always seek to possess it. Byron necessarily takes a Radcliffean perspective in relation to Newstead because it had become somewhat uninhabitable as well as too expensive to live in. He rented it out as a hunting lodge, while living with his widowed mother in an Anglican version of Radcliffe's *Emile*-influenced, Protestant community of virtue: the minster-dominated town of Southwell. But his language imitates Radcliffe in its 'pensive shades', 'pious voices' and praise for the house as defender of 'innocence from stern oppression' and lack of 'splendid vices'.[4] It is well known that Byron read Gothic fiction voraciously, and in *Childe Harold* IV attributes his love of Venice to 'Otway, Radcliffe, Schiller, Shakespeare's art' (18), all of which he claims to have known in boyhood.[5]

So although Byron's aristocratic radicalism and presentation of transgressive hero overreachers would most naturally ally him with Walpole's and Matthew Lewis's Whiggish and 'masculine' Gothic, he also acknowledges some Radcliffean influence (equally radical, if more middle class, since Radcliffe was raised in the liberal circle of Thomas Bentley and was enough of a Whig to visit the monument to the Glorious Revolution on her tour of the Lake District).[6]

Byron's use of Radcliffean Gothic is clearly shown in his unfinished epic, *Don Juan*, where the English scenes occur at a fictionalized Newstead Abbey and involve two ghost scenes, one of which ends with the ghost all too evidently explained. It is a characteristic of the Gothic fiction of Byron's friend, Matthew Lewis, and of Walpole himself that, although they often burlesque the very effects of terror they seek to evoke, so that the line between serious and parodic Gothic is difficult to draw, they nonetheless employ the supernatural as a mode of revelation and retribution. In *The Castle of Otranto*, Conrad is killed by a ghostly and yet material gigantic helmet, while other supernatural weapons suddenly appear and a portrait comes to life in order to seek vengeance. In Lewis's *The Monk*, demons are raised, and the seductive Matilda, who claimed to have donned a male disguise as a novice to be near Ambrosio, is revealed to have been an agent of Satan. *The Monk* ends with the devil carrying Ambrosio off to meet a violent death and eternal punishment. In the subplot, Agnes dresses as a ghostly nun, in order to elope with Raymond, but when he takes her away he finds an actual phantom of a nun has taken her place and claims him for her bridegroom.

Radcliffe and her imitators take a quite different attitude to the supernatural. As a devout Christian, Radcliffe does not seek to deny the existence of the afterlife and the possibility of apparitions. In an early novel, *A Sicilian Romance* (1790), she gives the following speech to the worthy governess of the Mazzini children:

> 'My children', said she, 'I will not attempt to persuade you that the existence of spirits is impossible. Who shall say that any thing is impossible to God? We know that he has made us, who are embodied spirits; he, therefore, can make disembodied spirits. If we cannot understand how such spirits exist, we should consider the limited powers of our minds, and that we cannot understand many things which are indisputably true.'[7]

Although the cautious Madame de Menon is reluctant to say that ghosts have actually appeared, she entertains their possibility, which is the position of all Radcliffe's heroines. Julia and her brother in *A Sicilian Romance* are haunted by strange groaning sounds coming from the ruinous part of their palace; Adeline in *The Romance of the Forest* similarly hears unexplained voices and has visions of a dying man and his corpse lying in its coffin, which she believes to be supernatural. Emily St Aubert is beset with unexplained voices and something possibly supernatural behind a black veil at the Castle of Udolpho; while the hero of *The Italian*, Vivaldi, continually encounters a spectral monk. The heroine of this last novel, Ellena Rosalba, is less prone to 'superstition' than her lover, but equally open to the supernatural.

In each of these examples of haunting, however, a natural explanation is eventually offered, except in the case of Adeline, where the dream state of her experience renders it already 'natural', if somewhat inexplicable, in its accurate prophecy of the discovery of her father's murdered body later in the novel. Critics have offered various explanations for Radcliffe's strategy, of which the most usual is that she was too much a woman of the Enlightenment to do more than dally with non-natural causes for phenomena. For others, the supernatural elements open up the unconscious, so that fears and desires that the conscious mind cannot acknowledge may be entertained. In *Ann Radcliffe: The Great Enchantress*, Robert Miles combines both explanations and adds to them the suggestion that the frequent false supernatural trails on which Radcliffe sends her readers inaugurates a new hermeneutics of reading, in which the meaning resides in the gaps that the reader must interpret for him or herself, with these dissonances often being signalled by unexplained or inexpressible phenomena.[8]

While it is true that Radcliffe's heroines do have to learn to detect and protect themselves against real physical threats to their persons, and the mistaking of natural for supernatural opponents is part of the educative process of her fiction, there is much more to the explained supernatural. Otherwise, why would she allow so much rein to these mistaken impressions? In *The Mysteries of Udolpho*, the title is accurate in that the novel's whole narrative drive is by means of a series of unexplained sights and sounds, of which the most celebrated is the mystery of what is behind the black veil in the picture chamber at the castle. When Emily first lifts the veil and looks within, all the reader is told is that 'what it had concealed is no picture', before Emily falls senseless to the floor, having passed rapidly through the aesthetic cycle of response from sublime terror to dampening horror.[9] It is no wonder that this scene so fascinated Jane Austen's Catherine Morland and Isabella Thorpe in *Northanger Abbey*, causing the latter to exclaim: "'Oh! I would not tell you what is behind the black veil for the world! Are you not wild to know?'" Catherine's answer is equivocal: "'Oh! Yes, quite; what can it be? – But do not tell me. I would not be told upon any account.'"[10] This interchange is instructive in terms of the effect of the postponement of the explanation for the mystery. Not until very late in the novel is the explanation casually revealed: Emily saw an emaciated skeleton crawling with worms, which she had taken (as did her faithful reader, Catherine Morland) for the skeleton of Signora Laurentini, murdered by Montoni. In the interim, the lack of explanation opens a space for the wildest possibilities to be entertained, whether natural or supernatural. Indeed, for Catherine Morland, the 'natural' explanation of a murdered corpse takes on a supernatural horror. Although the image proves to be a waxen *memento mori*, there is indeed a corpse behind another curtain in a recess of Udolpho, which Emily discovers and which again causes her to lose consciousness, as with her former discovery. And there are murders aplenty in the novel.

The effect of the lapse in explanation of these quasi-supernatural mysteries is not to engender Enlightenment rationalism in its readers, but rather to imbue the experience of the world of objects with a certain radiance. It is to offer something akin to the classic detective story of the early twentieth century. In that genre, a murder opens up a hermeneutics of suspicion, in which every character is found to have a motive or dark secret. The discovery of the actual murderer, while having a suitably cathartic effect in placing the guilt as it were on a scapegoat, who bears the sin of the little society infected, does not leave things as they were in primeval innocence. Rather, the non-murderers are granted forgiveness, but as part of a ritual in which they are revealed in their own guilt and propensity for evil actions and tendencies.[11] The Gothic novel is no less ethical in its concerns but links morality to epistemology: the heroine is to be educated in how to understand the nature of phenomena and also how to discern the relation between natural and supernatural. But just as the detective novel, as I have suggested, leaves all of its characters tainted yet forgiven, and with a deeper subjectivity, so the explained supernatural leaves all phenomena shadowed with the supernatural.

Although it is highly unlikely that Ann Radcliffe had read Kant, she is equally concerned with what he terms phenomena, the objects we apprehend, and noumena, those aspects of the thing-in-itself to which we have no access.[12] In her entertainment of the supernatural, she brings her heroine and reader up against the limits of human perception, but not quite in the same manner as Kant, for whom the inaccessibility of the noumena collapses the act of perception, so that all experience is confined within the mind. The novel would then become, as Terry Castle has indeed argued for the Gothic, a purely phantasmal revival of images in the brain.[13] If Radcliffe were to leave her heroines with the ghosts unexplained, they could be accused of imagining their fears, and the critique of power relations would thereby be lessened. In explaining the supernatural, Radcliffe confirms the reality of the heroine's fears: she really was the focus of murderous or seductive plotting, and Udolpho is verified as a massive instrument of oppression and usurpation. The various unexplained effects, then, were not mistakes so much as genuine aporias, in which the heroine is brought up against the limits of thought itself. Categories of dead/alive, natural/supernatural and natural/manufactured are brought together in all their impossibility, so that the heroine's fainting fits have a truly educative value.

Radcliffe was an appreciative reader of Schiller, and her explained supernatural is based on his fragmentary novel, *The Ghost-Seer*, which was translated into English in 1795.[14] A mysterious Armenian perplexes a superstitious Bohemian prince through a series of mysterious appearances, including the raising of the ghost of his dead friend. Although this last feat is uncovered as an imposture by means of complicated magic-lantern effects, the Armenian himself – an agent of the Inquisition – is not so easily explained in his supernatural ability to appear and disappear at will and to be invulnerable to bullets. Although the narrators believe that the various mysteries are all natural in origin and the plot of agents of the Catholic Church seeking a convert, as the text stands – it is still fragmentary and inconclusive – no full explanation is offered. Indeed, the unmasking of the sorcerer's impostures in precise detail only renders more mysterious the aims and ontological status of the mysterious Armenian. His quasi-supernatural quality does not preclude his office as an agent of the Inquisition and thus annul the radicalism of the story as critique, any more than the mysteries of Udolpho work to support rather than question the tyrannical behaviour of the villainous Montoni.

Radcliffe used *The Ghost-Seer* to structure her last published novel, *The Italian* (1797), in which the story moves from Venice to Naples, and the prince is a young count, Vivaldi, who is haunted by supernatural terrors through the agency of a mysterious monk (a source, perhaps, for the character and final scenes of Byron's *Giaour*), who has the power, like the Armenian, to appear and disappear at will. The monk acts in complicity with Vivaldi's mother to gain control over him and prevent his marriage to the poor Ellena. She, by contrast, is not subject to fears of the supernatural, although she is no materialist either. In her isolation she finds a relation to God through the sublime and uplifting effects of nature. As she reflects from her cell in an Appenine convent:

> Here, the objects seem to impart somewhat of their own force, their own sublimity to the soul. It is scarcely possible to yield to the pressure of misfortune while we walk as with the Deity, amidst His most stupendous works.[15]

Whereas the crafty monk creates sinister voices to mislead Vivaldi by concealing his own participation in their production, Ellena finds the objects of nature true and open mediations of the Divine. Indeed, walking with the Deity discloses the sublimity of nature and allies woman and the phenomenal world, with the noumenal (albeit conceived of as the Transcendent and thus ultimately unknowable) as their point of union.

Paradoxically, it is the 'male' Gothic protagonist, whose will-to-power is Sadean in its desire to penetrate and possess the phenomenal, who ends up trapped within the physical at the very point he seeks to reach beyond it, like Walpole's Conrad, who dies as the grotesquely gigantic helmet traps him inside. The Radcliffean 'female' Gothic heroine does not see the material as a blockage to thought but rather as its enabler, and she is thus able to escape the physical as blockage (in the form of the castle that entraps her) to enjoy it as true mediation of the divine, not as 'natural' so much as a Divine art: 'His most stupendous works.'

It is with this sense of the epistemological underpinnings of the Gothic that Byron's imitation of a Gothic haunting in *Don Juan* is concerned. Despite his friendship with Shelley, Byron was not at all an idealist. The flirtation with Bishop Berkeley at the beginning of Canto XI of *Don Juan* – 'What a sublime discovery 'twas to make the / Universe universal Egotism!' – is quickly interrupted by the realities of indigestion and a metaphorical stubbing of the toe on the particularities of a world of other people and independent objects.[16] If Juan is anything, he is a catalyst for revealing the complexity and vitality of existence apart from the self: in fact, his defining characteristic is one of happy passivity and a kind of negative capability that makes him all things to all men and, particularly, all women. Even Byron's Gothic overreachers are less omnivorous in their mental empire than those of Walpole, Lewis or Maturin. The Giaour, for example, is not only viewed from without by a variety of witnesses but is described as 'a noble soul' and has the acceptance of a melancholic ruin: 'Each ivied arch – and pillar lone, / Pleads haughtily for glories gone!' (*The Giaour*, 881–82). Not only does the Giaour accept his fate but, despite the criticism of organized religion in the poem, we learn at the end that he makes his confession to the priest, who 'shrived him on his dying day' (1332). The Giaour's thoughts revolve round the fate of the slave Leila, who was tied up in a sack and drowned by her master in vengeance for her affair with the Giaour. The Muslim curse put upon her lover for his own killing of Leila's murderer casts him as a future vampire and damns him to 'wander round lost Eblis' throne; / And fire unquench'd, unquenchable – / Around – within – thy heart shall dwell' (750–52), in imitation of William Beckford's oriental Gothic romance, *Vathek*, in which the Caliph's murderous greed and contract with a demonic Giaour bring this fate upon him.[17] Nevertheless, there is no suggestion in the text that this will actually be the fate of Byron's Giaour in the afterlife, although he suffers mental torments of guilt in his present existence. He is, however, primarily concerned for the salvation of his beloved. He argues, against Islamic tradition (as he understands it) that she must have a soul; he similarly discourses on the relation of heavenly and earthly love and his guilt for being the cause of Leila's death. With the poem's opening disquisition on Greece as a beautiful woman who may be a corpse, it is as full as any Radcliffe novel of contradictory ideas put into collision one with another: life and death, heaven and hell, soul and body, Islam and Christianity. The openness of the ending is a way of holding these binaries together and allowing the noumenal some articulation in the manner of Radcliffe.

Don Juan is based on a Spanish play that was later translated by Shadwell as *The Libertine* and performed as a puppet show and pantomime, in which last form Byron encountered it.[18] Its dénouement, as in Mozart's operatic version, occurs when Don Juan invites his murder victim – the governor or Commendatore – to dinner. The statue of the victim comes to life and drags Don Juan down to hell. A highly dramatic scene, it involves a whole series of opposed categories to be brought into collision: object/subject in the marble statue that takes on agency and volition, victim/aggressor, natural dinner invitation and supernatural 'invitation' to judgment. In Shadwell, the Don deliberately plays with these mixed categories: 'Here, Governour, your health! Friends, put it about! Here's excellent meat, taste of this ragout.'[19] My quotation is taken from Coleridge's discussion of the play in Chapter 23 of his *Biographia Literaria*, in which he uses the Don Juan play as a foil to Charles Maturin's Gothic *Bertram*, which Byron preferred over his own *Osorio (Remorse)* for performance at Drury Lane, having originally encouraged Coleridge to turn his talents to the revival of the blank-verse drama.[20] Although Coleridge's analysis has often been dismissed as prejudiced, it is philosophically interesting and probably the seed of Byron's own *Don Juan* and *Manfred*. Coleridge quotes from the banquet scene in order to show Don Juan's (John's) attitude to the supernatural, which is one of utter defiance:

> GHOST.—Monster! behold these wounds!
> D. JOHN.—I do! They were well meant, and well performed, I
>   see.[21]

After Don John has witnessed his friends being swallowed up, he is still unfazed:

> D. JOHN.—Think not to fright me, foolish ghost; I'll break your
>   marble body in pieces and pull down your horse.
>   (Thunder and lightning—chorus of devils, etc.)
> D. JOHN.—These things I see with wonder, but no fear.
> Were all the elements to be confounded,
> And shuffled all into their former chaos;
> Were seas of sulphur flaming round about me,
> And all mankind roaring within those fires,
> I could not fear, or feel the least remorse.[22]

Coleridge commends the portrayal of Don John as Promethean and specifically an example of 'the doctrine of a godless nature, as the sole ground and efficient cause not only of all things, events and appearances, but likewise of our thoughts, sensations, impulses and actions'.[23] Don John is the example of a pure materialism, a character who combines an unreal monstrousness in his single-minded pursuit of his own desires with the power of being loved by a woman for himself, no matter how badly he behaves. The only law Don John obeys is that of his own nature. Coleridge quotes from his own translation of Schiller's *Wallenstein* – 'Self-contradiction is the only wrong' – to delineate the 'self-subsistence' of the hero who unites 'great intellectual lordship with guilt', a combination, he argues, that has never been adequately represented.[24]

In his dramatic poem *Manfred*, written during 1817 – a year after Coleridge's *Biographia Literaria* – Byron seems to be taking up the challenge of presenting such a Promethean figure who combines those two qualities and seeks to live a life of utter self-consistency in his theurgic control of the lower spirits and defiance even of Arimanes – the Manichean evil principle himself – whom he forces to his will. Manfred appears to defy the supernatural, even as Don John does, but he is undone by his own desires, as his 'star', spiritual genius or double prophesies. Calling up Astarte from her tomb, he seeks forgiveness and a word of love from her, rather as Aeneas does from Dido in Virgil's epic. As in *The Giaour*, the ghost of the woman mediates between death and life, and opens up a space for possible forgiveness in her ambiguous replies to his requests:

> PHAN.   Manfred! To-morrow ends thine earthly ills.
>   Farewell!
> MAN.   Yet one word more – am I forgiven?

PHAN.   Farewell!
MAN.   Say, shall we meet again?
PHAN.   Farewell! (*Manfred*, II, iv, 152–54)

Her first speech might mean the ending of earthly ills but the beginning of unearthly ones, or it might mean the complete cessation of his suffering. Similarly, 'Farewell' might imply that Manfred will never see Astarte again, as in the triple repeat of Eurydice's name as she falls back into Hades in Ovid's version of the myth of Orpheus, in which he attempts to retrieve his wife from the underworld. Alternatively, it might be a literal 'fare well' blessing to her lover. When his own end comes, Manfred's 'Old man! 'tis not so difficult to die' evokes Don John's defiance, but it is prefaced by Manfred asking the abbot to take his hand, and wishing him also '[f]are thee well' in a more positive manner (III, iv, 148–51).

So in *Manfred*, the Don Juan overreacher, who sought to go beyond the confines of his own mortality, ends in a far less Promethean manner than the pantomime. Each of his Gothic anti-hero moments is arrested either by the phantom of his beloved or human physical contact in the form of the chamois hunter, whose arms prevent his suicide, or the abbot who holds his hand in his final death-throes. In both *Manfred* and *The Giaour*, the gnostic desire to break beyond the limits of the human and material and the Don Juan idealist self-subsistence and self-causation is questioned by the mediation of the ghostly woman and by human contact. The Don John/Juan removal to hell leaves its protagonist in eternal opposition to the supernatural, as in the 'male' Gothic, whereas the ambiguous and open endings of *Manfred* and *The Giaour* link their characters to both human and spiritual realities more in the manner of the 'female' Gothic. In that sense, these poems are true to Dante's original conception of Manfred, the godless Ghibelline leader whom the pilgrim encounters in ante-purgatory in *Purgatorio* III, who made his peace with God on the point of death and asserts that despite excommunication: 'none is so lost that the Eternal Love cannot return, so long as hope keeps aught of green'.[25]

Coleridge's description of Don Juan as possessing 'rank, fortune, wit, talent, acquired knowledge and liberal accomplishments, with beauty of person, vigorous health, and constitutional hardihood' seems to have gone straight into Byron's protagonist of his great epic, apart from the wit, most of which *Don Juan* reserves for its narrator.[26] Far different, however, is the willpower of Don Juan in Byron's poem. He really seems to lack this overreacher ambition, and instead seems more of an upper-class Joseph Andrews, who is borne along by events and the will of women: he is the seduced rather than the seducer, and thus his encounter with the supernatural must be far different from that of the traditional Don Juan figure. Any audience of the early nineteenth century, who would have been familiar with the legend of Don Juan, would have expected a great confrontation with a ghostly accuser, so Byron's Radcliffean presentation would have been doubly surprising.

Byron sets Cantos XIII to XVII in a Gothic abbey that is closely, indeed, exactly modelled on Newstead Abbey itself, and brings the ever youthful Juan to it as a sort of avatar of himself in the *Hours of Idleness* period, when he was trying out a range of poetic and social poses, among which, as we have already seen, was that of the true heir of the Gothic mansion. The Gothic elements of the house are at once announced in the Christian name of its chatelaine, Lady Adeline Amundeville, which is taken from Radcliffe's *Romance of the Forest*, in which Adeline finds refuge in a ruined abbey. Byron pulls out all the stops of the Whig genre, including a Druid oak, which stood 'like Caractacus', and foresters, standing for the Anglo-Saxon liberties of the British constitution. As Bernard Beatty points out: 'the Abbey is from the outset a substantial force in its own right which cannot be held within the narrator's controlling fluency'.[27] Whereas earlier settings from the harem to battlefield had been precisely rendered but passive settings that the hero moved through with ease, here the Abbey is truly Gothic in that it is both a protagonist in its own right and a building that is spatially and temporally active. Whereas the redouts of the 'male' Gothic overreacher are entrapping fortresses and engines of control, with the Radcliffean heroine finding herself incarcerated within such structures, the 'female' Gothic includes another sort of Gothic structure that has a positive valence. This second Gothic structure is usually ruined, so that it reveals the action of time upon it and it accepts its ruinous condition. It is the engenderer of reverence and awe in the virtuous protagonists of Radcliffean Gothic, allowing them to link nature and culture, past and present, and by the gaps in its walls, allow the noumenal some presence.

Byron achieves all these effects in his presentation of the Abbey in Canto XIII:

> A mighty window, hollow in the centre,
>   Shorn of its glass of thousand colourings,
> Through which the deepen'd glories once could enter,
>   Streaming from off the sun like seraph's wings,
> Now yawns all desolate: now loud, now fainter,

The gale sweeps through its fretwork, and oft sings
The owl his anthem, where the silenced quire
Lie with their alleluias quench'd like fire.

But in the noontide if the Moon, and when
    The wind is winged from one point of heaven,
There moans a strange unearthly sound, which then
    Is musical – a dying accent driven
Through the huge Arch, which soars and sinks again.
    Some deem it but the distant echo given
Back to the Night wind by the waterfall,
And harmonized by the old choral wall:

Others, that some original shape, or form
    Shaped by decay perchance, hath given the power
(Though less than that of Memnon's statue, warm
    In Egypt's rays, to harp at a fixed hour)
To this grey ruin, with a voice to charm.
    Sad, but serene, it sweeps o'er tree or tower:
The cause I know not, nor can solve; but such
The fact: – I've heard it, – once perhaps too much.
        (*DJ*, XIII, 62–64)

This is but a small section of the long description of the Abbey, but
it illustrates the Radcliffean approach very well in its emphasis on
the aperture – the hollowness in the arch where the glass has been
destroyed, which figures the action of time on culture and its overthrow
by nature, so that the wind howls through it and the owl takes over as
its tenant from the monks. The hollow arch also speaks of the building
as mediating between nature and culture, analogously to the mediation
of the light by the coloured glass formerly in its centre. This prepares
the way for further mediation in the next stanza, where the arch
becomes a sort of Aeolian harp, allowing a kind of æaetherial music that
orchestrates moon, waterfall and wind. The third stanza quoted above
gives another explanation, before moving abruptly into the present and
factual, with the narrator's declaration that he has heard the mysterious
sound 'once perhaps too much'.

   This is a shock in the narrative contract established with the reader
throughout the poem, which has always involved a deliberate and comic
distance from the events described. The narrator has knowledge of the
places and societies that he describes and a playful arbitrariness in
deploying his protagonist. Although the realism of his insider knowledge
of London society might seem to work against the fictionality of the

whole poem, the ironic distance serves to keep a certain balance. Here, however, all this is put at risk, as the narrator both describes his own house and then proceeds to insert himself into it, interrupting the flow of Gothicized description with the clipped monosyllables of his intervention, with the one two-syllabled word 'perhaps' only used to intensify the experience, not to question its veracity.

The narrator does not go on to explain what he heard on this occasion. The phrase 'too much' is his equivalent of Emily St Aubert's silence after raising the black veil. Her swoon on this occasion is a marker of excess of emotion and meaning in the same way that 'too much' is for Byron's narrator. Throughout the two cantos that separate this remark from the actual haunting scene, the narrator keeps the contradictions alive through metaphysical questioning, dark remarks about his own experience – 'For certain reasons, my belief is serious' (XV, 95) – and flippant asides: 'And now, that we may furnish with some matter all / Tastes, we are going to try the supernatural' (XV, 93). Even before Juan sees the ghostly friar, the reader is caught in a typically Gothic quandary about the reality of the supernatural.

The first haunting scene occurs in Canto XVI and is set up in Radcliffean rather than conventional 'male' Gothic style, with Juan's sighing over Aurora Raby and gazing at the moon. He feels 'pensive' and 'disposed / For contemplation', and his room '[l]et in the rippling sound of the lake's billow' (15), thus joining the natural to the social world. Like Emily St Aubert at Udolpho, he then wanders into the picture gallery and sees a ghost:

> It was no mouse, but lo! a monk arrayed
>   In cowl and beads and dusky garb, appeared,
> Now in the moonlight, and now lapsed in shade,
>   With steps that trod as heavy, yet unheard;
> His garments only a slight murmur made;
>   He moved as shadowy as the sisters weïrd,
> But slowly; and as he passed Juan by,
> Glanced, without pausing, on him a bright eye. (*DJ*, XVI, 21)

The monk is precisely observed and appears in both shade and moonlight, which betokens his reality, yet his steps are noiseless. Why his garments should make a sound and yet not his step is perplexing. He combines shadowiness with a bright eye. Mention of *Macbeth*'s weird sisters suggests a theatricality that conflicts with 'shadowy'. The next stanza sets out Juan's mixed feelings about the event and his reluctance to believe what he has seen, suspended between tradition and rationality in a truly post-Enlightenment hesitation, to which Tzvetan Todorov has appended the term the 'fantastic':

> In a world which is indeed our world, the one we know, a world without devils, sylphides, or vampires, there occurs an event which cannot be explained by the laws of this same familiar world. The person who experiences the event must opt for one of two possible solutions: either he is the victim of an illusion of the senses, of a product of the imagination – and laws of the world then remain what they are; or else the event has indeed taken place, it is an integral part of reality – but then this reality is controlled by laws unknown to us. [...]
>
> The fantastic occupies the duration of this uncertainty. Once we choose one answer or the other, we leave the fantastic for a neighbouring genre, the uncanny or the marvellous. The fantastic is that hesitation experienced by a person who knows only the laws of nature, confronting an apparently supernatural event.[28]

This is precisely Juan's situation: 'Doors there were many, through which, by the laws / Of physics, bodies whether short or tall / Might come or go; but Juan could not state / Through which the spectre seemed to evaporate' (XVI, 24). The Don Juan of the pantomime defies the supernatural statue; Byron's Don Juan is himself 'petrified' into stasis, as 'stands a statue' (XVI, 22; 23). He hesitates in an epistemological quandary, which is not helped by Lady Adeline and her husband claiming to have seen the same ghost and by the former singing a ballad in mock-medieval style about him.

The second haunting scene occurs at the end of Canto XVI and is prefaced with Byron's typical discussion of the relation of material and immaterial, body and soul, which ends with Juan having the courage to advance upon the spirit. At first he puts his arm through no spirit but touches an empty wall; however, on his second attempt, he puts his hand on 'a hard but glowing bust', the 'phantom of her frolic Grace – Fitz-Fulke' is revealed and the hesitation of the fantastic is resolved as the supernatural visitation is explained (XVI, 120–23).

And yet, as with Schiller's *Ghost-Seer* – which we know Byron had read[29] – all is not fully explained. The scene at breakfast following Juan's first encounter with the friar involved Fitz-Fulke staring hard at Juan as if surprised and calculating, which suggests that her own apparition was a response to take advantage of the ghost for erotic dalliance. Furthermore, when Juan and the Duchess come down to breakfast the next morning, they are not sleekly contented like lovers after a night of passion:

> Which best is to encounter – Ghost, or none,
>   'Twere difficult to say – but Juan looked
> As if he had combated with more than one,
>   Being wan and worn, with eyes that hardly brooked
> The light, that through the Gothic windows shone:
>   Her Grace, too, had a sort of air rebuked –
> Seemed pale and shivered, as if she had kept
> A vigil, or dreamt rather more than slept. (XVII, 14)

The poem ends there, due to Byron's own death, and we shall never know how it would have proceeded. What is clear, however, is that the explained supernatural was not being used by Byron to resolve the fantastic hesitation set up earlier by the ghost. We are not left with our noumena nicely disposed of. As with Schiller's Venetian tale, the human intervention presaged an even deeper mystery. Schiller had read Kant, and his tale may be left unfinished precisely in order to avoid entrapment by the self's inability to penetrate beyond its own perceptions, which a fully explained narrative would fall back upon. I have already suggested that the stories of Byron's Gothic overreachers tend to end in a similarly open and fragmentary fashion in order to avoid the fall back into philosophical idealism, but also to keep awake the possibility of the transcendent. Realism, even empiricism, however, requires some mediation between self and world, and these last cantos of *Don Juan* offer attempts at conceiving of the Gothic itself as a mediation by which the re-enchantment of the material may be achieved through the dramatization of loss and ruin. It is no accident that the statue of the Virgin Mary that survived the Reformation and is situated at the top of the Gothic arch at Newstead is described in Canto XIII: 'With her son in her blessed arms, look'd round [...] She made the earth below seem holy ground' (61). The modern mediatory figure who resembles her is Aurora Raby, an orphan and Gothic heroine in her Catholicism, which links past and present (just as her first name links day and night), and who with her sympathetic mode of being, sublime eyes and mournfulness for the crimes of others 'look'd as if she sat by Eden's door, / And grieved for those who could return no more' (XV, 45). In the Catholic prayer 'Salve Regina', Mary is addressed similarly: 'to thee do we cry, poor banished children of Eve'. Mary, as mediator of love, is the focus of stanzas 101–103 and 108 of Canto III, where twilight, the angelus and Dante's opening reference to both in *Purgatorio* VIII, 1–8 (which formed the opening to Gray's 'Elegy Written in a Country Churchyard') are all brought together to deepen and strengthen the love between Juan and Haidée.

In introducing this Mariological material, I am not claiming that Byron was a crypto-Catholic, although some of his contemporaries saw him tending in that direction, so much as suggesting that these mediatory women have a philosophical importance in the poem. It is a work that returns endlessly to questions of how we know anything and the nature of what we know, causing scholars like Terence Hoagwood to argue that Byron was a true sceptic in the classical sense.[30] This chapter has sought to show that his poetry is more concerned with the specifically post-Enlightenment problem of ascertaining the reality of our perceptions as well as of the transcendent: the natural is as hard to establish as the supernatural. Indeed, without the Divine in which to ground the contingent, things slip out of our conceptual grasp. So the problem for the guilt-ridden Manfred is theurgic: to reach the spiritual through the material. *Don Juan* is equally theurgic in sending its protagonist into the thick of society and various cultures to wrest meaning from them. He fails to do this throughout most of the poem because Don Juan remains untouched by what he undergoes: the ideal and the real are still completely separate. The use of Radcliffean Gothic, the fantastic and the explained supernatural all work together to reunite Juan with the world through fear, awe and stasis. The real – even the flesh of the voluptuous Duchess – is rendered deeper and more inexplicable through the opening of the supernatural as a possibility. The Virgin on the ruined arch and Aurora Raby mediate through their articulation of a lost history: like the Gothic Abbey itself, they speak of a displaced relation between faith and life. In the dramatization of that loss, the Gothic witnesses its importance and turns scepticism into a religious value. As *Don Juan*'s narrator puts it: 'He who doubts all things, nothing can deny' (XV, 88).

Notes

1 See Bernard Beatty, *Byron's 'Don Juan'*, especially pp. 137–211; Jerome McGann, Don Juan *in Context* (London: Croom Helm, 1976); and Terence Allan Hoagwood, *Byron's Dialectic: Skepticism and the Critique of Culture*.

2 Lady C[aroline] [Lamb], *Glenarvon* (London: Henry Colbourn, 1816) and John Polidori, *The Vampyre* (London: Henry Colbourn, 1819). Lord Grey de Ruthven was the name of the tenant of Newstead during Byron's school and college days, with whom he may have had a sexual relationship (see Fiona MacCarthy, *Byron: Life and Legend*, pp. 36–37). The Gothic plot thickens when one remembers that Sheridan Le Fanu's Gothic romance, *Uncle Silas* (1864), concerns the Ruthyn family, including the villain, Silas Ruthyn, who lives in a mouldering Gothic mansion in social isolation, because of his supposed murder of a friend and fellow

gambler, like Byron's grandfather at Newstead. The description of the portrait of
Silas as a child in Chapter 2 is reminiscent in its delicate and almost feminine
beauty combined with masculine resolution of descriptions of the young Byron
(Sheridan Le Fanu, *Uncle Silas: A Tale of Bartram-Haugh*, ed. W.J. McCormack
(Oxford: Oxford University Press, 1981), pp. 9–10).

3 On Newstead as a model for the Abbey of St Clair, see MacCarthy, *Byron: Life
and Legend*, p. 20. Radcliffe's source for the murderous and licentious Marquis de
Montalt in *The Romance of the Forest* might well have been Byron's grandfather,
the 'Wicked Lord' Byron, whose outrageous behaviour was a local legend. He was
believed to have murdered a friend and kinsman, William Chaworth (MacCarthy,
Byron: Life and Legend, pp. 16–17).

4 'Elegy on Newstead Abbey', pp. 4, 32, 24, 131.

5 Books III and IV of Byron's travelogue had the same value to a contemporary
audience as Radcliffe's novels, in that they allowed imaginative access to the
continent during a period when it was less easy to travel because of the Napoleonic
wars. The whole Venetian sequence in *Childe Harold* owes much to Radcliffe and
shares the 'fairy' language of *Mysteries of Udolpho*, vol. 2, Chapters 2 and 3.

6 Ann Radcliffe, *A Journey Made in the Summer of 1794, Through Holland and the
Western Frontier of Germany, With a Return Down the Rhine: To Which are Added
Observations During a Tour to the Lakes of Lancashire, and Westmoreland, and
Cumberland* (London: J. and G.G. Robinson, 1795), p. 389. On Radcliffe's politics,
see Robert Miles, *Ann Radcliffe: The Great Enchantress* (Manchester: Manchester
University Press, 1995).

7 Ann Radcliffe, *A Sicilian Romance*, ed. Alison Milbank (Oxford: Oxford University
Press, 1993), p. 36.

8 Robert Miles, *Ann Radcliffe: The Great Enchantress*, pp. 129–45.

9 Ann Radcliffe, *The Mysteries of Udolpho*, ed. Bonamy Dobrée, pp. 248–49.

10 Jane Austen, *Northanger Abbey*, ed. John Davie (Oxford: Oxford University Press,
1998), p. 23.

11 See W.H. Auden, 'The Guilty Vicarage', in *The Dyer's Hand and Other Essays*
(London: Faber, 1963).

12 Immanuel Kant, *Critique of Pure Reason*, trans. Norman Kemp Smith (London:
Macmillan, 1978), pp. 257–75.

13 Terry Castle, *The Female Thermometer: Eighteenth-Century Culture and the Invention
of the Uncanny* (New York, NY: Oxford University Press, 1995), p. 139.

14 *The Ghost-Seer; or, Apparitionist, an Interesting Fragment, Found Among the Papers
of Count O*****, From the German of Schiller*, trans. Daniel Boileau (London:
Vernor and Hood, 1795).

15 Ann Radcliffe, *The Italian: Or, The Confessional of the Black Penitents*, ed. Robert
Miles (Harmondsworth: Penguin, 2000), p. 75.

16 *DJ*, XI, 1–3.

17 William Beckford, *Vathek* in *Three Oriental Tales*, ed. Alan Richardson (Boston,
MA: Houghton Mifflin, 2002), p. 152.

18 [Charles Anthony Delpini], *Don Juan; Or, The Libertine Destroy'd: A Tragic
Pantomimical Entertainmen, in Two Acts: As Performed at the Theatres Royal,
Drury-Lane and Lyceum* (London: J. Roach, 1789).

19 Quoted in *Biographia Literaria*, vol. II, p. 189.

20 See *Byron: Life and Legend*, p. 248.

21 Coleridge, *Biographia Literaria*, vol. II, p. 190.

22 Ibid.

23 Ibid., p. 306.

24 Ibid., p. 307.

25 Dante Alighieri, *The Divine Comedy: Purgatorio*, trans. Charles S. Singleton, Bollingen Series LXXX (Princeton, NJ: Princeton University Press, 1973), *Purgatorio* III, 133–35, p. 31. On Byron's source for *Manfred* in Walpole, see Peter W. Graham, 'From the Alps to Otranto', in *Byron: A Poet for All Seasons*, Proceedings of the 25th Byron Conference and Tour, 1–8 September 1999, ed. Marios Byron Raizis (Messolonghi: Messolonghi Byron Society, 2000), pp. 171–77.

26 Coleridge, *Biographia Literaria*, p. 307.

27 Beatty, *Byron's 'Don Juan'*, p. 143.

28 Tzvetan Todorov, *The Fantastic: A Structuralist Approach to a Literary Mode*, trans. Richard Howard (Cleveland, OH: Case Western Reserve University Press, 1973), p. 25.

29 Letter to Murray, 2 April 1817 (*BLJ*, V, p. 203).

30 Hoagwood, *Byron's Dialectic: Skepticism and the Critique of Culture*, pp. 35–37, *passim*.

CHAPTER EIGHT

The Haunting of *Don Juan*

Peter W. Graham

'What is a ghost?' Stephen said with tingling energy. 'One who has faded into impalpability through death, through absence, through change of manners.'

(James Joyce, *Ulysses*)

The mighty dead return, but they return in our colors, and speaking in our voices, at least in part, at least in moments, moments that testify to our persistence, and not to their own.

(Harold Bloom, *The Anxiety of Influence*)

The past is never dead. It's not even past.

(William Faulkner, *Requiem for a Nun*)

The haunting of Don Juan, a spectral visit at the heart of the last episode in Byron's unfinished mock epic, has haunted me for a long time. I first encountered this ghost story, so Gothic and yet so rational, as a graduate student. The haunting made its way into my dissertation and, years later, into *'Don Juan' and Regency England*, where the last essay, 'Don Juan in England', leaves the charismatic seduced or seducer suspended in a Schlegelian hovering.[1] Byron also left the poem's protagonist hovering, wandering between two worlds and tempted by three women, one of whom has just impersonated the spectral Black Friar and paid him a midnight call. Writing that chapter, I followed the Byronic narrator's injunction and considered Don Juan's first encounter with the Black Friar an actual haunting of some sort. But I could never totally exorcize the other possibility – that both visits might be instances of the fictively material impersonating the immaterial – an enactment of the multi-layered Platonism that it amuses Byron to represent elsewhere in his poem, for instance towards the end of Canto II, as the narrator speaks of being at a masquerade with Philosophy, 'masqued then as a fair Venetian', and his partner, a palpable and particular woman, simultaneously incarnates the abstraction and disguises herself as the muse imagined to embody it (II, 209–11). In the years that followed, I've been revisited, at midnight moments and others, by the shape-shifting practical and critical problems the Black Friar poses. Writing the ensuing essay has given me occasion to look very closely at the Black Friar's visit and its immediate contexts – not so much to lay to rest a ghost whose visits have never been unwelcome but rather to see and say how Byron, brilliantly successful at crafting an ambiguous narrative, can tease readers from beyond the grave.

*

The archetypal Don Juan tale, appropriated and renovated by Byron, can be considered a ghost story in various ways. The protagonist, Don Juan, is himself a particular embodiment of a revenant more closely related to Harold Bloom's idea of a ghost than to Stephen Dedalus's. Persistent rather than impalpable and vibrant rather than faded, Don Juan keeps coming back in many and diverse literary and subliterary guises, always coloured by the assumptions and preoccupations of the particular cultures and sensibilities reviving him but invariably trailing clouds of the archetypal hue. Among the ancestral revenants most immediately relevant to Byron's title character are Mozart's Don Giovanni and the protagonists of the Don Juan pantomimes and extravaganzas that held the London stage post-Mozart and pre-Byron. When the spectacular climax of Mozart's version and many others shows the scoffing, worldly Don being dragged down to hell, the immediate crime for which he is being punished is not seduction and abandonment. Rather, he has failed to honour the dead. The agent of his retribution is not a woman scorned but the spirit-animated statue of the commandant he's killed. The sceptical, worldly Don has mockingly disrespected a memorial effigy and thereby implied that he doesn't believe in ghosts or – at least doesn't fear them.

Part of this revenant tradition, Byron's *Don Juan* is itself a poem haunted in several other senses. Spectres of Byron's personal past and cultural heritage haunt the poem as half-real, unstable blends of selective and associative memory, imagination, disarming candour, figure-cutting, allusion, illusion and other equally protean qualities. In a chronotopic form whereby different times saturate place, the spectral past pervades the English Cantos in particular. Norman Abbey – Don Juan's final destination in the unfinished poem as we have it – is said to be haunted by the spectral Black Friar, a dispossessed, otherworldly watcher of the Abbey's successive generations of worldly incumbents. As Byron contrives things, the reality or unreality, ghostliness or physicality of the Black Friar remains tantalizingly up for grabs – or indeed, as I aim to argue, constantly shifting. The spectral Friar may actually haunt the halls of the Abbey. He may also be conjured up in the individual imaginations of the Norman Abbey house-party guests by their hostess's strategically deployed ballad, 'Beware! beware! of the Black Friar'. He is certainly impersonated or incarnated by the Duchess of Fitz-Fulke, a shrewdly mundane erotic opportunist. This chapter will look closely at the Norman Abbey episode and the mutable spectrality of the Black Friar. Whether he's a ghostly presence, a ghostly costume, or both and yet neither, the Friar is an unbodied embodiment of Byron's undying fascination with his personal and cultural pasts – and, less historically but more philosophically, with the spirit-flesh amalgam that for him distinctively constitutes humanity. This liminal leitmotif is stated most succinctly in *Manfred* – 'half dust half deity, alike unfit / To sink or soar' (I, ii, 40–41) – but it also makes important appearances throughout *Don Juan* and several other Byronic texts.

*

When Byron does a mental Odysseus or Lambro or Beppo act and returns in company with his narrator and Juan to Newstead (alias Norman) Abbey, his *nostos* entails an unusually complicated sort of spectral haunting. The Norman Abbey episode, for the most part a country-house comedy of the sort that Thomas Love Peacock or Anthony Trollope might present in prose, progressively focuses in on an unworldly theme: the tale of a revenant – the ghostly Black Friar stalking the cloisters-turned-into-country-house that once belonged to his order. The Black Friar is merely Norman Abbey's most obvious returning phenomenon though. Byron also brings back, revised and improved through the retrospective lens of expatriate nostalgia, an improved version of his ancestral estate – Newstead as it would have been if its park had not been harvested by the Wicked Lord and if the house and its furnishings had been in much better repair. Himself a spectral presence haunting, by report and repute, both a house and a social circle now spectral to him, Byron conjures up the dead or altered people he knew during his Years of Fame. These lost people are themselves revenants in two further senses. Revised and remembered, these friends, enemies and acquaintances resemble characters encountered in *Don Juan*'s earlier cantos and, along with the protagonist, reconstitute patterns of experience already established within the poem. Furthermore, they are contingent English incarnations of transcendent truths of character and situation embodied in classical myth and elsewhere.

Byron's narrator suggests his awareness of this chronotopic blend of real experience and illusion, personal embodiment of universal form in stanzas 21–22 of Canto XIV, which Cecil Lang refers to as 'the richest lode in all *Don Juan*'.[2] These stanzas include the Latin tag '*Pars* parva *fui*', which hints that Byron himself took part in the resurrected and recorded past events.[3] Perhaps, we might speculate, Byron takes part once again by imaginatively donning the friar's black robes and walking the halls of memory. Perhaps the nostalgic author and former incumbent of Newstead himself could be that first spectral haunter of Norman Abbey – a presence that Bernard Beatty rightly sees as ultimately mysterious, though it later suggests the practical possibilities of impersonation to the erotic opportunist Fitz-Fulke.[4] Byron did not live for long under Newstead's roofs, nor was he a particularly responsible absentee lord of the manor. But the idea that he 'held the sway of Newstead' was important to him in adolescence – as his prefatory remarks to *Hours of Idleness* testify – and mentally travelling home in verse to the ancestral hall was an irresistible temptation, the last completed act of his sprawling poem's unfinished narrative. Throughout the English Cantos but particularly at Norman Abbey, Byron eloquently, if inadvertently, reveals himself in love with what passes and what endures – and with how he remembers what he's left behind.

The justly acclaimed *ubi sunt* stanzas of the English Cantos owe much of their power and pathos to the Byronic narrator's awareness that all's changed amongst the particular English gentlemen and ladies he invokes and remembers. A key to the passage's nostalgic effect is found in its first stanza:

> 'Where is the world', cries Young, 'at *eighty*? Where
> The world in which a man was born?' Alas!
> Where is the world of *eight* years past? '*Twas there* –
> I look for it – 'tis gone, a Globe of Glass!
> Cracked, shivered, vanished, scarcely gazed on, ere

> A silent change dissolves the glittering mass.
> Statesmen, chiefs, orators, queens, patriots, kings,
> And dandies, all are gone on the world's wings. (XI, 76)

In *Don Juan* and elsewhere, Byron's pyrotechnic allusiveness has resurrected many otherwise faded verbal ghosts that, coloured by his art, memorably haunt the literary landscape – a prime example being four forgettable lines beginning 'Go, little book, from this thy solitude!' that Byron liberated from Southey's *Lay of the Laureate* – today, we'd call this act 'sampling' – appropriated for the valedictory noises of *Don Juan*'s first canto, then blatantly announced as a crib and condemned as trash in the concluding couplet of the very stanza that guarantees the pilfered lines' poetic immortality: 'The first four rhymes are Southey's every line / For God's sake, reader! take them not for mine.' Canto XI's 'Globe of Glass' passage offers a contrasting kind of riff on revenance. It invokes and blends a trio of cultural ghosts – two of them from texts so familiar as perhaps to be better termed immortal or undead – and refreshes the spectral appearance by permuting and combining his allusive samplings and inextricably blending them with the 'repertory of fact' that runs through the English Cantos.

Byron's vanished 'Globe of Glass' passage, with its retrospective vision of '*eight* years past', verbally echoes Young's *Resignation* ('Where is the world at *eighty*?') and Shakespeare's *Hamlet*, Act I, Scene i ("'Tis here!' "'Tis here!' "'Tis gone!', the respective speeches of Barnardo, Marcellus and Horatio as the ghost of old Hamlet vanishes before their eyes), as McGann's commentary to the Oxford edition of *Don Juan* points out.[5] It also calls up Macbeth's final encounter with the three witches in Act IV, Scene i. Here, the last vision shown to Macbeth is a spectral parade: '*A show of eight* KINGS, *[the eighth] with a glass in his hand, and* BANQUO *last*.'[6] Unlike Byron's 'crack'd, shivered, vanished' globe that reflected a palpable past spectrally shadowing the nostalgic mind of a half-Scots, nonchalantly crowned king of 'foolscap subjects', the self-styled 'grand Napoleon of the realms of rhyme', the eighth king's globe offers a prophecy to an ambitiously worldly yet superstitious wholly Scots usurper – a character at least as haunted as Byron. Immaterial and thus unable to be shattered, this Shakespearean glass displays futurity's dynastic revenge on a monarch, self-made, like Byron and Shakespeare, who thought to take fate into his own hands – hands stained blood-red, rather than taking 'all colours – like the hands of dyers' as the *Don Juan* narrator has said a poet's hands do (III, 87) – and as Keats's remarks on 'negative capability' suggest that Shakespeare's hands and whole self had notably done. Whereas Byron's reflected and vanished notables – an enjambed parade of 'Statesmen, chiefs, orators, queens, patriots, kings, / And dandies' – is passively dispersed, scattered like windblown leaves 'on the world's wings', Banquo's crowned and sceptred descendants deliberately present themselves, the first eight spectrally embodied and many more visible in the glass at which their blood-bolter'd progenitor proprietarily points. The haunting-in-advance that shows childless Macbeth the ironic futility of his bloody ambition both contrasts Byron's *ubi sunt* image re-invoking the now-broken globe that reflected a recent yet irrevocably *past* past and parallels, in a half wistful and half triumphant way, the poet-peer's own partially dead-end fate. In realms of rhyme, Byron can re-member both the barony that, because his marriage had produced no son, will descend to another branch of the family and the unentailed ancestral property that he had at last successfully sold (to Colonel Wildman). Materially bereaved like Macbeth, Byron can haunt the lost dominion that haunts him precisely because he wields the pen as well as wearing the coronet. His power, like Shakespeare's and unlike Macbeth's, is imaginative rather than material.

*

The chronotopic haunting of *Don Juan* is a much mediated matter. The palpable past is recaptured impalpably, through the sort of recalled impression beautifully characterized by the vanished Globe of Glass, a verbal figuration of a memory of visual images that are themselves reflections of real but vanished beings displayed and presumably distorted on the curved surface of an imagined, no-longer-extant object. The poem's inextricable union of word or image with thing or fact emerges memorably in Canto IX, where the narrator claims to 'have forgotten what he meant to say' (IX, 36) but takes consolation that his 'lost advice' will one day come to light. The passage fancifully imagines a physical retrieval of what's been lost in terms of the naturalist Georges Cuvier's view of successive world-destroying catastrophes followed by re-creations on ever-impoverished scales:

> But let it [the 'lost advice'] go: – it will one day be found
>   With other relics of 'a former world',
> When this world shall be *former*, underground,
>   Thrown topsy-turvy, twisted, crisped, and curled,
> Baked, fried, or burnt, turned inside-out, or drowned,

> Like all the worlds before, which have been hurled
> First out of and then back again to Chaos,
> The Superstratum which will overlay us. (IX, 37)

The narrator goes on to imagine a future time when the remains of
George IV might be unearthed as a gigantic buried treasure by the 'new
worldlings of the then new East', much as during George's regency and
reign '[m]ammoths, and your winged Crocodiles' were being discovered
and marvelled at by fossil hunters. (The 'winged Crocodiles', coinci-
dentally, were mainly found at Lyme Regis, a site etymologically easy
to associate with the former Regent.) As the bones of plesiosaurs and
mammoths seemed titanic to the Georgians, so George IV's would to
the diminutive denizens of this imagined new creation, for, says Byron,
following Cuvier, '[m]en are but maggots of some huge Earth's burial'
(IX, 39). This digression on mortality might seem blatantly materialist,
yet it's neatly bracketed by the narrator's lament for his lost idea and
observation: 'But I am apt to grow too metaphysical' (IX, 41). This
coexistence of material and spiritual, physical and metaphysical, which
is broadly characteristic of Byron's way of thinking and of the haunting
of *Don Juan* the poem, is crucial to the haunting of Don Juan the
protagonist.

*

Don Juan's haunting dominates Canto XVI, but it begins at the close of
Canto XV and occupies the final composed stanza of the fragmentary
Canto XVII. Canto XV, like most of the others, closes with digressive
narratorial remarks that sound close to, if not indistinguishable from,
Byron's authorial voice. Having defended himself from potential charges
of self-contradiction – 'But if a writer should be quite consistent, /How
could he possibly show things existent?' (XV, 87) – semi-facetiously
affirmed his moderation in metaphysics and theology alike, and claimed
that his business is moral, 'to *dress* society, / And stuff with *sage* that
very verdant goose', the narrator asserts that he will give up argument
and instead 'that we may furnish with some matter all / Tastes, we are
going to try the supernatural' (XV, 93):

> Grim reader! Did you ever see a ghost?
>   No; but you have heard – I understand – be dumb!
> And don't regret the time you may have lost,
>   For you have got that pleasure still to come:
> And do not think I mean to sneer at most

> Of these things, or by ridicule benumb
> That source of the sublime and the mysterious: —
> For certain reasons, my belief is serious.
>
> Serious? You laugh: — you may, that will I not;
>   My smiles must be sincere or not at all.
> I say I do believe a haunted spot
>   Exists [...]. (XV, 95–96)

Beginning with the narrator's by now familiar jocoserious tone, the passage subtly modulates to something more sombre, at least to my ear — though as ensuing details suggest and has several times been made clear in earlier passages, such as the digression characterizing the 'Chinese nymph of tears, green tea' as his muse of pathos, the narrator asserts that his 'higher' states of mind and spirit are at least partly shaped by 'lower' somatic contingencies. Thus the seriousness concerning supernatural events may or may not be undercut by the suggestive details that he sings by night ('sometimes an owl, / And now and then a nightingale'), as old portraits scowl down from old walls and 'dying embers dwindle in the grate' — a Gothic scenario that makes the narrator, striking the same pose that will twice characterize Don Juan in the next canto, aware that he has 'sate up too late' (XV, 97) and is hence, subject to 'chilly midnight shudderings' (XV, 98). The canto leaves the Byronic narrator musing, much as Don Juan will shortly be doing, but far more philosophically:

> Between two worlds life hovers like a star,
>   'Twixt night and morn, upon the horizon's verge:
> How little do we know that which we are!
>   How less what we may be! The eternal surge
> Of time and tide rolls on, and bears afar
>   Our bubbles; as the old burst, new emerge,
> Lash'd from the foam of ages; while the graves
> Of Empires heave but like some passing waves. (XV, 99)

This meditation on liminality, mutability and the limits of epistemology in the 'half dust half deity' human condition implicitly encourages the reader to discard rigid preconceptions and cultivate an open-minded, self-doubting attitude that's receptive to all possibilities yet also sceptical about them. Such a mindset, at once critical and sympathetic, is ideal for enjoying and appraising the particular variants on the spectral themes of fading into impalpability and returning in the colours and voices of the haunted that will dominate Canto XVI.

But as this canto opens, the narrator overtly demands his reader's credulity, though his demands have the air of paradox about them. He claims that his Muse is 'the most sincere that ever dealt in fiction' (XVI, 2) and that his comprehensive 'tale is / "De rebus cunctis et quibûsdam aliis"' (of all things that are and of other things as well) (XVI, 3). Continuing in the superlative mode, he asserts that 'of all truths which she has told, the most / True is that which she is about to tell. / I said it was the story of a ghost – / What then? I only know it so befell' (XVI, 4). This pronouncement from a Byronic-sounding narrator who's very recently observed 'I do believe a haunted spot / Exists' and who's about to give his readers a fully observed twenty-four hours of Don Juan's life at Newstead, alias Norman Abbey, encourages us to think that Byron believed his ancestral home was haunted. And to be sure, he knew its cloisters had been haunted by himself, Hobhouse, and their set in monks' robes, though he may also have a supernatural haunting in mind. The narrator extends his demands for credulity while playfully undermining his case through its absolutist phrasing in such imperatives as 'therefore, mortals, cavil not at all; / Believe: – if 'tis improbable, you *must* / And if it is impossible, you *shall*: / 'Tis always best to take things upon trust' (XVI, 6). What to take on trust in the ensuing narrative? The testimony of this engaging but demonstrably slippery raconteur? Our own perceptions, so recently described as both limited and mutable? The facts and fictions dealt by that Muse called 'most sincere'?

*

The Canto XVI ghost story is a narratological hybrid. It draws upon at least two essentially different sets of conventions: those of the Gothic supernatural tale and those of the civilized comedy of manners. This is precisely the blend of conventions that Jane Austen exploits to fine parodic effect in *Northanger Abbey*, and like Austen, Byron enjoys evoking and then subverting Gothic *frissons*. But Don Juan's experiences of spectrality at an abbey are far less easy to dismiss than Catherine Morland's self- and fiction-generated Gothic horrors are. Juan's first spectral visitation, like Catherine's, occurs in his bedroom at the end of a full day's incident. Again as in Catherine's case, erotic arousal contributes to the day's eventfulness in creating unease. Having found the virginal Aurora Raby's eyes 'more bright' than his social mentor Lady Adeline would advise, he 'felt restless, and perplexed, and compromised' (XVI, 12) on retiring for the night, 'somewhat pensive, and disposed

/ For contemplation rather than his pillow' (XVI, 15) in the 'Gothic chamber' lit by moonlight, but also by the light of a bright lamp 'Upon his table or his toilet, – *which* / Of these is not exactly ascertained – / (I state this, for I am cautious to a pitch / Of nicety, where a fact is to be gained)' (XVI, 16), as the narrator insists with a comically smug self-conscious exactitude. His materialist precision also explains the inclusion of a motive, 'as the night was clear though cold', for why Juan throws open his door and, presumably for warming exercise, prowls the sombre portrait-lined gallery where, inspired by the pale smiles of dead beauties, he 'mused on mutability, / Or on his mistress – terms synonymous' (XVI, 19). As ripe for supernatural visitation as is the Gothic-primed Catherine Morland or, more profoundly, Byron's Cain and Goethe's Faust when Lucifer and Mephistopheles respectively appear to them, Juan 'heard, or thought so' what either he registers or the narrator characterizes as '[a] supernatural agent – or a mouse' (XVI, 20). Whether the blend of spiritual credulity and material common sense that poses the pair of alternatives is Juan's or the narrator's is not exactly certain, though we are looking into Juan's mind as the spectral episode begins. But wherever the alternatives arose, the next stanza directly discards one of them:

> It was no mouse, but lo! A monk, arrayed
>   In cowl and beads and dusky garb, appeared,
> Now in the moonlight, and now lapsed in shade,
>   With steps that trod as heavy, yet unheard;
> His garments only a slight murmur made;
>   He moved as shadowy as the sisters weïrd,
> But slowly; and as he passed Juan by,
> Glanced, without pausing, on him a bright eye. (XVI, 21)

Juan, 'petrified', remembers having heard 'a hint / Of such a spirit in these halls of old' and, though dismissive of ancient superstition, still wonders '*did* he see this? or was it a vapour?' (XVI, 22). Whichever it is and whatever its origin, the 'thing of air, / Or earth beneath, or heaven, or t'other place' (XVI, 23) passes him three times and then vanishes, its going as materially ambiguous as had been its coming: 'Doors were there many, through which, by the laws / Of physics, bodies whether short or tall / Might come or go; but Juan could not state / Through which the spectre seemed to evaporate' (XVI, 24). Again the narrator comically lays out all the material alternatives – bodies of all sizes can come or go through any of these doors – but avoids weighing in on whether the presence was embodied or not. Juan cannot say whether physics or metaphysics account for this experience, but it leaves him shaken on his return to a prosaically material environment, where the indeterminately placed lamp, now referred to as a 'taper / Burnt, and not *blue*', as should fire in a spirit's presence, according to Coleridge's *Christabel* and other Gothic narratives, and where there is an old newspaper to offer banal prose as a refuge and soporific: 'He read an article the king attacking, / And a long eulogy of "Patent Blacking"' (XVI, 26) and then a paragraph 'I think, about Horne Tooke, / Undrest, and rather slowly went to bed' (XVI, 27). Some of the detail reported here may seem irrelevant to some readers. The inclusion of 'I think' may attract the notice of others, who might question why a narrator inspired by this Muse who deals in fiction can't be sure whether Tooke or someone else was the subject of the third article. Is the reassuringly mundane detail meant to imply that this is not a realm for supernatural goings on, whatever an ingénue like Catherine Morland might believe about properties called abbeys? At this point, Byron's protagonist and his readers are equally perplexed.

Next morning, Juan wakes, wonders whether to report 'his visitant or vision' and risk 'being quizzed for superstition' (XVI, 28) and somewhat slights his customary toilet, though perhaps not terribly much. His hair, which during the spectral visitation he had felt 'twine like a knot of snakes around his face' (XVI, 23), by morning light falls in negligent curls over his forehead – the potential effect of indifference or of the art that conceals art – and 'His very neckcloth's Gordian knot was tied / Almost a hair's breadth too much on one side' (XVI, 29). Certain other elements of Juan's being less totally under his own control are more deranged. His mind is more 'distrait' than his neckcloth is, and this distraction makes his fellows at breakfast see that something's wrong – 'Adeline the first', whether because of her astute perceptiveness or her interest in Juan. Adeline's awareness is followed by a physical change echoing his:

> She looked, and saw him pale, and turned as pale
>   Herself; then hastily looked down, and muttered
> Something, but what's not stated in my tale.
>   Lord Henry said his muffin was ill buttered;
> The Duchess of Fitz-Fulke played with her veil,
>   And looked at Juan hard, but nothing uttered.
> Aurora Raby, with her large dark eyes,
> Surveyed him with a kind of calm surprise. (XVI, 31)

This stanza, showing us the reactions of Juan's host and the three women already characterized as very different and very differently interested in him, conforms to several patterns already seen at work within the episode. The passage is detailed, but selectively and ambiguously so. It blends generic conventions so as to scramble the signals that, unmixed, would indicate how readers should appraise the details. Lacking a single set of signals, are we to respond under the rubrics of Gothic to a spectral visitation or under those of a comedy of manners to a move in a country-house seduction? When Juan and Adeline both go pale, they somatically (and, in her case, sympathetically) register an emotional response and an indication of sensibility under stress. Are we to infer that these blanchings, reported without any explanation, indicate an erotic affinity between Juan and Adeline (earlier called 'the fair most fatal Juan ever met')? Or that the two are spiritual kindred in their sensitivity to supernatural phenomena – phenomena that Adeline, as mistress of the Abbey, may understand more fully than Juan does? Or both? And if so, in what proportions? Or is it something else altogether? The precisely rendered responses of the other two women and the self-absorbed non-response of the man are equally enigmatic. The lines contain evidence that clearly might suggest many things, but how poor mortal readers are to judge it is far less clear. Our credulous or sceptical response to Canto XVI's ghostly incident shapes our understanding of the Duchess's playing with her veil – an accessory that seems odd for morning wear and calls up a fanciful association with the idea of nuns, who in turn call up the idea of monks. Undoubtedly a distracting or distracted gesture, its motive might be that the Duchess knows something of why Juan is upset. That is how it would look to readers who take the previous night's haunting sceptically, as a country-house prank or amorous strategy. Or perhaps the distracted or distracting gesture arises from Fitz-Fulke's realizing that she can put Juan's haunting to her own use, an interpretation based on believing in the spectral nature of the haunting, as readers are meant to in a Gothic ghost tale. Aurora's 'calm surprise' and 'large, dark eyes' might signal that she has nothing to do with what's going on but at least some interest in Juan. But earlier in the canto those eyes were remembered by Juan as 'more bright / Than Adeline (such is advice) advised' (XVI, 12) – and this brightness of eye links Aurora, like Adeline and the Duchess, with the ghost, whose 'bright eye' is the only body part overtly mentioned as visible to the haunted Juan. Lord Henry's muffin complaint might signify only that he's a self-centred materialist who doesn't care about this matter – or it might, as a Catherine Morland would over-ingeniously hypothesize, be a cool bit of misleading intended to throw everyone off the scent of his complicity in a well-staged prank on Juan (whatever its motivation) or to hide his own anxiety about the visit of a spectre that appears 'when aught is to befall / That ancient line', as Adeline's ballad of the Black Friar puts it. But although we're given details of the reactions and are perhaps tempted to understand them in light of some things we have learned in the previous Norman Abbey cantos, what is largely uninflected is bound to remain ambiguous, like a Delphic prophecy. We can't confidently interpret without knowing what interpretive conventions to apply.

*

Whether we view the spectral visitation credulously or sceptically, according to the narrative conventions of the ghost story or those of the comedy of manners, the remainder of the canto's twenty-four hours of Norman Abbey life are chronicled by a moral satirist, the narrator, stuffing 'with *sage* that very verdant goose' society, as he had promised to do. But amidst the worldly comedy-of-manners details float vaporous remnants of the ghostly visit. Once Don Juan has acknowledged that while not exactly well he has no need of a physician, it's the earthbound Lord Henry who says: '"You look [...] as if you had had your rest / Broke in upon by the Black Friar of late"' (XVI, 35). This hypothesis makes Juan 'still more pallid' as he asks '"What Friar?"' in an attempt to seem 'sedate / Or careless' (XVI, 35), thereby allowing Henry, something of an impresario, briefly to mention his Abbey's resident ghost, of late 'not [...] oft perceived', and to set the stage for showcasing his wife's triple talents as poet, harpist and singer of the ballad 'Beware! beware of the Black Friar' – the song that along with 'The isles of Greece!' is the only lyric interruption of *Don Juan*'s *ottava rima* narrative. Performing her composition, Adeline is linked to the unnamed writer-performer of 'The isles of Greece!' and the Byronic narrator. They are the only three poets explicitly permitted to play Apollo's sacred instrument in an allusive work that mentions many poets, both good and bad. These three versatile improvisers are, as I have argued elsewhere, liars with lyres[7] – even if the narrator claims fidelity to a sincere Muse – and Lady Adeline brilliantly deploys her lyric performance to serve current needs. Having Adeline sing her ballad of the Black Friar allows Byron, the meta-contriver of the scene, to haunt his former home. The performance permits Adeline at once to gratify her husband's request, to amplify for her guests the ghost story evoked by Don Juan's pallor, and also perhaps to insinuate in a delicate way meant to be perceptible to Juan alone a certain disaffection from her husband and attraction towards him.

Whether or not Juan makes this inference, Adeline's song has drawn attention away from him and allowed him to 'rally / His spirits' and jest about the spectral visit – which causes the Duchess in her turn to wish for 'a still more detailed narration / Of this same mystic Friar's curious doings, / About the present family's deaths and wooings' (XVI, 53). The conversation becomes general, sceptics versus believers: 'But Juan, when cross-questioned on the vision, / Which some supposed (though he had not avowed it) / Had stirred him, answered in a way to cloud it' (XVI, 54). There's more than one strategic obfuscator present at the Norman Abbey breakfast table, but as in other matters it is easier to detect the phenomenon than to understand its cause.

After a day's country-house life gives way to an electioneering open-house dinner, mingling high-born house guests with local squires and their ladies, Don Juan is again confused and distrait, seeming unconscious 'of all passing there' (XVI, 87). Although we are reminded 'that he the night before had seen a ghost', we are not exactly told that he's haunted by the memory – only that

> what confused him more than smile or stare
> From all the 'squires and 'squiresses around,
> Who wondered at the abstraction of his air [...]
> Was, that he caught Aurora's eye on his,
> And something like a smile upon her cheek. (XVI, 91–92)

This pattern of cause and effect links Aurora with the Black Friar. Finding or remembering himself the object of either being's gaze makes Juan change colour like a hero of sensibility: pale at breakfast, he is 'carnation with vexation' at dinner. But Aurora, unlike Adeline at the breakfast recently past and Fitz-Fulke at the breakfast yet to come, does not display somatic sympathy with him:

> But what was bad, she did not blush in turn,
>   Nor seemed embarrassed – quite the contrary;
> Her aspect was as usual, still – *not* stern –
>   And she withdrew, but cast not down, her eye,
> Yet grew a little pale – with what? concern?
>   I know not; but her colour ne'er was high –
> Though sometimes faintly flushed [...]. (XVI, 94)

Byron and his narrator understand as much about the psychology of paling and colouring as the narrator of any Jane Austen novel – or indeed as Charles Darwin in his chapter on blushing in *The Expression of the Emotions in Man and Animals*. The narrator's ability to read a countenance is hardly in doubt; but even if it were, the coyly evasive nature of his professed failure to interpret Aurora's failure to blush is clearly evident because, only thirty stanzas earlier, he has concisely, if tentatively, assigned meaning to the facial colour of the pregnant 'country girl in a close cap / And scarlet cloak' (XVI, 61) awaiting an encounter with Lord Henry in his capacity as Justice of the Peace. Unlike Aurora in both social class and sexual experience, this girl resembles her in having bright black eyes and in not blushing at a moment when she might conventionally be expected to do so:

> The present culprit was extremely pale,
>   Pale as if painted so; her cheek being red
> By nature, as in higher dames less hale
>   'Tis white, at least when they just rise from bed.
> Perhaps she was ashamed of seeming frail,
>   Poor soul! for she was country born and bred,
> And knew no better in her immorality
> Than to wax white – for blushes are for quality. (XVI, 64)

This guilty girl, 'a poacher upon Nature's manor' (XVI, 62), is herself a kind of spectre for the narrator. Directly after speaking of her first appearance 'in a close cap / And scarlet cloak', he observes parenthetically and elliptically: '(I hate the sight to see, since – / Since – since – in youth, I had the sad mishap – / But luckily I have paid few parish fees since)' (XVI, 61). Who knows what colour, red or white, the narrator, if embodied, would have turned at this haunting by his past? Whichever, his description of the unblushing red-cloaked girl and of the memory she evokes in him deftly accomplishes at least three tasks. It provides a visual parallel for Aurora, who's pale as Juan colours. It indicates that the narrator, if he chooses, knows how to interpret complexions. And, I believe, it slyly raises the possibility that, as was the case in the ruling-class narrator's past, Lord Henry could be the male accomplice in the country girl's natural crime.

*

When Juan retires to his chamber at the end of this eventful day, he seems readier for a tryst with a woman than a visit from a ghost. Although the night is once again 'clear but cold', he is already unclothed and sitting in his room rather than walking the gallery:

> The night was as before: he was undrest,
>   Saving his night gown, which is an undress;

Completely 'sans coulotte', and without vest;
   In short, he could be hardly clothed with less;
But apprehensive of his spectral guest,
   He sate, with feelings awkward to express,
(By those who have not had such visitations)
Expectant of the ghost's fresh operations. (XVI, 111)

As was true the night before, there comes an ambiguous sound, here announced with mock-epic suspense that's a rhetorical ghost of the way Byron had introduced the cannon roar that breaks up the Duchess of Richmond's ball in *Childe Harold*, Canto III:

            – Hush! what's that?
I see – I see – Ah, no! –'tis not – yet 'tis
Ye powers! it is the – the – the – Pooh! The cat!
   The devil may take that stealthy pace of his!
So like a spiritual pit-a-pat,
   Or tiptoe of an amatory Miss [...] (XVI, 112)

Ghost or girl? Again the Gothic and the comedy of manners alternatives are balanced against one another. And again the apparent sound of footsteps, but this time 'It is the sable Friar as before' (XVI, 113). At present only narrator and reader have ocular proof, for Juan's on the other side of his closed door. Still, the 'awful footsteps' and a 'noise like to wet fingers drawn on glass' make Juan's ear understand what his eye cannot yet conclude. His blood curdles at the sounds suggesting a repeat performance. Juan is open-eyed and open-mouthed as the door opens with 'a most infernal creak', and although there's no indication whether the knob moves or not, and thus if the door opens naturally or supernaturally, readers might remember from the previous night's physics lesson that immaterial spectres have no need of material portals. Perhaps Juan also reaches this empirical conclusion, for 'His own internal ghost began to awaken / Within him' and to hint, very sensibly, 'that soul and body on the whole / Were odds against a disembodied soul' (XVI, 118).

A brave man of the sword-wielding class, Don Juan, 'his veins no longer cold, but heated / Resolved to thrust the mystery carte and tierce' (XVI, 119). He backs the Black Friar against a wall. The narrator's fencing terms simultaneously suggest the commandant's death in the traditional Don Juan legend, the sexual prowess associated with the Don Juan archetype and its current incarnation alike, and the penetrating disdain for supernatural intimidation also found in the archetypal legend, where it's crucial to Don Juan's demise. Juan thrusts forth his unarmed arm in this flesh-spirit encounter and at first hits only the wall, as if his stalker were immaterial. The ghost, however, betrays signs of material vitality: blue eyes glaring 'rather variably for stony death', 'a remarkably sweet breath', a fair curl, and 'a red lip, with two rows of pearls beneath'. The thrust of Juan's second arm, which traps the Friar in an embrace, 'pressed upon a hard but glowing bust, / Which beat as if there was a warm heart under' (XVI, 121–22). And the mystery resolves as the sable robe falls back to reveal 'In full voluptuous, but *not o'er*grown bulk, / The phantom of her frolic Grace – Fitz-Fulke!' (XVI, 123). Almost uniquely for *Don Juan*, the canto ends amidst the action rather than after easing into increasingly Byronic-sounding digressions: having pondered the natural and supernatural throughout the canto, readers are left – as is Don Juan – with the immanence of (Her) Grace. But that immanence is all that we know for sure: the fragmentary Canto XVII begins, as is the general case, with narratorial digression, and only in its last two completed stanzas does it return to the Duchess and Juan, who are the last two arrivals at next morning's breakfast. How had they passed their night? The narrator is, as he has heretofore been in the Black Friar episode, scrupulously descriptive but cryptically non-committal:

> Which best is to encounter – Ghost, or none,
>   'Twere difficult to say – but Juan looked
> As if he had combated with more than one,
>   Being wan and worn, with eyes that scarcely brooked
> The light, that through the Gothic windows shone:
>   Her Grace, too, had a sort of air rebuked –
> Seemed pale and shivered, as if she had kept
> A vigil, or dreamt rather more than slept. (XVII, 14)

The voice of practical common sense that prevails in the comedy of manners would argue that, narratological ambiguities aside, there is nothing erotically uncertain here. Given the proven nature of Don Juan and the reputed nature (and name) of the Duchess, there is only one way in which their nocturnal embrace could have ended, and what they show at breakfast are signs of their ardently sleepless night. But the voice of a more visionary sensibility – the sort of mind that believes in what's unseen and listens to what's unsaid – might wonder if perhaps the Black Friar, real the first night, came back again and haunted not one person but two. A mind bent toward burlesque could go in the opposite direction, towards even more comic carnality, and imagine a trio of Black Friars visiting Juan that night, unrobing and giving him a delightful yet fateful dilemma, a Gothic equivalent of the Judgment of Paris.

*

As the preceding pages have shown, I'm no ghost-buster – and no ghost-prover either. For me, anyway, close reading of the Black Friar episode raises more questions than it answers. What's certain, at the end, is that being denied certainty in Byron's spectral tale feels right. The *Don Juan* narrator asks his readers to take things on trust but also encourages them to use their minds. He encourages both willing suspension of disbelief and unremitting attention to nuances, details, and shifts of shape and tone. He wallows in nostalgia yet detaches himself from his class, kind, and ancestral place. He both exploits and subverts the power of the Don Juan legend. His artfully mixed signals are perhaps the best way of ensuring that we the readers remain haunted in varied and provocative ways.

Notes

1 Peter W. Graham, '*Don Juan' and Regency England* (Charlottesville, VA: University of Virginia Press, 1990), pp. 195–96.

2 Cecil Y. Lang, 'Narcissus Jilted: Byron, *Don Juan*, and the Biographical Imperative', in *Historical Studies and Literary Criticism*, ed. Jerome J. McGann (Madison, WI: University of Wisconsin Press, 1985), pp. 168–69.

3 'The first Latin phrases, cleverly adapted from the *Aeneid* (2.91, 6), "Haud ignara loquor" and "these are Nugae, quarum / Pars parva fui", can be rendered as "I know whereof I speak" and "these are trifling matters [which I myself saw and] in which I played a small part."' Ibid.

4 See Bernard Beatty, *Byron's 'Don Juan'*, pp. 87–92.

5 *CPW*, V, p. 751, n. 604.

6 Act IV, scene i.

7 '*Don Juan' and Regency England*, p. 140.

CHAPTER NINE

Being neither Here nor There: Byron and the Art of Flirtation

Corin Throsby

Byron was a flirt. Everyone from John Cam Hobhouse to Augusta Leigh commented on the poet's ability to ensnare would-be lovers with an artful combination of meaningful looks and studied aloofness. Augusta wrote to Lady Byron in 1816: 'he has been *flirting* [underlined twice] if not worse at the Theatre tonight – to say the truth I think flirting is ye *worst* for everybody talks and stares of course'.[1] Byron's sister recognizes the performance-making and attention-getting nature of the poet's dalliances, which were an integral part of Byron's public persona. Byron makes many references to his own flirtations in his letters, making it sound as if flirting was a natural and commonplace part of his life. He refers, for example, to 'the every-day flirtation of every-day people' that occurred between him and Lady Adelaide Forbes, a friend of Thomas Moore. Byron writes in his typically non-committal style that he may have 'very possibly married' Lady Adelaide were it not for an overwhelming sense of indifference. It is this indifference, he adds, that makes him 'so uncertain and apparently capricious. [...] nothing impresses me sufficiently to *fix*'.[2] According to Thomas Medwin, Byron believed, especially after his own failed marriage, that 'those are wisest who make no connexion to wife or mistress'.[3]

If we take Adam Phillips's definition of flirtation as 'the (consciously or unconsciously) calculated production of uncertainty', we might say that not only Byron's persona, but also his poetic style was inherently flirtatious.[4] The poet's disinclination to '*fix*' relationships in his personal life and flirtatiously keep things in a state of pre-matrimonial suspension was mirrored in his capricious poetic style. While Byron was involved in countless real-life flirtations – his non-committal stance apparently making him all the more desirable to potential admirers – his flirtatious poetry enticed his readers to purchase his work with ever-increasing fervour. Typically, Byron created a highly intimate poetic voice, which encourages his readers to feel that they are in a gripping personal dialogue with the author. In particular, he flirted with his reader through a process of disclosure and veiling or by revealing himself in his work and then denying that such an exposure occurred. This flirtatious 'apparitional' presence gave readers enough of a glimpse to excite their curiosity, but left enough gaps to enable them to interpret 'Byron' in whatever way they pleased.

Byron's poetry is filled with glances, glimpses, flickering presences, deferred endings, contradictions, ellipses and suggestive dashes. His self-defined 'mobility', fast-paced meter and well-documented habit of simultaneous 'scorching and drenching' all contribute to his flirtatious elusiveness.[5] Byron also flirted with his readers by including just enough biographical information in his poetry to encourage them to believe that his characters were thinly disguised versions of himself. As we can see from the following passage, the poet recognizes the allure of an outline and a suggestion of meaning, as opposed to explicitly detailed description:

> Would that I were a painter! to be grouping
>   All that a poet drags into detail!
> Oh that my words were colours! but their tints
> May serve perhaps as outlines or slight hints. (*DJ*, VI, 109)

Jerome McGann has described Byronic heroes as 'masked men', arguing that 'Byron was operating *en masque* from his first appearance in print.'[6] McGann suggests that the poet used a 'semi-private code' of 'autobiographical references', in which '"realities" are represented in the form of conscious pseudodisguise'.[7] According to McGann, Byron 'puts on the mask' of his heroes in order to 'tell certain truths about the life he has known and lived' and in doing so 'becomes the principal subject of his own fictions'.[8] The reader does not, however, 'stand at a remove from the action', but is instead 'forced to play a role'. Although he does not mention Wolfgang Iser's reader-response theory directly, McGann argues that the 'mystery' and 'abyss' of meaning in Byron's poetry (reminiscent of Iser's notion of a hermeneutic 'gap') acts as a 'temptation and threat, promise and invitation' to the reader to create meaning, so that 'every reader becomes like "Every Poet", his *own* Aristotle'.[9]

I would suggest that a better metaphor for Byron's 'mask' is the rather more ghostly, less tangible image of the veil.[10] A mask suggests an impenetrable barrier between interior and exterior, a solid demarcation between private and public, whereas a veil only partially conceals that which it covers and, in doing so, actually draws attention to whatever is underneath. If someone is wearing a mask, there is an emphasis on the character being portrayed – the mask itself – rather than the identity of the actor behind the mask. The blankness of the veil, however, together with the glimpses it offers of that which it conceals, arouses a curiosity as to the form beneath. In post-Saidian studies of the veil as a cultural and ideological signifier of Orientalist 'Otherness', much has been made of the veil's permeable nature – the fact that 'while it demarcates the line between public and private space, it does not multilaterally impede the flow of light, air or vision'.[11] Since it only partially obscures that which it covers, a veil allows eroticized glimpses of the private self. Georg Simmel discusses the veil in relation to flirtation, arguing that 'by ornamenting ourselves or part of ourselves, we conceal what is adorned' and through this very act of concealing the body, 'we draw attention to it and its attractions'.[12] These erotic connotations of the veil accord better with McGann's description of Byron's 'textual seductions and manipulations' than the less obviously titillating mask.[13]

Byron's poems are filled with images of half-concealment and partial-revelation. Many of the female characters in the Oriental tales wear both literal and metaphorical veils, and other characters continually play with both disguises and masks.[14] Much of this imagery is suggestively erotic. In *Don Juan*, Byron describes the petticoat as 'that chaste and goodly veil, / Which holds a treasure, like a Miser's hoard, / And more attracts by all it doth conceal' (XIV, 27). Here, Byron alludes to a fundamental characteristic of Simmelian flirtation – the idea that the 'refusal and the withdrawal of the self are fused with the phenomenon of drawing attention to the self'.[15] When something is partially concealed, it becomes all the more alluring. Byron continued to write about the fascination of the veil in *Marino Faliero* (1820):

> The veil which blackens o'er this blighted name
> And hides, or seems to hide, these lineaments,
> Shall draw more gazers than the thousand portraits
> Which glitter round it in their pictured trappings [...]. (V, i,
> 501–04)

The veil only 'seems to hide' that which is underneath. It is this semi-concealment that draws attention far more than something that brazenly 'glitters' for all to see.

Due in part to the increasing popularity of all things Oriental in the late eighteenth and early nineteenth centuries, veiled women are frequently to be found in the literature immediately preceding Byron's career. One of the most influential instances of veiling in the early Romantic period occurs in the opening scenes of Matthew Lewis's *The Monk* (1796), in which the two protagonists see a heavily veiled woman.[16] Critical reception of *The Monk* foreshadowed the conservative reaction to Byron's poetry. Coleridge's review of the novel, for example, is brimming with scandalized outrage that British female readers should be exposed to such erotically charged, flirtatious material: 'Many of the narratives can only tend to excite ideas the worst calculated for a female breast.'[17] The erotic potential of the semi-veiled 'Other' is in part the basis of Coleridge's disgust, as he describes, with almost lasciviously detailed abhorrence, the 'Corinthian harlot, clad from head to foot in the transparent thinness of the Coan vest'.[18] The use of veiling in the opening scene of *The Monk* epitomizes the idea of flirtatious semi-concealment:

> The voice came from a female, the delicacy and elegance of whose figure inspired the Youths with the most lively curiosity to view the face to which it belonged. This satisfaction was denied to them. Her features were hidden by a thick veil; But struggling through the crowd had deranged it sufficiently to discover a neck which for symmetry and beauty might have vied with the Medicean Venus. It was of the most dazzling whiteness, and received additional charms from being shaded by the tresses of her long fair hair [...] Her bosom was carefully veiled. Her dress was white; it was fastened by a blue sash, and just permitted to peep out from under it a little foot of the most delicate proportions. A chaplet of large grains hung upon her arm, and her face was covered with a veil of thick black gauze.[19]

It is the denial of a full view of the woman's face that makes her so attractive and heightens those fleetingly visible parts of her body – her neck and her foot – into fetishized objects of desire. Her neck is not merely pale but 'of the most dazzling whiteness', paradoxically because it is 'shaded' by the veil of her hair. The emphasized blackness and thickness of the veil draws attention to, rather than disguises, the delicacy, lightness and fairness of her features.

Byron uses a similar contrast in one of his early poems, 'Remind Me Not, Remind Me Not' (1808), in which a woman's eyelids become the veil that draws attention to her eyes:

> And then those pensive eyes would close,
> And bid their lids each other seek,
> Veiling the azure orbs below;

> While their long lashes' darkening gloss
> Seemed stealing o'er thy brilliant cheek,
> Like raven's plumage smooth'd on snow. (19–24)

Just as the somewhat sinister image of the raven's feathers serves to emphasize the purity of the partially covered snow, so the dark veil of the woman's lashes illuminates the brilliance of her pale cheek. Keats observed this technique of partial-obscurantism in his sonnet 'To Lord Byron' (1814):

> As when a cloud a golden moon doth veil,
> Its sides are tinged with a resplendent glow,
> Through the dark robe oft amber rays prevail,
> And like fair veins in sable marble flow […].

Byron's poetry is filled with such 'veilings', though its narrative absences, paratextual layers and teasing ambiguities only serve to draw attention to the spectral presence of the poet behind them.

*

If flirtation is the 'production of uncertainty', then *The Giaour* is arguably the most flirtatious of all Byron's works. The poem is made up of numerous disjointed fragments told by different narrators with often conflicting points of view and with chronologically inconsistent transitions from one fragment to the other. The first edition of *The Giaour*, described by Michael G. Sundell as 'a good adventure story', was published in February 1814 and had a relatively linear plot, with no one character developed more than another.[20] But by the seventh edition at the end of 1815, Byron had transformed it into his most fragmented and confusing work yet published. Rather than the process of clarification that one might expect, Byron's revisions instead consciously or unconsciously mystified his poem, fragmenting the plotline and obscuring the supporting characters, lending everything a shadowy, furtive quality.

This is a poem defined as much by its absences as by what is present. In his Advertisement preceding the tale, Byron notes not only that his poem is comprised of 'disjointed fragments' but also that these snippets are based on a tale that is in itself incomplete. He states that 'the story, when entire, contained the adventures of a female slave', immediately drawing attention to the fact that the broader narrative is destined to remain beyond the grasp of the reader.[21] As the story progresses, it becomes clear that the principal narrator knows as little about the other characters as the reader does, with the fisherman asking questions almost every twenty lines. Byron continually draws attention to the fact that there is a complete story, but then emphasizes its elusiveness. He says, for example, of the story: 'That tale can only Hassan tell', just before Hassan dies, frustrating the reader's chances of ever possessing the whole truth (446). The poem is crowded with questions without answers ('but who and what art thou / Of foreign garb and fearful brow?' (230–31)) and contradictory interpretations ('Strange rumours in our city say'; 'But others say, that on that night' (447; 467)).

The role that the reader has to play in the creation of meaning in this unstable work has been recognized since its first publication. A reviewer in the *Antijacobin Review* argued that the danger of *The Giaour* was not due to an absence of religious or moral principle, but to the fact that 'there is a doubt left on the reader's mind by the loose and ambiguous manner in which allusions are made, in different places'.[22] Walter Scott, on the other hand, described the critics who complained about *The Giaour*'s 'obscurity' as the kind of readers 'who run over poetry as a cat does over a harpsichord'.[23] Scott writes in a letter to Byron:

> every real lover of the art [of poetry] is obliged to you for condensing the narrative, by giving us only striking scenes [...] and leaving to the imagination the says I's and says he's, and all the minutiae of detail which might be proper in giving us evidence before a court of justice. The truth is, I think poetry is most striking when the mirror can be held up to the reader [...].[24]

Byron carries out the Simmelian process of flirtatious 'semi-concealment' that entices the reader to create his or her own narrative in order to fill in the poem's deliberately obscure 'outline'.

The Giaour himself is flirtatious from the outset, in the earliest sense of the word: he is almost never still. He is called into fugitive being by a question – 'Who thundering comes on blackest steed?' (180) – and teasingly pauses only once in ninety-nine lines, before exiting in as swift and oblique a fashion as he came – 'the Giaour is gone, / And did he fly or fall alone?' (277–78). He is obscure – 'His faith and race alike unknown' (807) – and riddled with contradictions. The heroine, Leila, is as flitting as her lover. She is a ghostly presence or manifest absence at the centre of *The Giaour*, providing the impetus for the poem's action, in spite of the fact that her death occurs before its narrative begins. Her ghost haunts the poem, paradoxically 'shining in her white symar', veiled in her shroud and yet still visible for the Giaour and the reader to 'gaze on' (1273–75). In the fragment describing Leila's descent into her 'watery grave', the sea becomes, to borrow David Seed's term, a 'matrix of concealment', which mirrors the obfuscation of Byron's narrative structure.[25] Indeed, this is a multi-layered veiling, as Leila's form is not only obscured by the sea and then by the sack-shroud – in which we assume she was placed by her executioners – but also by the curtain of asterisks on either side of this tantalizingly brief fragment. This veiling only serves to excite the fisherman's – as well as the reader's – curiosity. Despite the layers of concealment, we are still allowed teasing glimpses of the form beneath, prompting the fisherman to continue to gaze on 'it' (we are never given an actual description of what 'it' is, but must deduce from the hints in Byron's Advertisement and earlier in the poem that this is Leila), even after 'it' vanishes from view, leaving behind a beguiling 'speck of white' which 'mock'd the sight' (382–83).

Leila is the embodiment of the uncertainty of flirtation, which, as Phillips observes, 'puts into disarray our sense of an ending'.[26] Not even her drowning draws Leila's presence in the poem to a certain end, as her shade appears to the Giaour in a vision: 'I saw her – yes – she liv'd again' (1272). In this passage, Leila is both a presence and an absence, hovering uncertainly 'between two worlds'. When the Giaour tries to embrace her, the apparition disappears – 'my arms [...] shrink upon my lonely breast' – but he immediately insists: 'Yet still –'tis there' (1294–98).[27] The allure of Leila's absent presence is illustrated by the butterfly of Kashmir, which is linked to Leila by its 'rising' immediately after the fragment describing her descent into the sea (388). The butterfly is a symbol of unattainable beauty, which flirtatiously '[i]nvites the young pursuer near', but then 'leads him on [...] A weary chase' and, ultimately, 'leaves him, as it soars on high' (391–94).[28] Byron identifies the elusive quality of the butterfly as the essence of its appeal: 'The lovely toy so fiercely sought / Has lost its charm by being caught' (404–05). Similarly, Leila, a shrouded ghost, her presence veiled by her death, is all the more alluring because she remains beyond the grasp of the Giaour – and beyond the full perception of the reader.

Flirtation involves an invitation as well as a withdrawal and, although Byron creates textual absences in the poem, he also gives the reader plenty of physical detail upon which to gaze. Indeed, like a veil, the very concealment of certain elements in the poem serves to draw attention to other details. After passing the fisherman in a blur of speed, the Giaour pauses for, as Byron emphasizes, just an instant:

A moment checked his wheeling steed –

> A moment breathed him from his speed –
> A moment on his stirrup stood –
> Why look he o'er the olive wood? (218–21)

Although the Giaour's actions are still mysterious, the fleeting moment allows the fisherman to catch a glimpse of the hero and invites the reader to imagine his physical form. The Giaour's corporeal form – even if always partially obscured – is one of the few tangible elements of the poem, and the reader is continually invited to glimpse it. Stolen glances and partial sightings are central to Byron's aesthetic of flirtation. And this is a poem riddled with imagery associated with looking. Eyes are presented as giving access to a person's essence. A corpse is described by its lifeless eyes – 'that sad shrouded eye, / That fires not – wins not – weeps not – now' (78–79) – while an elaborate description of the 'dark charm' of Leila's eyes, '[b]right as the jewel of Giamschid', is used as an explanation of why, contrary to the Islamic belief that women are 'nought but breathing clay', she has a soul (473–90).[29]

Yet if eyes offer access to the soul, then Byron teases the reader with partial glimpses. It was not until the third edition of the poem that Byron expanded the physical description of the Giaour to include the supremely Byronic features:

> See – by the half-illumin'd wall
> His hood fly back – his dark hair fall –
> That pale brow wildly wreathing round [...]. (893–95)

The fact that the Giaour is only 'half-illumin'd' and cloaked in a hood makes this glimpse of the 'pale brow' particularly alluring. Byron would have written these lines around the same time as he was sitting for Thomas Phillips's famous portrait of 1813, which cemented the dark curl and pale skin as Byron's signature look. Many readers would have been familiar, too, with Byron's 'pallid brow' (611), 'dark hair' (894) and 'lip' that will 'curl' (853) from the numerous copies of George Sanders's portrait of 1809.[30] So when Byron invites the reader to 'See [...] that pale brow' of the Giaour, pushing back the hooded veil to reveal his form beneath, he is implicitly conjuring an image of his own physical form. Jerome McGann similarly draws attention to a ghostly reflexivity that connects the poet and his fictional characters. Byron's poetry, he writes,

> lies exactly in the relation, in the dialectical play between corresponding apparitional forms: on the one side, the spectacular poet – the man cut into a Keatsian figure, the person translated into what the Byronic texts call 'a name'; [...] on the other, the various fictional and historical selvings.[31]

Yet this is not a public gaze he is inviting, but a private, intimate one. It is only 'the close observer' that 'can espy / A noble soul, and lineage high' – that is, the ghost of Lord Byron – when they look upon the Giaour (868–69). He gives us the impression that such readers are separate from the 'common crowd', who only 'see the gloom' (866). These lines read like a flirtatious challenge: only a select few will ever truly understand the poet, though there is a possibility that any particular reader could be one of those distinguished few.

Byron's apparitional presence in *The Giaour* is enhanced further by a story that playfully rests just on the border of the text itself. Byron states in his Advertisement at the beginning of *The Giaour* that the tale was inspired by the story of a slave girl who, 'in the Mussulman manner', was thrown 'into the sea for infidelity' and later avenged by her lover.[32] A rumour circulated at the time the poem was published that Byron had witnessed this incident first-hand and had in fact saved the girl from death. By all accounts, the rumour appears to have been true; although, thanks to a masterful system of 'concealment and revelation' on the part of the poet, the story took on a life of its own. The rumour was started by Lord Sligo, who had arrived in Athens a few days after Byron left and was told the story of the girl's rescue by locals. Somehow the tale got back to England and was repeated by Caroline Lamb, among others. On Byron's request, Sligo wrote the poet a lengthy letter, explaining what he had heard:

> As you were returning from bathing in Piraeus, you met the procession going down to execute the sentence of the Waywode on this unhappy girl. Report continues to say, that on finding out what the object of their journey was, and who was the miserable sufferer, you immediately interfered; and on some delay in obeying your orders, [...] you drew a pistol, and told him, that if he did not immediately obey your orders [...] you would shoot him dead.[33]

Byron claimed that he thought the story 'had been *unknown*', adding, 'and I wish it were'.[34] Yet his actions suggest otherwise. Byron circulated Lord Sligo's letter among some of his most influential – not to mention notoriously gossipy – friends and acquaintances, including Lewis, Moore, Samuel Rogers, Lord Holland, Edward Daniel Clark and Lady Melbourne. Byron was well aware that the story was an exaggeration of the truth. He describes it to Clark and Moore, as if he had never heard it before, as 'a strange [...] story', a 'report of the reports' and a 'curious letter', noting to Lady Melbourne that the story 'differs from our friend C[aroline]'s as much as from mine'.[35]

Byron was careful to distance himself from the rumour while simultaneously facilitating its circulation. An extended version of the story, based on Sligo's letter and including a description of the poet's supposed affair with the girl before he saved her, was published in Medwin's *Conversations* (1825). Sligo's letter is now reproduced in almost every edition of the poem. Marchand indexes the letter as 'the origin of *The Giaour*' and in his biography cites it as the 'episode from which the *Giaour* was later derived', while McGann notes that it is the story on which 'the central incident in *The Giaour* is based'.[36] What has rarely been addressed, however, is how *different* this story is from Byron's poem. In *The Giaour*, Leila *is* actually drowned; there is no one there to save her. Sligo's report is more of a 'good adventure story' than any of the editions of *The Giaour*, with Byron as the gun-slinging hero who saves the damsel in distress. This rumour enabled Byron to become, like Leila, both a presence and an absence in the poem. As he leaves so many gaps in his texts, he also plants a suggestion as to how those gaps may at least be partially filled – with semblances of himself.

Byron's first, relatively straightforward version of *The Giaour* was not published; rather, it was circulated among friends and associates only.[37] It was only after he decided to extend *The Giaour*'s readership from this private coterie to the general public that he started his reworking and destabilizing of the poem. And the more he concealed or removed from the poem, the greater the reading public's fascination seemed to be. Murray published seven editions of the poem, each with teasingly brief additions, which served to expand the story but also engendered new gaps and new ghosts, which only heightened the public's curiosity. This strategy of flirtation worked: the poem was phenomenally successful, and Byron decided to repeat and build upon this winning formula in his next poem, *The Corsair*, which famously sold 10,000 copies on its first day of publication.[38]

Many years later, Byron made playful reference to his 'haunting' of *The Giaour* in *Don Juan*. In the cross-dressing harem sequence of Canto VI, Katinka tries to convince the Matron to let her share her bed with the disguised 'Juanna' because she has a 'fear of ghosts':

> 'I am sure I see
> A phantom upon each of the four posts;
> And then I have the worst dreams that can be,
> Of Guebres, Giaours, and Ginns, and Gouls in hosts.' (VI, 48)

Byron here acknowledges the spectral nature of the Giaour and the erotic potential of a ghostly vision. The curtains on the bed become shadowy veils and 'phantom' visions, and a feigned fear of ghosts is used as a playful tool for bedroom farce. By evoking the name of the Giaour in his list of hosts, Byron is, in Susan Wolfson's words, 'conjuring his fame' and once again haunting – now literally as a ghost – the narrative of his own poem.[39] In the same way that 'Juanna' ultimately evades Katinka's grasp, the spectre of Byron remains distinctly uncertain, partially 'conjured', yet always leaving the reader wanting more.

Notes

1 Augusta Leigh to Lady Byron, 26 January 1816, Deposit Lovelace Bodleian 79, pp. 173–76.

2 *BLJ*, III, p. 121. Emphasis in the original.

3 Thomas Medwin, *Medwin's Conversations of Lord Byron*, ed. Ernest J. Lovell, Jr (Princeton, NJ: Princeton University Press, 1966), p. 73.

4 Adam Phillips, *On Flirtation* (London: Faber, 1994), p. xvii.

5 Byron talks of mobility in *Don Juan*, including a note about '*mobilité*' in European culture, describing it as a 'vivacious versatility' which is 'false – though true' (XVI, p. 97). The 'forward press', 'speed' and 'breeziness' of Byron's poetry has been discussed by a number of critics, including Susan J. Wolfson, *Formal Charges: The Shaping of Poetry in British Romanticism* (Stanford, CA: Stanford University Press, 1997), p. 134; and Camille Paglia, *Sexual Personae: Art and Decadence from Nefertiti to Emily Dickinson* (New Haven: Yale University Press, 1990), p. 357. Byron's technique of simultaneous 'scorching and drenching' is discussed in the first chapter of Jane Stabler's, *Byron, Poetics and History*. Byron discusses the state of being both scorched and drenched in response to a review by the critic Francis Cohen, see *BLJ*, VI, p. 207.

6 Jerome J. McGann, *Byron and Romanticism*, p. 141.

7 Ibid., pp. 143–44.

8 Ibid., p. 148.

9 Ibid., pp. 156–57.

10 Andrew Rutherford, among others, has used the term 'thinly-veiled self-portrait' to describe Byron's poetry. See Andrew Rutherford, *Byron the Best-Seller* (Byron Foundation Lecture; Nottingham: University of Nottingham, 1964), p. 17.

11 David A. Bailey and Gilane Tawadros, 'Introduction', in *Veil: Veiling, Representation and Contemporary Art*, eds. David A. Bailey and Gilane Tawadros (London: Institute of International Visual Arts, 2003), p. 22.

12 Georg Simmel, *Georg Simmel: On Women, Sexuality, and Love*, trans. Guy Oakes (New Haven, CT: Yale University Press, 1984), p. 137.

13 McGann, *Byron and Romanticism*, p. 148.

14 In *The Corsair*, for example, Gulnare is covered by both a headdress of some description and her 'dark far-floating hair, / That nearly veiled her face and bosom fair' (III, 410–11). There is a nice flirtatious ambiguity in these lines, as the word 'nearly' flickers between veiling closely and not quite veiling.

15 Simmel, *On Women*, p. 137.

16 Byron and Lewis were friends not only as part of the London literary scene but also

later when Lewis visited Italy and they spent time together at the Villa Diodati and also in Venice. The two often read each other's work, and Byron acknowledged that Lewis's translation of Goethe's *Faust* was somewhat of an influence on *Manfred*, see *BLJ*, V, p. 268. Byron almost certainly read *The Monk*, and Canto II of *Don Juan* borrows from 'The Exiles' – a poem that was inserted into the second edition of Lewis's novel. The influence of 'The Exiles' on *Don Juan* was first suggested by Hoxie N. Fairchild, 'Byron and Monk Lewis', in *Times Literary Supplement*, 11 May 1946.

17 Samuel Taylor Coleridge, 'Review of Matthew G. Lewis, *The Monk*', in *The Critical Review* (February 1797), pp. 194–200.

18 Ibid.

19 Matthew Lewis, *The Monk: A Romance*, ed. Howard Anderson (London: Oxford University Press, 1973), p. 10.

20 Michael G. Sundell, 'The Development of *The Giaour*', in *Studies in English Literature 1500–1900*, 9:4 (1969), p. 590.

21 *CPW*, III, p. 39.

22 *Antijacobin Review* (August 1813), in *The Romantics Reviewed: Contemporary Reviews of British Romantic Writers*, 5 vols., ed. by Donald H. Reiman (New York and London: Garland Publishing, Inc., 1972), vol. 1, p. 30.

23 Walter Scott, *The Letters of Sir Walter Scott, 1811–1914*, ed. H.J.C. Grierson (London: Constable, 1932), p. 374.

24 Ibid.

25 See David Seed, '"Disjointed Fragments": Concealment and Revelation in *The Giaour*', in *The Byron Journal*, 18: (1990), p. 21.

26 Phillips, *On Flirtation*, p. xvii.

27 We find a similar episode in *Manfred*, in which the identity of the apparition – as well as her relationship with the eponymous protagonist – is teasingly withheld:

> SEVENTH SPIRIT. [*appearing in the shape of a beautiful female figure*].
>   Behold!
> MAN.   Oh God! if it be thus, and *thou*
>   Art not a madness and a mockery,
>   I yet might be most happy. – I will clasp thee,
>   And we again will be – [*The figure vanishes*]
>   My heart is crush'd! (I, i, 187–91)

28 Byron also uses the flirtatiously 'uncertain' image of a flitting butterfly to describe his Muse in *Don Juan*: 'My Muse, the butterfly hath but her wings, / Not stings, and flits through ether without aim, / Alighting rarely' (XIII, 89); and 'March! / March, my Muse! If you cannot fly, yet flutter; / And when you may not be sublime, be arch, / Or starch, as are the edicts statesmen utter' (XV, 27).

29 Tom Mole develops the idea of 'scopophilia' in *The Giaour* in Tom Mole, *Byron's Romantic Celebrity: Industrial Culture and the Hermeneutic of Intimacy*, pp. 65–74.

30 For a discussion of Byron's portraits, see Christine Kenyon Jones, 'Fantasy and Transfiguration: Byron and His Portraits', in *Byromania: Portraits of the Artist in Nineteenth- and Twentieth-Century Culture*, ed. Frances Wilson (London: Macmillan, 1999), pp. 130–36. William St Clair notes that Murray 'put on sale sets of engravings for binding into his books', with a portrait of Byron leading

the series. See William St Clair, *The Reading Nation in the Romantic Period* (Cambridge: Cambridge University Press, 2004), p. 331.

31 McGann, *Byron and Romanticism*, p. 106.

32 *CPW*, III, p. 39.

33 *CPW*, III, p. 414.

34 *BLJ*, III, p. 230.

35 *BLJ*, III, pp. 206, 104, 102.

36 *BLJ*, III, p. 283; Leslie A. Marchand, *Byron: A Biography*, vol. 1 (London: John Murray, 1957), p. 257; *CPW*, III, p. 414.

37 See *CPW*, III, p. 413.

38 For accounts of *The Corsair*'s unprecedented commercial success, see *CPW*, III, pp. 444–45 and Marchand, *Byron: A Portrait*, p. 162.

39 Susan J. Wolfson, 'Byron's Ghosting Authority', p. 778.

AFTERWORD

Blowing on a Dead Man's Embers: Byron's Biographical Ghosts

Peter Allender

'Every great man', observed Oscar Wilde, 'has his disciples and it is always Judas who writes the biography.'[1] Wilde was fortunate to have Richard Ellman as his eventual biographer, but the genre continues to be held in a bad light, especially by poets and novelists. John Updike considered that 'even the best biographies are too long' and asked: 'what is the point of them anyway?'[2] Playing the devil's advocate in the opening essay from his *Works on Paper: The Craft of Biography and Autobiography*, Michael Holroyd stated that he can see how, for some, biographers seem like parasites feeding off 'pre-digested carrion', attempting either to replace literature or 'rob us of its enchantment'.[3]

W.H. Auden believed that what every author hopes to receive from posterity is justice – a hope, he believed, that is usually disappointed. Larkin, reviewing Peter Ackroyd's biography of T.S. Eliot, believed that 'If Eliot wished to live quietly, succeeding in avoiding notice, living and partly living, without making his life a continual allegory, then he had a right to do so.' But, he concludes: 'Truly it is not worth putting people off, they will get you whatever precautions you take.'[4] Larkin's diaries, it will be recalled, were destroyed soon after his death, according to his instructions, rather than contrary to them, as was famously the case with the burning of Byron's memoirs. When Andrew Motion 'got' Larkin, it was to describe attitudes and opinions that resulted in his poetry being withdrawn from some university syllabuses. Phoning Motion, Larkin would announce in his distinctive and lugubrious baritone: 'This is your subject speaking.'[5] If posthumous long-distance communication were possible, what kind of conversation would Byron have with his appointed biographer? Perhaps to keep the imaginative possibility of such a conversation in mind is the first duty of the life writer. Without such interaction, Holroyd warns in his essay 'Smoke with Fire: On the Ethics of Biography', the biographer does not 'stretch out a hand to his subject and invite him, invite her, to write one more work posthumously and in collaboration', but can become dangerously over-absorbed in a dead world.[6] Robert Graves also delivers something of a warning when he writes:

> To bring the dead to life
> Is no great magic.
> Few are wholly dead:
> Blow on a dead man's embers
> And a live flame will start.
>
> ('To Bring the Dead to Life', 1–5)

There is no difficulty in imagining whose embers Graves had in mind here, as he goes on to declare that it becomes 'natural' to '[l]imp as he limped, / Swear by the oaths he swore.'

At its best, there is a conversation in a literary biography: the subject seems to ask to be heard and remembered and have, perhaps, his or her largely misunderstood voice again made intelligible. Larkin felt that a writer's reputation is twofold: what we think of his work and what we think of him; 'What's more, we expect the two halves to relate: if they don't, one or other of our opinions will alter until they do.'[7] It is not true, then, to say that death confers a protective immortality or, as Hazlitt wrote of Shelley, '[e]ven detraction has been silent at his tomb'.[8] Do poems, in fact, resist biography? And are poets in particular likely to discourage biographical speculation? We like to feel that a poet lives a 'continual allegory'. But life, especially if it ends early, tends not to be novel-shaped and, even for a poet, is not consistently poetic. Ultimately, then, can biography ever be more than fiction of a depleted kind, if only because we usually know the inevitable conclusion?

The question is what kind of flame is being kept alight in literary biography and in what and whose interest? Chekhov admitted to 'autobiographophobia' when asked to provide details of his life for a periodical. But he managed, nevertheless, to supply twenty-five lines of information, including the sentence: 'I have also sinned in the realm of drama, although moderately', concluding with the heartfelt remark: 'However this is all rubbish. Write what you want. If there are no facts, substitute something lyrical.'[9]

What do we allow ourselves to make of the following lyrical response to Byron's death in Greece written in 1856?

Who that has a spark of generous feeling that rejoices in the good in a fellow-being, has not dwelt with pleasure on the thought that Lord Byron's career was ennobled and purified towards its close by a high and sympathetic purpose, by honest and energetic efforts for his fellowmen? Who has not read with deep emotion those last pathetic lines, beautiful as the afterglow of a sunset, in which love and resignation are mingled with something of a melancholy heroism? Who has not lingered with compassion over the dying scene at Messolonghi – the sufferer's inability to make his farewell message intelligible and last long hours of silent pain.[10]

Are we comfortable with phrases like 'generous feeling', 'high and sympathetic purpose', 'ennobled and purified', 'deep emotion' and 'melancholy heroism'? Do we begin to think in terms of fine writing, even purple passages? Or oratory? A politician's or a fellow freedom fighter's perhaps? Does it make any difference that these words of enlightened sympathy are those of a writer one would have thought hard indeed to impress: George Eliot? What accounts for the diminished and tarnished version published 141 years later?

Byron [in Greece] faced a challenge that no human being could have matched up to. He found himself in a black comic opera to which he had fled out of boredom, only to be engulfed by chaos and helplessly apotheosised into a myth.[11]

Noble tragedy has become black farce in Phyllis Grosskurth's *Byron: The Flawed Angel* (1997) – the first of several recent biographies of Byron.

The aim in this Afterword is to reflect on the idea of a biographer 'blow[ing] on a dead man's embers' – or those of a subject not 'wholly dead' – and, in theory, keeping the flame alight. Ian Hamilton's astute 1992 study of literary estates and the rise of biography is entitled *Keepers of the Flame*. He practised the craft himself, of course. The poet Paul Muldoon has claimed that the biography of Robert Lowell, which is perhaps Hamilton's masterpiece, is, for him, preferable to Lowell's poetry. We might also remember that Hamilton was pursued angrily down the street by one of his subjects, J.D. Salinger. In *Keepers of the Flame*, he begins the chapter 'Byron and the Best of Friends' by noting how disdainful Byron can seem to be of literary reputation. He frequently confesses how tired he is of 'the vanity of authorship'. In 1823, he wrote from Cephalonia to his sister Augusta, anxiously enquiring about his daughter, Ada:

Is she social or solitary – taciturn or talkative – fond of reading or otherwise? And what is her *tic*? – I mean her foible – is she passionate? I

hope that the Gods have made her any thing save *poetical* – it is enough
to have one such fool in a family.[12]

Hamilton opens with Byron's well-known view of Robert Burns, which
he acknowledges as a kind of self-portrait: 'what an antithetical mind!
tenderness, roughness – delicacy, coarseness – sentiment, sensuality
– soaring and grovelling, dirt and deity – all mixed up in that one
compound of inspired clay'.[13] For Hamilton, John Cam Hobhouse was
the first and ideal keeper of the Byron flame, despite the fact that he
made a conflagration of the memoirs. And it was to Hobhouse that
Byron – however disdainful he seemed about reputation – revealed his
anxiety about posterity. He confessed:

> Will not my life (it is egotism – but you know this is true of all men who
> have *had* a name even if they survive it) be given in a false and unfair
> point of view to others? I mean to *praise* as well as *censure*.[14]

Between 1824 and 1825, immediately after the poet's death, over ten
lives of Byron appeared. Already there was a divergence evident between
what Thomas Love Peacock described as works by 'small Boswells of
the eavesdropping genus' and those by someone Hamilton characterizes
as an 'arch-manipulator [...] bewildering his spectators with a surfeit
of information'. Hamilton goes on to contrast those 'chroniclers' who
were 'ready to misreport for profit or in order to settle an old score',
and the biographer, with his or her subject seemingly safely dead, who
has to deal with 'calculated mood shifts and inconsistencies' and is
overwhelmed by 'a mass of "material" but unable to make sense of it'.[15]

Byron's 'small Boswells' are no more, but there are still difficulties
with some representations of Byron discernible in recent lives and studies,
especially those which labour under a 'surfeit of information'. How is
Byron, the writer, now praised and censured? Although disdainful
of literary reputation, for Hamilton, Byron 'never seems free of the
suggestion, that a measure of imposture, a degree of carefully planned
theatricality, was essential to any successful cultural performance'.[16]
Theatricality, with its implication of insincerity, is a term used frequently
against Byron. Jerome McGann, in *Byron and Romanticism* (2002),
notes John Gibson Lockhart's comment – 'Stick to *Don Juan*: it is the
only sincere thing that you have ever written' – as one which 'nicely
captures the problem of Byron's sincerity'. But he later adds how *Childe
Harold's Pilgrimage*, rather than *Don Juan*, would 'make the drama
of "Consciousness awaking to her woes" world-famous'.[17] The view of
Byron's wife is surprisingly sympathetic with his intensity of feeling,

however misplaced; even after the separation, she wrote: 'It is unhappily your disposition to consider what you *have* as worthless, what you have *lost* as invaluable.'[18] That he was self-divided and his mind 'antithetical' is indisputable, as Byron was only too aware himself. But more interesting than his apparent theatricality are his sincerity and common sense. His 'authenticity' is how Stephen Cheeke describes these qualities in his 2003 study *Byron and Place*, in which he sympathetically explores how 'the recovery of lived experience' was so important to Byron and how 'place' in particular 'was central to Byron's fashioning of himself, and Byron's places were constantly changing'.[19] In light of this, it might be said that Byron was haunted by a sense of place, just as he was by the perpetually changing inner landscape of his own moods.

As is evident, lives of Byron continue to be written: three in the five years from 1997 to 2002 and another in 2009, all by women.[20] The writer of one, Fiona MacCarthy, in a very curious article in the *Guardian Review* in November 2003, admitted to feeling threatened by Byron's ghost as she sat researching in John Murray's at 50 Albemarle Street under the famous Thomas Phillips portrait. What kind of disquiets and insecurities is she actually confessing to when she claims to believe in 'Byron operating a posthumous vendetta' aimed at preventing her from finishing the biography, on which she worked for eight years, as she was plagued by a succession of accidents and illnesses? She knows that Byron loathed all 'scribbling women' and targeted them in his poem 'The Blues'. MacCarthy can see that what she calls her 'cool appraisal' by a twenty-first-century professional biographer might seem like the last straw to the man who had insisted that educating women 'only served to turn their heads with conceit' and wishes that she had taken more notice of the present John Murray's father, who wrote: 'Ah me, what perils do environ / The man who meddles with Lord Byron.'[21] One is tempted to suggest that her appraisal might have been made a warmer one – perhaps even have included something lyrical or, better still, engaged in a more intimate way with her haunting subject. She seemed to have no problem with the subject of her first biography, the sculptor and engraver, Eric Gill, whose appetite for sex she describes as 'unusually avid'.[22] So it was and often quaintly illegal, too.

MacCarthy asks a disconcerting question in her introduction to *Byron: Life and Legend* (2002): 'Does Byron matter these days? After what amounts to a five year pilgrimage' (or was it eight?):

> I would argue that he does. His poetry may sometimes seem to be grossly uneven in quality, his thought processes slipshod. Goethe was

right when he judged that Byron as a thinker was almost on the level of a child.[23]

Can her representation of Byron recover from this negative assessment, which, like most introductions, was evidently written after the main work was completed? MacCarthy tries hard to give a balanced account of Byron's final achievement, even going so far as to announce, without much direct evidence, that Byron might have been crowned King of Greece. But like her foreword – or is it afterword? – her approach remains cool, even forensic, throughout. She warms neither to the poet nor, in any sustained sense, to his poems. Here is how she characterizes Byron: 'if not a great thinker he is a great voicer, a conduit of feeling. He has a quality of empathy, a flow of human sympathy extending through the generations and the centuries.'[24] Her biography, rather than a 'conduit', is an overwhelming deluge of information, which actually submerges any sense of genuine sympathy that there might be with her subject. Fittingly, the concluding three pages of her final chapter, 'The Byronic Englishman', are a detailed, even prurient account of the exhumation of Byron's body at Hucknall in 1938. 'There are always private reasons behind the choice of a biographical subject',[25] MacCarthy declares in her conclusion, without in the preceding 564 pages ever giving any developed indication of why Byron was her choice, either as a personal quest or an imaginative attempt to 'bring the dead to life'.

Benita Eisler's *Byron: Child of Passion, Fool of Fame* (1999) at first seems more at ease with the poems. *Childe Harold*, in particular, informs most of her even longer study. She also seems more sensitive towards those Byronic oppositions, describing how

> all contradictions converged, hypersensitivity to status, yearning to be loved for himself alone, the 'craving void' he described within himself, which made him require constant diversion, and the strains he felt playing a social role – all were aspects of his troubled identity. As his ties with England loosened [...] these divisions seemed to deepen.[26]

Oddly, or perhaps inevitably, her contradictory view of Byron becomes more and more apparent. Like MacCarthy, she has blown on the embers, but finds it difficult to be warmed by the ensuing flames. When she reaches page 709, and a description of the funeral rites for Shelley, Eisler quotes Byron's view of him as 'the best and least selfish man I ever knew', adding her own unsubstantiated comparison between the two: 'For his part, Byron could never escape the little lame boy living above an Aberdeen perfumer's shop; Shelley's aristocratic courage and moral certainties beyond his means.'[27] Seven hundred and nine pages have resulted in an infantilized subject, and there are still fifty more pages to go. And this is a biography about which Andrew Motion wrote: 'Byron's story has never been so well handled. [...] The tale itself seems always fascinating, occasionally astonishing, and intermittently horrific; the telling is uniformly shrewd, confident and non-judgmental.'[28] Perhaps; but the image of the little lame boy seems pretty judgmental. Horrific – where? Uniformly shrewd? Again, maybe; but her concluding pages are increasingly erratic. Was Eisler in a rush to finish and move on to her next subject – or victim? (Chopin, by the way.) In her conclusion, Messolonghi is travestied as 'a swampy pest-hole of the Peloponnese' (it is in central Greece). Disraeli's *Vivian Grey* is ascribed to Edward Bulwer-Lytton. (As Peter Levi once remarked on errors in books: 'The mistakes are the plums in the pudding.') Newstead Abbey is misrepresented as an 'all-purpose theme-park of England's past, falling somewhere between Graceland and a generic "stately home"'.[29] Byron now is Elvis Presley – indeed, the 'fool of fame'. This biographer, as with MacCarthy, does not exactly become her subject; rather, the subject seems to become her naïve victim. Finally, Eisler accuses Byron of being one of the few poets who have 'spawned such proprietorial [sic] commentary: He has been claimed by labour politicians, queer theorists, and specialists in manic depression'.[30] Michael Foot's *Debts of Honour* is thus swiftly dealt with – along with the politician, who knew more, and understood more, about the Romantics than Eisler ever will.

Likewise Kay Redfield Jamison, whose *Touched with Fire* (1994) is a personally informed discussion of 'manic depressive illness and the artistic temperament'. Jamison shows a sympathetic understanding of the 'underlying mobility' of Byron's own actual temperament, which, from her own experience of what is now called bipolar disorder, she describes as 'frequently seasonal' and subject to 'September melancholias', 'winter depressions', 'mixed states' and 'pronounced diurnal rhythms'.[31] All of which led him to experience not only abrupt changes of mood, but to display apparent irrationality – evidenced, for instance, by his superstitiousness (Byron would never start any venture on a Friday or a Sunday, for example, and even on other days of the week he tended to look out for portents and would often experience a deep sense of unexplained foreboding). Frequent 'melancholias' might also explain his morbid fascination with physical decay. He could be especially tormented by the horrors of bodily decomposition after burial, and his fascination with the ghostly and supernatural perhaps stems from this obsession. Jamison might be accused of making Byron's 'mixed states' and the lives of other artists she treats in *Touched with Fire* too clear-cut and clinically convenient for the argument she wants to present concerning 'manic depressive illness', rather than about 'the artistic temperament' as such, whatever that might be. However, she does also develop a humanely corrective perspective on what can still be a received view of Byron as

> theatrical [...] brooding, mock-heroic, posturing, cynical, passionate, [and] sardonic [which] suggests an exaggerated or even insincere quality; minimising the genuine degree of suffering and overlooking the extraordinary intellectual and emotional discipline he exerted over a kind of pain that brings most who experience it to their knees.[32]

Jamison explores with sympathy and insight how Byron 'in the end [...] brought a deeply redemptive spirit to the problems of despair, ennui, uncertainty, and disillusionment'.[33] Byron concludes his journey across the Alps in 1816 by confessing to his sister that he had 'seen some of the noblest views in the world',

> But in all this – the recollections of bitterness [...] which must accompany me through life – have preyed upon me here – and neither the music of the Shepherd – the crashing of the Avalanche – not the torrent – the mountain – the Glacier – the Forest – not the Cloud – have for one moment – lightened the weight upon my heart – nor enabled me to lose my own wretched identity.[34]

Here, Byron reveals his exceptional sensitivity towards all his experience, whether physical or psychological, with that dramatic sense of how real his own moods and fears were to him. Even amidst the beauties of the Alps, he cannot escape his own 'wretched identity' as a self-exiled inner émigré and a fate where 'each is tortured in his separate hell – / For we are crowded in our solitudes.'[35]

Byron had as ambivalent an attitude towards ghosts as he had to much else. In 'The Blues', they can reflect the effects of enthusiasm or 'enthusymusy', as would-be poets are intoxicated by the powers of their own inspiration:

> 'Tis the source of all sentiment – feeling's true fountain:
> 'Tis the Vision of Heaven upon Earth; 'tis the gas
> Of the soul: 'tis the seizing of shades as they pass,
> And making them substance: 'tis something divine [...]
>   ('The Blues', Eclogue Second, 138–141)

At other times, 'shades' represent both hell on earth and Hades beyond it, as when he imagines the Burgundian dead after the battle of Morat:

Here Burgundy bequeath'd his tombless host,
A bony heap, through ages to remain,
Themselves their monument;– the Stygian coast
Unsepulchred they roam'd, and shriek'd each wandering ghost.
(*CHP*, III, 63)

Byron was also, of course, in a very real sense haunted by his own thoughts and moods, more vivid as they could be to him than the mountains themselves, and was acutely self-analytical. How much more meaningful and sympathetic are Jamison's responses to this passionate process than the dry chronologies of conventional biographers and their obsessions with minutiae and oft-repeated anecdotes.

Phyllis Grosskurth's concluding sentence to her *Byron: The Flawed Angel* merely expresses the hope that Byron 'finally paid for the Napoleonic coach he had built in London in 1816' – a comment that reveals her own limitations and how little she has been changed by her 'journey'.[36] The distinction that Peacock noted now seems to be a widening one between academic studies and professional biography. From the latter it is a relief to turn to *On a Voiceless Shore: Byron in Greece* (1998), an engaging and insightful work by Stephen Minta, who, in the manner of Bruce Chatwin, evokes the significance of place and landscape as he travels. From the beginning, we are with a writer who knows Greek and loves Greece, seeing beneath the tarnished myths regarding Byron and the country. Similarly, David Roessel's *In Byron's Shadow: Modern Greece in the English and American Imagination* (2002) provides a corrective view of Byron's actions that represent his hopes for 'a new, spiritual, political, or cultural revival' in Greece. At the heart of Roessel's argument is Jerome McGann's proposal in *The Beauty of Inflections* that Byron is deeply concerned with 'the renewal of the value of the individual person, and the renewal of Greece as a political identity [which] becomes Byron's "objective correlative" of this idea'.[37] Roessel recalls Lawrence Durrell, who begins *Prospero's Cell* with the belief that 'other countries may offer you discoveries in manners or love or landscape; Greece offers you something harder – the discovery of yourself'.[38]

Minta describes how, during his last months, Byron has been made to appear

> a pathetic, indecisive figure, a futile actor, a helpless spectator who returned to Greece almost by accident, caught out of his depth in a situation he neither foresaw nor understood. Whereas Greece offers an alternative vision, a country where the generosity of Byron's act is still sincerely celebrated.

Messolonghi itself has been given a bad name as the ultimate outpost at the end of the world somehow itself responsible for Byron's demise.[39]

Edward Trelawny, untrustworthy as ever and perhaps both a 'small Boswell' and an 'arch-manipulator', called 'Messolonghi a miserable mean place in which to spend eternity.'[40] Minta reminds us of how it is still remembered as 'the centre of resistance to the Turks in the Independence struggle [and] home of five future prime ministers of an independent Greece'.[41] As we have seen, some writers do not appear even to have looked at a map of Greece, but Minta knows the real Messolonghi and movingly describes how, in the Garden of Heroes, 'Byron's statue appears as natural as the palm trees that surround it, more natural certainly than either would appear in England': an England that no longer knows how to deal with its heroes.[42] Byron might well have chosen to fight for a Latin American or Italian cause. As Minta repeats, the Greek Byron now seems natural to us, but he does seem to underplay Byron's sense of being fated to return to Greece and die there:

> Given the early deaths of both his parents, Byron was probably destined to die young. But there was nothing inevitable about his death in Messolonghi. That, in the end, was simply bad luck, perhaps simply the chance of the weather. Once he was dead, however, everything begins to look fated. The failure of ideals, the disappointments, betrayals, all the threads of life inexorably unwinding.[43]

Byron had written to Thomas Moore in July 1821: 'There is no such thing as a life of passion any more than a continuous earthquake, or an eternal fever. Besides, who would ever *shave* themselves in such a state?'[44] But when he writes to Edward Blaquiere in August 1823, aboard the brig *Hercules* en route to Cephalonia, the immediacy and authenticity of the experience, the sense of adventure, is very striking. Blaquiere was the London Greek Committee's roving correspondent, who did not wait to meet Byron in Genoa, but rushed, without apology, to London to be the first to write about the Greek war. 'Here am I – but where are *you*?' Byron exclaims, and adds a PS: 'Excuse haste I write on the binnacle of a ship by the light of a lanthorn and a squall blowing.'[45] The *Hercules* was a ship that Trelawny described as 'a collier-built tub, on the lines of a baby's cradle'. She would do anything but sail a straight course, as 'the least touch of Neptune's foot set her rocking'.[46] Perhaps Trelawny, as a 'small Boswell', is partly responsible for the childish view of Byron's achievement. Not only is the ship a baby's cradle, but the poet behaved like a 'boy cornet' aboard it, Trelawny writes in his *Records of Shelley, Byron, and the Author*, displaying 'dawdling habits' with his 'plotting – planning – shilly-shallying' and seeming to lack energy and a real sense of purpose.[47] However, Byron's flame burns clearest in his own writing. The Greek venture was, for him, both genuine and purposeful, but – as he also seems to have sensed – a valedictory one. For Byron was superstitious, he believed in fate. He knew that more than ever he was living at the edge of his physical and mental strength and saw portents all around him. 'We have had strange weather', he writes, 'and strange incidents – natural, moral, physical, martial and political.'[48] It is possible to read the last volume of his journals and letters and gain an overpowering sense that Byron knew what was going to happen to him.

In the end, Byron has to survive his biographers. Jerome McGann, in a concluding dialogue to the essays collected in *Byron and Romanticism*, sees him as an 'emblem' of difference. McGann states that for 'scholars and educators' (he might also have included biographers and readers), 'I can hardly imagine a better model in a world [...] where even difference is administered and becomes what Byron grieved to see himself become, partly at his making: a "name", a word.' For McGann, Byron is a figure, like Blake and Shelley, for whom 'creative doubt' becomes a matter of 'public prophecy and not simply [...] a psychical condition'. They are therefore enabled to write 'histories' that 'can be multiple and self-contradictory'.[49] This is something McGann believes Byron captures with 'exquisite precision' in 'the great closing couplet' of *The Corsair*:

> He left a Corsair's name to other times,
> Linked with one virtue, and a thousand crimes.

The conclusion has to be that, however haunted by it MacCarthy claims to have felt, Byron's spirit eludes conventional chronological biography. For the over-reliable, omniscient narrator, whether deliberately judgmental or not, the subject becomes a child – the child of an unforgiving and over-controlling parental figure. There is, as a result, little sense of the depth of significance of that creative doubt. Too often we are left, amid the certainties and surfeit of detail, with an echo of Byron's question: 'Here am I – but where are *you*?'

Notes

1 Oscar Wilde, 'The Critic as Artist', in *The Artist as Critic: Critical Writings of Oscar Wilde*, ed. Richard Ellmann (Chicago, IL: University of Chicago Press, 1969), p. 342.

2 Updike, 'One Cheer for Literary Biography', in *The New York Review of Books*, 4 February 1999.

3 Holroyd, *Works on Paper: The Craft of Biography and Autobiography* (London: Abacus, 2003), pp. 4, 6.

4 Ian Hamilton, *Keepers of the Flame: Literary Estates and the Rise of Biography* (London: Hutchinson, 1992), p. 304.

5 Andrew Motion, 'This Is Your Subject Speaking', in *An Enormous Yes: In Memoriam Philip Larkin*, ed. Harry Chambers (Calstock: Peterloo Poets, 1986), p. 25.

6 Holroyd, *Works on Paper*, p. 19.

7 Hamilton, *Keepers of the Flame*, p. 305.

8 William Hazlitt, 'Shelley's Posthumous Poems', *Edinburgh Review* (July 1824), in *CWWH*, vol. XVI, p. 270.

9 Janet Malcolm, *Reading Chekhov: A Critical Journey* (London, Granta, 2001), pp. 15–16.

10 David Crane, *The Kindness of Sisters: Annabella Milbanke and the Destruction of the Byrons* (London: Harper Collins, 2002), p. 275.

11 Phyllis Grosskurth, *Byron: The Flawed Angel* (London: Hodder and Stoughton, 1997), p. 462.

12 Byron to Augusta Leigh, 12 October 1823, *BLJ*, XI, p. 47.

13 Hamilton, *Keepers of the Flame*, p. 109.

14 Byron to John Cam Hobhouse, 23 November 1821, *BLJ*, IX, p. 68. Emphasis in the original unless otherwise stated.

15 Hamilton, *Keepers of the Flame*, p. 142.

16 Ibid., p. 109.

17 Jerome McGann, *Byron and Romanticism*, pp. 139, 273.

18 Hamilton, *Keepers of the Flame*, p. 111.

19 Stephen Cheeke, *Byron and Place: History, Translation, Nostalgia*, pp. 13, 20.

20 The last of these – Edna O'Brien's *Byron in Love* (London: Weidenfeld & Nicolson, 2009) – was published after the writing of this piece. [Editor's note.]

21 Fiona MacCarthy, 'The Curse of Byron', *The Guardian*, 15 November 2003.

22 Fiona MacCarthy, *Eric Gill* (London: Faber, 1989), p. v.

23 Fiona MacCarthy, *Byron: Life and Legend*, p. xiv.

24 Ibid., p. xiv.

25 Ibid., p. 565.

26 Benita Eisler, *Byron: Child of Passion, Fool of Fame* (New York, NY: Alfred A. Knopf, 1999), p. 265.

27 Ibid., p. 709.

28 Andrew Motion, extract from review of Eisler (1999), in *Financial Times*, reprinted in the American Vintage paperback edition (2000).

29 Eisler, *Byron: Child of Passion, Fool of Fame*, pp. 753, 758.

30 Ibid., p. 761.

31 Kay Redfield Jamison, *Touched with Fire: Manic Depressive Illness and the Artistic Temperament* (New York, NY: Simon and Schuster, 1994), pp. 156–57.

32 Ibid., pp. 165

33 Ibid., pp. 165, 190.

34 'Alpine Journal', *BLJ*, V, pp. 104–05.

35 'Lament of Tasso', 86–87.

36 Grosskurth, *Byron: The Flawed Angel*, p. 427.

37 David Roessel, *In Byron's Shadow: Modern Greece in the English and American Imagination* (New York, NY: Oxford University Press, 2002), p. 5.

38 Lawrence Durrell, *Prospero's Cell* (London: Faber, 1962), p. 11.

39 Stephen Minta, *On a Voiceless Shore: Byron in Greece* (New York, NY: Henry Holt, 1998), p. 211.

40 Ibid., p. 99.

41 Ibid.

42 Ibid., p. 280.

43 Ibid., p. 255.

44 Byron to Thomas Moore, July 1821, *BLJ*, IX, p. 146.

45 Byron to Edward Blaquiere, August 1823, *BLJ*, XI, p. 15.

46 Edward John Trelawny, *Records of Shelley, Byron, and the Author* (1858; Harmondsworth: Penguin, 1973), p. 227.

47 Ibid., p. 239.

48 Byron to John Kinnaird, 30 March 1824, *BLJ*, XI, p. 145.

49 McGann, *Byron and Romanticism*, pp. 291–92.

Bibliography

Abraham, Nicolas, and Maria Torok. *The Shell and the Kernel*, vol. 1: *Renewals of Psychoanalysis*, trans. Nicholas T. Rand (Chicago, IL: Chicago University Press, 1994).

Abrams, M.H. *Natural Supernaturalism: Tradition and Revolution in Romantic Literature* (New York, NY: W.W. Norton, 1971).

Agamben, Giorgio. *Profanations*, trans. Jeff Fort (New York, NY: Zone Books, 2007).

——. *Stanzas: Word and Phantasm in Western Culture*, trans. Ronald L. Martinez (Minneapolis, MN: University of Minnesota Press, 1993).

——. *Homo Sacer: Sovereign Power and Bare Life*, trans. Daniel Heller-Roazen (Stanford, CA: Stanford University Press, 1995).

Aquinas, St. Thomas. *Commentary on Aristotle's* Metaphysics, trans. John P. Rowan (Notre Dame, IN: Dumb Ox Books, 1961).

Arscott, Caroline, and Katie Scott, eds. *Manifestations of Venus: Art and Sexuality* (Manchester: Manchester University Press, 2000).

Auden, W.H. *The Dyer's Hand and Other Essays* (London: Faber, 1963).

Augustine, St. *Confessions*, ed. James J. O'Donnell (Oxford: Oxford University Press, 1992).

Austen, Jane. *Northanger Abbey*, ed. John Davie (Oxford: Oxford University Press, 1998).

Bailey, David A., and Gilane Tawadros, eds. *Veil: Veiling, Representation and Contemporary Art* (London: Institute of International Visual Arts, 2003).

Balthasar, Hans Urs von. *The Theology of Henri de Lubac*, trans. Susan Clements (San Francisco, CA: Ignatius Press, 1983).

——. *The Glory of the Lord*, vol. 4: *The Realm of Metaphysics in Antiquity*, trans. Brian McNeil, CRV, Andrew Louth, John Saward, Rowan Williams and Oliver Davies (Edinburgh: T&T Clark, 1991).

——. *Glory of the Lord*, vol. 5: *The Realm of Metaphysics in the Modern Age*, trans. Oliver Davies, Andrew Louth, Brian McNeil, John Saward and Rowan Williams (Edinburgh: T&T Clark, 1991).

Barbour, Brian. "'Between Two Worlds': The Structure of the Argument in "Tintern Abbey"", in *Nineteenth-Century Literature*, 48:2 (1993).

Barfoot, C.C. 'Hauntings 2: Byron's Phantoms', in *Centennial Hauntings: Pope, Byron and Eliot in the Year 88*, eds. C.C. Barfoot and Theo D'Haen (Amsterdam: Rodopi, 1990).

Barth, Karl. *Die Kirchliche Dogmatik* (Zurich: TVZ, 1932–1970).

Batchen, Geoffrey. 'Spectres of Cyberspace', in *The Visual Culture Reader*, ed. Nicholas Mirzoeff (London: Routledge, 1998).

Baudrillard, Jean. *Seduction* (New York, NY: St Martin's Press, 1979).

Bauman, Zygmunt. *Intimations of Postmodernism* (London: Routledge, 1992).

Beatty, Bernard. *Byron's 'Don Juan'* (Kent: Croon Helm, 1985).

———. *'Don Juan' and Other Poems* (Harmondsworth: Penguin, 1987).

———, and Vincent Newey, eds. *Byron and the Limits of Fiction* (Liverpool: Liverpool University Press, 1988).

———. 'Byron and the Romantic Sublime', in *Revue de l'Université de Moncton: Des Actes Sélectionnés du 30ᵉ Congrès International sur Byron*, ed. Paul M. Curtis (Moncton: Université de Moncton, 2005).

———. 'Milk and Blood, Heredity and Choice: Byron's Readings of *Genesis*', in *Eve's Children: The Biblical Stories Retold and Interpreted in Jewish and Christian Traditions*, ed. Gerard P. Luttikhuizen (Leiden: Brill, 2003).

Beckford, William. 'Vathek', in *Three Oriental Tales*, ed. Alan Richardson (Boston, MA: Houghton Mifflin, 2002).

Benchimol, Alex. 'Remaking the Romantic Period: Cultural Materialism, Cultural Studies and the Radical Public Sphere', in *Textual Practice*, 19:1 (2005).

Benjamin, Walter. *Selected Writings, Volumes 1-4*, eds. Marcus Bullock and Michael W. Jennings (Cambridge, MA: Harvard University Press 1996–2003).

Bennett, Andrew. *Romantic Poets and the Culture of Posterity* (Cambridge: Cambridge University Press, 1999).

Bernhard Jackson, Emily. *The Development of Byron's Philosophy of Knowledge: Certain in Uncertainty* (Basingstoke: Palgrave Macmillan, 2010).

Bloom, Harold. *The Visionary Company: A Reading of English Romantic Poetry* (New York, NY: Cornell University Press, 1961).

Bolla, Perter de. *The Discourse of the Sublime: Readings in History, Aesthetics and the Subject* (London: Blackwell, 1989).

Bone, Drummond. 'A Sense of Endings: Some Romantic and Postmodern Comparisons', in *Romanticism and Postmodernism*, ed. Edward Larrissy (Cambridge: Cambridge University Press, 1999).

———, ed. *The Cambridge Companion to Byron* (Cambridge: Cambridge University Press, 2004).

Brown, David. *God and Enchantment of Place: Reclaiming Human Experience* (Oxford: Oxford University Press, 2004).

Buber, Martin. *I and Thou*, trans. Ronald Gregor Smith (New York, NY: Charles Scribner's Sons, 1958).

Bultmann, Rudolf. *Kerygma and Myth: A Theological Debate*, trans. Reginald H. Fuller (London: SPCK, 1954).

Burke, Edmund. *A Philosophical Enquiry into the Origin of Our Ideas of the Sublime and the Beautiful*, ed. Adam Phillips (Oxford: Oxford University Press, 1990).

Buse, Peter, and Andrew Stott, eds. *Ghosts: Deconstruction, Psychoanalysis, History* (Basingstoke: Macmillan Press, 1999).

Butler, Judith. *Bodies that Matter: On the Discursive Limits of 'Sex'* (London: Routledge, 1993).

Caputo, John D. 'Spectral Hermeneutics: On the Weakness of God and the Theology of the Event', in *After the Death of God*, eds. John D. Caputo and Gianni Vattimo (New York, NY: Columbia University Press, 2007).

Carlyle, Thomas. *Sartor Resartus* (Oxford: Oxford University Press, 1987).

Castle, Terry. *The Female Thermometer: Eighteenth-Century Culture and the Invention of the Uncanny* (New York, NY: Oxford University Press, 1995).

Certeau, Michel de. *The Mystic Fable*, vol. 1: *The Sixteenth and Seventeenth Centuries*, trans. Michael B. Smith (Chicago, IL: University of Chicago Press, 1992).

——. *The Practice of Everyday Life*, trans. S. Rendall (Berkeley, CA: University of California Press, 1999).

Cheeke, Stephen. *Byron and Place: History, Translation, Nostalgia* (Basingstoke: Palgrave Macmillan, 2003).

Chesterton, G.K. 'Wonder and the Wooden Post', in *The Coloured Lands* (London: Sheed and Ward, 1938).

——. *Orthodoxy* (New York, NY: Doubleday, 1959).

Churchill, Charles. *The Poetical Works of Charles Churchill with Memoir etc by the Rev. George Gilfillan* (Edinburgh: James Nichol, 1855).

Chrétien, Jean-Louis. *The Call and Response*, trans. Anne A. Davenport (New York, NY: Fordham University Press, 2004).

Christensen, Jerome. *Lord Byron's Strength* (Baltimore, MD: Johns Hopkins University Press, 1993).

Cixous, Hélèna. 'Fiction and Its Phantoms: A Reading of Freud's *Das Unheimlich* ("The Uncanny")', in *New Literary History*, 7:3 (1976).

Clark, David L., ed. *Romanticism and the Legacies of Jacques Derrida*, Special Issue of *Studies in Romanticism*, 46:2 (2007).

Clarke, Susanna. *Jonathan Strange and Mr Norrell* (London: Bloomsbury, 2004).

Cochran, Peter, ed. *Byron and Women (and Men)* (Newcastle upon Tyne: Cambridge Scholars Publishing, 2010).

——. *The Gothic Byron* (Newcastle upon Tyne: Cambridge Scholars Press, 2009).

Coleridge, Samuel Taylor. *Biographia Literaria*, 2 vols, ed. J. Shawcross (Oxford: Clarendon Press, 1907).

——. 'Review of Matthew G. Lewis, *The Monk*', *The Critical Review* (February 1797).

Cooke, Michael G. *The Blind Man Traces the Circle: On the Patterns and Philosophy of Byron's Poetry* (Princeton, NJ: Princeton University Press, 1969).

Cooper, Tracy. *Palladio's Venice: Architecture and Society in a Renaissance Republic* (New Haven, CT: Yale University Press, 2005).

Cooppan, Vilashini. *Worlds Within: National Narratives and Global Connections in Postcolonial Writing* (Stanford, CA: Stanford University Press, 2009).

Cottingham, John. *The Spiritual Dimension: Religion, Philosophy and Human Value* (Cambridge: Cambridge University Press, 2005).

Crane, David. *The Kindness of Sisters: Annabella Milbanke and the Destruction of the Byrons* (London: HarperCollins, 2002).

Culler, Jonathan. 'Apostrophe', in *The Pursuit of Signs: Semiotics, Literature, Deconstruction* (Ithaca, NY: Cornell University Press, 1981).

Davis, Colin. 'État Présent: Hauntology, Spectres and Phantoms', in *French Studies*, 59:3 (2005).

———. *Haunted Subjects: Deconstruction, Psychoanalysis and the Return of the Dead* (Basingstoke: Palgrave Macmillan, 2007).

———. 'The Skeptical Ghost: Alejandro Amenábar's *The Others* and the Return of the Dead', in *Popular Ghosts: The Haunted Spaces of Everyday Life*, eds. María del Pilar Blanco and Esther Peeren (New York, NY: Continuum, 2010).

[Delpini, Charles Anthony.] *Don Juan; Or, The Libertine Destroy'd: A Tragic Pantomimical Entertainmen, in Two Acts: As Performed at the Theatres Royal, Drury-Lane and Lyceum* (London: J. Roach, 1789).

Derrida, Jacques. 'The Ghost Dance: An Interview with Jacques Derrida', trans. Jean-Luc Svoboda, in *Public*, 2 (1989).

———. *Specters of Marx: The State of the Debt, the Work of Mourning, and the New International*, trans. Peggy Kamuf (New York, NY: Routledge, 1994).

———. 'Marx c'est Quelqu'un', in *Marx en Jeu*, eds. Jacques Derrida, Marc Guillaume and Jean-Pierre Vincent (Paris: Descartes & Cie, 1997).

———. 'The Rhetoric of Drugs', in *Points ... Interviews, 1974–1994*, trans. Peggy Kamuf, Pascale-Anne Brault and Michael B. Naas (Stanford, CA: Stanford University Press, 1995).

———. *Limited Inc*, trans. S. Weber and J. Mehlman (Evanston, IL: Northwestern University Press, 1988).

———. 'Force of Law: The Mystical Foundation of Authority', in *Deconstruction and the Possibility of Justice*, eds. Drucilla Cornell, Michel Rosenfeld and David Gray Carlson (New York, NY: Routledge, 1992).

———. *On Cosmopolitanism and Forgiveness*, trans. Mark Dooley and Michael Hughes (New York, NY: Routledge, 2001).

———. *Writing and Difference*, trans. Alan Bass (Chicago, IL: University of Chicago Press, 1978).

———. *On the Name*, trans. David Wood, John P. Leavey, Jr. and Ian McLeod (Stanford, CA: Stanford University Press, 1995).

———. *The Truth in Painting*, trans. Geoff Bennington and Ian McLeod (Chicago, IL: University of Chicago Press, 1978).

Descartes, René. *Meditations on First Philosophy*, trans. F.E. Sutcliffe (London: Penguin, 1968).

Desmond, William. *Being and the Between* (New York, NY: SUNY, 1995).

———. *Ethics and the Between* (New York, NY: SUNY, 2001).

———. *God and the Between* (Oxford: Wiley-Blackwell, 2007).

Dickens, Charles. *Our Mutual Friend* (Oxford: Oxford University Press, 1989).

Durrell, Lawrence. *Prospero's Cell* (London: Faber, 1962).

Eckhart, Meister. *Selected Writings*, trans. Oliver Davies (London: Penguin, 1994).

Eisler, Benita. *Byron: Child of Passion, Fool of Fame* (New York, NY: Vintage, 2000).

Eliot, T.S. *Inventions of the March Hare: Poems 1909–1917*, ed. Christopher Ricks (New York, NY: Harvest Books, 1998).

Elledge, Paul. 'Byron's Separations and the Endings of Pilgrimage', *Texas Studies in Literature and Language*, 37:1 (Spring 1995).

———. *Byron and the Dynamics of Metaphor* (Nashville, TN: Vanderbilt University Press, 1968).

Empson, William. *Seven Types of Ambiguity* (London: Chatto & Windus, 1930).

Ensslin, Felix. 'Between Two Deaths: From Mirror to Repetition', in *Between Two Deaths*, eds. Felix Ensslin and Ellen Blumenstein (Berlin: Hatje Cantz, 2007).

Evans, Bergen. *The Psychiatry of Robert Burton* (New York, NY: Columbia University Press, 1944).

Fairchild, Hoxie N. 'Byron and Monk Lewis', *Times Literary Supplement*, 11 May 1946.

———. 'Romantic Faith', in *Religious Trends in English Poetry*, vol. III: 1780–1830 (New York, NY: Columbia University Press, 1949).

Foucault, Michel. *Aesthetics, Method and Epistemology*, in *The Essential Works of Michel Foucault, 1954–1984*, vol. 2, ed. James D. Faubion, trans. Robert Hurley (Harmondsworth: Penguin, 1998).

Freccero, Carla. *Queer / Early / Modern* (Durham, NC: Duke University Press, 2006).

Freud, Sigmund. 'The "Uncanny"', in *The Standard Edition of the Complete Works of Sigmund Freud*, vol. 17, trans. James Strachey (Harmondsworth: Penguin, 1985).

Fuller, David. 'Keats and Anti-Romantic Ideology', in *The Challenge of Keats: Bicentenary Essays 1795–1995*, eds. Allan Christensen, Lilla Crisafulli, Giuseppi Galigani and Anthony Johnson, *Studies in Literature*, 28 (Amsterdam: Rodopi, 2000).

Gamer, Michael. *Romanticism and the Gothic: Genre, Reception, and Canon Formation* (Cambridge: Cambridge University Press, 2000).

Germain, Gil. *Spirits in the Material World: The Challenge of Technology* (Maryland, MD: Lexington Books, 2009).

Gleckner, Robert. *Byron and the Ruins of Paradise* (Baltimore, MD: Johns Hopkins, 1967).

Gonsalves, Joshua. 'Byron – In-Between Sade, Lautreamont and Foucault: Situating the Canon of "Evil" in the Nineteenth Century', *Romanticism on the Net*, 43 (2009), available at: http://id.erudit.org/revue/ron/2006/v/n43/013591ar.html?vue=resume (accessed 7.15.2013).

Graham, Elaine. *Representations of the Post/Human: Monsters, Aliens and Others in Popular Culture* (Manchester: Manchester University Press, 2002).

Graham, Peter W. *'Don Juan' and Regency England* (Charlottesville, VA: University of Virginia Press, 1990).

Grosskurth, Phyllis. *Byron: The Flawed Angel* (London: Hodder and Stoughton, 1997).

Guccioli, Teresa. *Lord Byron's Life in Italy*, ed. Peter Cochran, trans. Michael Rees (Newark, NJ: University of Delaware Press, 2005).

Hamilton, Ian. *Keepers of the Flame: Literary Estates and the Rise of Biography* (London: Hutchinson, 1992).

Harmless, William, S.J. *Desert Christians* (Oxford: Oxford University Press, 2004).

Hawkes, David. 'Against Materialism in Literary Theory', in *The Return of Theory in Early Modern English Studies: Tarrying with the Subjunctive*, eds. Paul Cefalu and Bryan Reynolds (Basingstoke: Palgrave Macmillan, 2011).

Haywood, Ian. *Bloody Romanticism: Spectacular Violence and the Politics of Representation, 1776–1832* (New York, NY: Palgrave Macmillan, 2006).

Hénaff, Marcel. 'Naked Terror: Political Violence, Libertine Violence', in Special Issue of *SubStance* 86: 'Reading Violence', eds. David F. Bell and Lawrence R. Schehr, 27:2 (1998).

———. *Sade: The Invention of the Libertine Body* (Minneapolis, MN: The University of Minnesota Press, 1999).

Hervey, James. *Meditations and Contemplations* (London: Cornish, 1855).

Hirsch, E.D. 'Byron and the Terrestrial Paradise', in *From Sensibility to Romanticism*, eds. Frederick Hilles and Harold Bloom (Oxford: Oxford University Press, 1965).

Hirst, Wolf Z. *Byron, the Bible, and Religion* (London and Toronto: Associated University Presses, 1991).

Hoagwood, Terence Allan. *Byron's Dialectic: Skepticism and the Critique of Culture* (Toronto: Bucknell University Press, 1993).

Hobhouse, John Cam. *Historical Illustrations of the Fourth Canto of Childe Harold: Containing Dissertations on the Ruins of Rome, and an Essay on Italian Literature* (London: John Murray, 1818).

Hogle, Jerrold E. 'The Gothic Ghost as Counterfeit and Its Haunting of Romanticism: The Case of "Frost at Midnight"', in *European Romantic Review*, 9:2 (Spring 1998).

Holroyd, Michael. *Works on Paper: The Craft of Biography and Autobiography* (London: Abacus, 2003).

Hopps, Gavin. '"Eden's Door": The Porous Worlds of *Childe Harold's Pilgrimage* and *Don Juan*', in *The Byron Journal*, 37:2 (2009).

———, and Jane Stabler, eds. *Romanticism and Religion from William Cowper to Wallace Stevens* (Aldershot: Ashgate, 2006).

Hudson, Arthur Palmer. 'The "Superstitious" Lord Byron', in *Studies in Philology*, 63:5 (1966).

Hulme, T.E. 'Romanticism and Classicism', in *Speculations*, ed. Herbert Read (London: Routledge, 1936).

Hyman, Gavin. *A Short History of Atheism* (London: I.B. Tauris & Co., 2010).

Jackson, Ken, and Arthur F. Marotti. 'The Turn to the Religious in Early Modern English Studies', in *Criticism*, 46:1 (2004).

Jameson, Fredric. 'Marx's Purloined Letter', in *Ghostly Demarcations: A Symposium on Jacques Derrida's Specters of Marx,* ed. Michael Sprinker (New York, NY: Verso, 1999).

Jamison, Kay Redfield. *Touched with Fire: Manic Depressive Illness and the Artistic Temperament* (New York, NY: Simon and Schuster, 1994).

Jarvis, Simon. *Wordsworth's Philosophical Song* (Cambridge: Cambridge University Press, 2007).

Johnson, Barbara. *A World of Difference* (Baltimore, MD: Johns Hopkins, 1987).

Joseph, M.K. *Byron the Poet* (London: Gollancz, 1964).

Kant, Immanuel. *Critique of Pure Reason*, trans. Norman Kemp Smith (London: Macmillan, 1978).

Kearney, Richard. *The God Who May Be: A Hermeneutics of Religion* (Bloomington, IN: Indiana University Press, 2001).

Keats, John. *The Poems of John Keats*, ed. Jack Stillinger (London: Heinemann, 1978).

Kenyon Jones, Christine. 'Fantasy and Transfiguration: Byron and His Portraits', in *Byromania: Portraits of the Artist in Nineteenth – and Twentieth-Century Culture*, ed. Frances Wilson (London: Macmillan, 1999).

Kierkegaard, Søren. *Works of Love*, trans. Howard V. and Edna H. Hong (Princeton, NJ: Princeton University Press, 1995).

Knight, G. Wilson. *Poets of Action* (London: Methuen, 1967).

Kompridis, Nikolas, ed. *Philosophical Romanticism* (London: Routledge, 2006).

Lacan, Jacques. *The Ethics of Psychoanalysis, 1959–1960*, trans. Dennis Porter (New York, NY: W.W. Norton, 1992).

———. *The Ethics of Psychoanalysis 1959–1960*, trans. Dennis Porter (New York & London: W.W. Norton, 1992).

———. 'Kant Avec Sade', trans. James B. Swenson, *October*, 51 (Winter 1989).

———. 'Desire and the Interpretation of Desire in *Hamlet*', trans. J. Hulbert and ed. J.A. Miller, in *Yale French Studies*, 55:56 (1977).

Landy, Joshua, and Michael Saler, eds. *The Re-Enchantment of the World: Secular Magic in a Rational Age*, (Stanford, CA: Stanford University Press, 2009).

Lang, Cecil Y. 'Narcissus Jilted: Byron, *Don Juan*, and the Biographical Imperative', in *Historical Studies and Literary Criticism*, ed. Jerome J. McGann (Madison, WI: University of Wisconsin Press, 1985).

Leigh, David, S.J., '*Infelix Culpa*: Poetry and the Skeptic's Faith in *Don Juan*', in *Keats-Shelley Journal*, 28 (1979).

Levinas, Emmanuel. *Otherwise than Being or Beyond Essence*, trans. Alphonso Lingis (Pittsburgh, PA: Duquesne University Press, 1998).

———. *Autrement qu'être ou au-dela' de l'essence* (The Hague: Martinus Nijhoff, 1974).

Lewis, Mathew. *The Monk: A Romance*, ed. Howard Anderson (Oxford: Oxford University Press, 1973).

Lonsdale, Roger, ed. *The New Oxford Book of Eighteenth-Century Verse* (Oxford: Oxford University Press, 1987).

Lovell, Earnest J. *Byron: The Record of a Quest* (Hamden, CT: Archon Books, 1966).

Lubac, Henri de. *The Mystery of the Supernatural*, trans. Rosemary Sheed (Montreal: Palm Publishers, 1967).

Luckhurst, Roger. 'The Contemporary London Gothic and the Limits of the "Spectral Turn"', in *Textual Practice*, 16:3 (2002).

MacCarthy, Fiona. *Byron: Life and Legend* (New York, NY: Farrar, Strauss and Giroux, 2002).

Makdisi, Saree. *Palestine Inside Out: An Everyday Occupation* (New York, NY: W.W. Norton, 2008).

Malcolm, Janet. *Reading Chekhov: A Critical Journey* (London, Granta, 2001).

Man, Paul de. *The Rhetoric of Romanticism* (New York, NY: Columbia University Press, 1984).

———. 'Autobiography as De-facement', in *MLN*, 94:5 (December 1979).

Mansini, Guy. 'The Abiding Theological Significance of Henri de Lubac's Surnaturel', in *The Thomist*, 73:4 (2009).

Marchand, Leslie A. *Byron: A Portrait* (London: Cresset, 1987).

Marion, Jean-Luc. *God Without Being: Hors Texte*, trans. Thomas A. Carlson (Chicago, IL: University of Chicago Press, 1991).

———. 'The "End of Metaphysics" as a Possibility', trans. Daryl Lee, in *Religion after Metaphysics*, ed. Mark A. Wrathall (Cambridge: Cambridge University Press, 2003).

Maritain, Jacques. *Creative Intuition in Art and Poetry* (New York, NY: Pantheon, 1953).

Marjarum, Edward Wayne. *Byron as Skeptic and Believer* (New York, NY: Russell & Russell, 1962).

Martin, Philip. 'Reading *Don Juan* with Bakhtin', in *Don Juan: Theory in Practice*, ed. Nigel Wood (Buckingham: Open University Press, 1993).

Martin, Philip W. *Byron: A Poet before His Public* (Cambridge: Cambridge University Press, 1982).

Mathias, T.J. *The Pursuits of Literature: A Satirical Poem. Part the Fourth and Last* (London: Printed for T. Becket, 1797).

McCalman, Iain, ed. *An Oxford Companion to the Romantic Age: British Culture 1776–1832* (Oxford: Oxford University Press, 1999).

McGann, Jerome. Don Juan *in Context* (London: Croom Helm, 1976).

———. *The Romantic Ideology: A Critical Investigation* (Chicago, IL: University of Chicago Press, 1983).

———. *Byron and Romanticism* (Cambridge: Cambridge University Press, 2002).

Medwin, Thomas. *Medwin's Conversations of Lord Byron*, ed. Ernest J. Lovell, Jr (Princeton, NJ: Princeton University Press, 1966).

Melchiori, Barbara. 'Lord Byron Among the Ghosts', in *Arte e letteratura: Scritti in ricordo di Gabriele Baldini* (Rome: Edizioni di Storia e Letteratura, 1972).

Mellor, Anne. *English Romantic Irony* (Cambridge, MA: Harvard University Press, 1980).

Milbank, Alison. 'Apologetics and the Imagination: Making Strange', in *Imaginative Apologetics: Theology, Philosophy and the Catholic Tradition*, ed. Andrew Davidson (London: SCM Press, 2011).

Milbank, John. 'Scholasticism, Modernism and Modernity', in *Modern Theology*, 22:4 (2006).

———. 'Sublimity: The Modern Transcendent', in *Transcendence: Philosophy, Literature, and Theology Approach the Beyond*, ed. Regina Schwartz (New York, NY: Routledge, 2004).

———. *The Suspended Middle: Henri de Lubac and the Debate Concerning the Supernatural* (London: SCM, 2005).

———. *Being Reconciled: Ontology and Pardon* (London and New York, NY: Routledge, 2003).

Miles, Robert. *Ann Radcliffe: The Great Enchantress* (Manchester: Manchester University Press, 1995).

Milton, John. *The Poems of John Milton*, ed. John Carey and Alastair Fowler (London: Longman, 1968).

Minta, Stephen. *On a Voiceless Shore: Byron in Greece* (New York, NY: Henry Holt, 1998).

Mole, Tom. *Byron's Romantic Celebrity: Industrial Culture and the Hermeneutic of Intimacy* (Basingstoke: Palgrave Macmillan, 2007).

Motion, Andrew. 'This Is Your Subject Speaking', in *An Enormous Yes: In Memoriam Philip Larkin*, ed. Harry Chambers (Calstock: Peterloo Poets, 1986).

Newey, Vincent. 'Authoring the Self: *Childe Harold* III and IV', in *Byron and the Limits of Fiction*, eds. Bernard Beatty and Vincent Newey (Liverpool: Liverpool University Press, 1988).

Nietzsche, Friedrich. *The Birth of Tragedy*, trans. Francis Golffing (New York, NY: Doubleday, 1956).

O'Brien, Edna. *Byron in Love* (London: Weidenfeld & Nicolson, 2009).

O'Connor, Flannery. 'Novelist and Believer', in *Mystery and Manners* (New York, NY: Farrar, Straus & Giroux, 1970).

Pafford, Ward. 'Byron and the Mind of Man: *Childe Harold III-IV* and *Manfred*', in *Studies of Romanticism*, 1:2 (Winter 1962).

Paglia, Camille. *Sexual Personae: Art and Decadence from Nefertiti to Emily Dickinson* (New Haven: Yale University Press, 1990).

Partridge, Christopher. *The Re-Enchantment of the West*, vol. 1: *Alternative Spiritualities, Sacralization, Popular Culture and Occulture* (London: T&T Clark, 2004).

Peacock, Thomas Love. *Memoirs of Shelley and Other Essays and Reviews*, ed. Howard Mills (London: Rupert Hart-Davis, 1970).

Phillips, Adam. *On Flirtation* (London: Faber, 1994).

Pickstock, Catherine. *After Writing: On the Liturgical Consummation of Philosophy* (Oxford: Blackwell, 1998).

Pieper, Josef. *Leisure: The Basis of Culture* & *the Philosophical Act*, trans. Alexander Dru (New York, NY: Pantheon, 1952).

Praz, Mario. *The Romantic Agony* (New York, NY: Oxford University Press, 1970).

Procházka, Martin. 'History and Ruins in Canto IV of *Childe Harold's Pilgrimage*', *Litteraria Pragensia*, 7:14 (1997).

Quevedo, Redivivus. *Spiritual Interview with Lord Byron. In Which His Lordship Gave His Opinions and Feelings About His New Monument and Gossip about the Literature of His Own and the Present Day, With Some Interesting Information About the Spirit World. With Notes Explanatory and Elucidatory* (London: Samuel Palmer and Sons, n.d.).

Rabaté, Jean-Michel. *The Ghosts of Modernity* (Florida, FL: University Press of Florida, 1996).

Radcliffe, Ann. *The Mysteries of Udolpho*, ed. Bonamy Dobrée (London: Oxford University Press, 1966).

——. *A Sicilian Romance*, ed. Alison Milbank (Oxford: Oxford University Press, 1993).

——. *A Journey Made in the Summer of 1794, Through Holland and the Western Frontier of Germany, With a Return Down the Rhine: To Which are Added Observations During a Tour to the Lakes of Lancashire, and Westmoreland, and Cumberland* (London: J. and G.G. Robinson, 1795).

——. *The Italian: Or, The Confessional of the Black Penitents*, ed. Robert Miles (Harmondsworth: Penguin, 2000).

Rawes, Alan. *Byron's Poetic Experimentation: Childe Harold, The Tales, and the Quest for Comedy* (Aldershot: Ashgate, 2000).

Reiman, Donald H., ed. *The Romantics Reviewed: Contemporary Reviews of British Romantic Writers*, 5 vols. (New York and London: Garland Publishing, Inc., 1972).

Ricoeur, Paul. *The Symbolism of Evil*, trans. Emerson Buchanan (Boston, MA: Beacon Press, 1967).

Riffaterre, Michael. 'Prosopopeia', in *Yale French Studies*, 69 (1985).

Roessel, David. *In Byron's Shadow: Modern Greece in the English and American Imagination* (New York, NY: Oxford University Press, 2002).

Rubenstein, Mary-Jane. *Strange Wonder: The Closure of Metaphysics and the Opening of Awe* (New York, NY: Columbia University Press, 2008).

——. 'Of Ghosts and Angels: Derrida, Kushner, and the Impossibility of Forgiveness', in *JCRT*, 9:1 (2008).

Ruskin, John. *Modern Painters*, vol. III (London: George Allen, 1906).

——. 'Fiction, Fair and Foul', in *The Works of John Ruskin*, vol. XXXIV, eds. E.T. Cook and A. Weddeburn (London: George Allen, 1903–1912).

Rutherford, Andrew. *Byron the Best-Seller* (Byron Foundation Lecture; Nottingham: University of Nottingham, 1964).

Sade, Marquis de. *Justine, Philosophy in the Bedroom and Other Writings*, trans. Richard Seaver and Austryn Wainhouse (New York, NY: Grove Press, 1965).

——. *The Misfortunes of Virtue and Other Early Tales*, trans. David Coward (Oxford: Oxford University Press, 1992).

Saint-Amand, Pierre. 'The Immortals', in *Yale French Studies*, 94 (1998).

Schiller, Friedrich. *The Ghost-Seer; Or, Apparitionist, An Interesting Fragment, Found Among the Papers of Count O******, from the German of Schiller*, trans. Daniel Boileau (London: Vernor and Hood, 1795).

——. *Sämtliche Werke*, vol. 1, eds. Gerhard Fricke and Herbert G. Göpfert (München: Carl Hanser Verlag, 1965).

Scott, Sir Walter. *The Letters of Sir Walter Scott, 1811–1914*, ed. H.J.C. Grierson (London: Constable, 1932).

Scribner, Robert W. *Religion and Culture in Germany (1400–1800)*, ed. Lyndal Roper (Leiden: Brill, 2001).

Sedley, David L. *Sublimity and Skepticism in Montaigne and Milton* (Ann Arbor, MI: University of Michigan Press, 2005).

Seed, David. '"Disjointed Fragments": Concealment and Revelation in *The Giaour*', in *The Byron Journal*, 18 (1990).

Shaw, Philip. 'Wordsworth and Byron', in *The Byron Journal*, 31 (2003).

Shelley, Mary. *The Novels and Selected Works of Mary Shelley*, eds. Nora Crook and Pamela Clemit, 8 vols. (London: Pickering & Chatto, 1996).

Shelley, Percy Bysshe. *The Poems of Shelley*, vol. 1, eds. Geoffrey Matthews and Kelvin Everest (London: Longman, 1989).

Sherry, Patrick. 'Disenchantment, Re-Enchantment, and Enchantment', in *Modern Theology*, 25:3 (2009).

Simmel, Georg. *Georg Simmel: On Women, Sexuality, and Love*, trans. Guy Oakes (New Haven, CT: Yale University Press, 1984).

Slocombe, Will. *Nihilism and the Sublime Postmodern: The (Hi)Story of a Difficult Relationship from Romanticism to Postmodernism* (New York & London: Routledge, 2006).

Smith, Nichol D., ed. *Jeffrey's Literary Criticism* (London: Froude, 1910).

Spence, Joseph. *Observations, Anecdotes, and Characters of Books and Men*, ed. Edmund Malone (London: John Murray, 1820).

St Clair, William. *The Reading Nation in the Romantic Period* (Cambridge: Cambridge University Press, 2004).

Stabler, Jane, ed. *Palgrave Advances in Byron Studies* (Basingstoke: Palgrave Macmillan, 2007).

———. '"Awake to Terror": The Impact of Italy on Byron's Depiction of Freedom's Battles', in *Byron and the Politics of Freedom and Terror*, eds. Matthew J.A. Green and Piya Pal-Lapinski (Basingstoke: Palgrave Macmillan, 2011).

———. *Byron, Poetics and History* (Cambridge: Cambridge University Press, 2002).

Steiner, George. *Real Presences* (Chicago, IL: University of Chicago Press, 1989).

Sundell, Michael G. 'The Development of *The Giaour*', in *Studies in English Literature 1500–1900*, 9:4 (1969).

Tanner, Tony. *The Reign of Wonder: Naivety and Reality in American Literature* (Cambridge: Cambridge University Press, 1965).

Taylor, Charles. *A Secular Age* (Cambridge, MA: Harvard University Press, 2007).

Tertullian. *Tertullian's Treatise on the Incarnation*, trans. Ernest Ewans (London: SPCK, 1956).

Thomson, James. *The Castle of Indolence*, ed. James Sambrook (Oxford: Clarendon Press, 1986).

Todorov, Tzvetan. *The Fantastic: A Structuralist Approach to a Literary Mode*, trans. Richard Howard (Cleveland, OH: Case Western Reserve University Press, 1973).

Townshend, Dale. 'Gothic and the Ghost of *Hamlet*', in *Gothic Shakespeares*, eds. J. Drakakis and D. Townshend (Abingdon: Routledge, 2008).

Trelawny, Edward John. *Records of Shelley, Byron, and the Author* (Harmondsworth: Penguin, 1973).

Ulmer, William A. *The Christian Wordsworth, 1798–1805* (New York, NY: SUNY Press, 2001).

Vattimo, Gianni. *Nihilism and Emancipation* (New York, NY: Columbia University Press, 2004).

Wall, Geoffrey. 'Thinking With Demons: Flaubert and De Sade', in *The Cambridge Quarterly*, 36:2 (2007).

Ward, Graham. *Cities of God* (London: Routledge, 2000).

——. *Theology and Contemporary Critical Theory* (Basingstoke: Macmillan, 2000).

——. 'Transcendence and Representation', in *Transcendence: Philosophy, Literature, and Theology Approach the Beyond*, ed. Regina Schwartz (London: Routledge, 2004).

——. *True Religion* (Oxford: Blackwell, 2002).

Watkins, Daniel P. *A Materialist Critique of English Romantic Drama* (Florida, FL: University Press of Florida, 1993).

——. 'Violence, Class Consciousness and Ideology in Byron's History Plays', in *ELH*, 48:4 (Winter 1981).

Weber, Max. *The Protestant Ethic and the Spirit of Capitalism*, trans. Talcott Parsons (London: Unwin Hyman, 1989).

Williams, Rowan. *Grace and Necessity: Reflections on Art and Love* (London: Continuum, 2005).

Wolfreys, Julian. *Victorian Hauntings: Spectrality, Gothic, the Uncanny and Literature* (Basingstoke: Palgrave, 2002).

——, ed. *Introduction to Criticism at the 21st Century* (Edinburgh: Edinburgh University Press, 2002).

Wolfson, Susan. 'Byron's Ghosting Authority', in *ELH*, 76:3 (Fall 2009).

——. *Formal Charges: The Shaping of Poetry in British Romanticism* (Stanford, CA: Stanford University Press, 1997).

Woolf, Virginia. *A Writer's Diary*, ed. Leonard Woolf (New York, NY: Harcourt, 1953).

Wordsworth, William. *The Poetical Works of William Wordsworth*, eds. E. de Selincourt and H. Darbishire, 5 vols. (Oxford: Clarendon Press, 1940–1949).

Young, Edward. *Night Thoughts*, ed. Stephen Cornford (Cambridge: Cambridge University Press, 1989).

Žižek, Slavoj, and John Milbank. *The Monstrosity of Christ: Paradox or Dialectic?*, ed. Creston Davis (Cambridge and London: MIT Press, 2009).

——. *The Sublime Object of Ideology* (New York & London: Verso, 1989).

——. *The Fragile Absolute – Or, Why is the Christian Legacy Worth Fighting For?* (New York & London: Verso, 2000).

——. *The Indivisible Remainder: Essays on Schelling and Related Matters* (New York & London: Verso, 1996).

——. *Violence* (London: Profile Books, 2008).

Zupančič, Alenka. 'Kant with Don Juan and Sade', in *Radical Evil*, ed. Joan Copjec (London: Verso, 1996).

Notes on Contributors

Peter Allender taught English in secondary schools for over twenty-five years. Until, with great good fortune, he became a student again in his fifties on the MA in Romanticism course at the University of Bristol and was privileged to be taught about Byron with enthusiasm and imagination by Stephen Cheeke, Andrew Nicholson and Tim Webb. He went on to complete a PhD thesis on William Hazlitt – a writer not always as inimical towards Byron as he is sometimes considered to be. Peter continues to teach part-time at the University of Bristol.

Bernard Beatty is Senior Fellow in the School of English at the University of Liverpool and Associate Fellow in the School of Divinity at the University of St Andrews. He is the author of *Byron's 'Don Juan'* (London: Croom Helm, 1985) and *Byron's 'Don Juan' and Other Poems* (Harmondsworth: Penguin, 1987). He has edited three collections of essays on Byron and written on Romanticism, the Bible and aspects of literary theory. His most recent work has been on Shelley and the Bible, Byron and the Bible, Byron and Venice, the psalms, the theology of beauty and two essays – one on Browning and Newman and the other on Pope, Byron and Newman. He was Editor of *The Byron Journal* from 1988 to 2005 and remains on the Editorial Board. He is Vice-President of both the Byron Society and the Newstead Abbey Byron Society, and he is on the Board of Directors of the International Byron Society.

Peter W. Graham is Professor of English at Virginia Tech. His particular scholarly interest is nineteenth-century British literature and culture. Among his book publications are: *Byron's Bulldog: The Letters of John Cam Hobhouse to Lord Byron*; *'Don Juan' and Regency England*; *Articulating the Elephant Man* (with Fritz Oehlschlaeger); and *Jane Austen & Charles Darwin: Naturalists and Novelists*.

Gavin Hopps is Lecturer in Literature and Theology and Director of the Institute for Theology, Imagination and the Arts at the University of St Andrews. He has published numerous articles on Romantic writing and has co-edited a collection of essays on Romanticism and religion. He is currently working on a monograph on the levity of *Don Juan* and is also working with Jane Stabler on a new edition of Byron's complete poetical works.

Mary Hurst completed her PhD at the University of Liverpool in 2006 and has worked at the University of Manchester and Edge Hill, where she now lectures in English Literature. She has written on Byron and religion and the aestheticization of confession in Byron's poetry. She is currently writing on Byron's desire for, and understanding and exploitation of, solitude in his poetry.

Alison Milbank studied Theology and English Literature at the University of Cambridge and then completed a doctorate at the University of Lancaster. She was the John Rylands Research Institute Fellow at the University of Manchester and, after temporary lectureships at Cambridge and the University of Middlesex, taught in the English department at the University of Virginia for five years. Her research and teaching focuses on the relation of religion to culture in the post-Enlightenment period, with particular literary interest in non-realist literary and artistic expression, such as the Gothic, the fantastic, horror and fantasy. She is the author of *Dante and the Victorians* (Manchester: Manchester University Press, 2009); *Chesterton and Tolkien as Theologians: The Fantasy of the Real* (London: T&T Clark, 2009); and, with Andrew Davison, *For the Parish: A Critique of Fresh Expressions* (Norwich: SCM, 2010).

Piya Pal-Lapinski is Associate Professor of English at Bowling Green State University, where she teaches nineteenth-century British Literature and Critical Theory. She is the author of *The Exotic Woman in Nineteenth Century British Fiction and Culture: A Reconsideration* (New Hampshire: University of New Hampshire Press, 2005). She has recently co-edited the essay collection *Byron and the Politics of Freedom and Terror* (London: Palgrave, 2011) and is currently working on a book-length project on fashion and the state in the nineteenth-century novel.

Philip Shaw is Professor of Romantic Studies at the University of Leicester. He maintains research interests in Romantic poetry and prose and the visual arts. His publications include: *Suffering and Sentiment in Romantic Military Art* (2013), *The Sublime* (2006) and *Waterloo and the Romantic Imagination* (2002). He is reviews editor of *The Byron Journal*.

Corin Throsby currently teaches at the University of Cambridge. She was recently named one of the Arts and Humanities Research Council's 'New Generation Thinkers' and has been appearing regularly on BBC radio to talk about her research. She is writing a book on the correspondence between readers and authors in the nineteenth century.

Dale Townshend is Senior Lecturer in Gothic and Romantic Literature at the University of Stirling, Scotland. His publications include: *The Orders of Gothic: Foucault, Lacan, and the Subject of Gothic Writing, 1764–1820* (New York: AMS, 2007); four volumes in the *Gothic: Critical Concepts in Literary and Cultural Studies* series (with Fred Botting) (London: Routledge, 2004); *Gothic Shakespeares* (with John Drakakis) (London: Routledge 2008); and *Macbeth: A Critical Guide* (with John Drakakis) (London: Arden, 2013). He is currently at work on three major projects: a monograph entitled *Gothic Antiquity: History, Romance and the Architectural Imagination, 1760–1840*; *Ann Radcliffe, Romanticism and the Gothic* (with Angela Wright) (Cambridge: Cambridge University Press, 2014); and *The Gothic World* (with Glennis Byron) (London: Routledge, 2013).

Index